Through No Fault of Their Own?

Through No Fault of Their Own?

The Fate of Those Who Have Never Heard

Edited by

William V. Crockett
and
James G. Sigountos

Preface by Kenneth S. Kantzer

BAKER BOOK HOUSE
Grand Rapids, Michigan 49516

Copyright 1991 by
Baker Book House Company

Library of Congress Cataloging-in-Publication Data

Through no fault of their own? : the fate of those who have never heard / edited by
William V. Crockett and James G. Sigountos : preface by Kenneth S. Kantzer.
        p.   cm.
    Includes bibliographical references and index.
    ISBN 0–8010–2562–1
    1. Salvation outside the church. 2. Christianity and other religions. 3. Univer-
salism.   I. Crockett, William V.   II. Sigountos, James G. (James George), 1956–   .
BT759.T47   1991
234—dc20   91-28526
                                                           CIP

Printed in the United States of America

Unless otherwise indicated, Scripture references are from the Holy Bible: New
International Version. Copyright 1973, 1978, 1984 by the International Bible Society.

Dedicated to

G. Linwood Barney,

missionary, educator, and friend

Contents

Part 3 Missiological Issues

Part 4 Concluding Remarks

Foreword

A few years ago several of us were discussing the question addressed in this book—the fate of those who have never heard the gospel. This issue has vexed the church from the beginning, but lately it has grown more acute. Many books and articles by liberal scholars and church leaders have concluded that traditional evangelism and missionary activity are no longer necessary, and, in fact, may even be harmful. These ideas are beginning to surface even in evangelical circles, and many wonder whether we still need to be concerned about the Great Commission's call to "make disciples of all nations" (Matt. 28:16–20).

In Plato's *Apology of Socrates*, Socrates says he is the wisest person on earth because he does not pretend to know every phase of human knowledge. We think it would be similarly foolish to pretend we can write authoritatively on a subject requiring such broad knowledge. From Old Testament studies to modern church history, from ancient Hellenistic religions to the current religions of the world—each area must be consulted.

In this volume, a group of solid evangelical scholars—specialists in their fields—discuss the crucial questions raised by this topic. Each chapter is up-to-date, and represents the best of evangelical scholarship.

This book is divided into three major sections. The first covers theological issues, and discusses how scholars past and present have dealt with the fate of those who have never heard. The chapters in this section also explore important theological ideas, such as the nature of hell or whether God might change his mind about eternal punishment.

The second section explores what the Bible says about those who have never heard. Scholars who challenge the evangelical position have tried to argue that the Bible is more "open-minded" than we have traditionally thought. They claim, for example, that Israel thought her religion was only one among many valid religions, and that Jesus' teaching about the kingdom of God included other religions, rather than excluding them. This section of the book shows that the Bible draws a sharp line between Christianity and other religions. Several chapters address related issues, such as the nature of eternal punishment and the meaning of Acts 4:12.

The final section deals with missiological questions. It explores "cutting-edge" questions such as how missionaries should deal with other religions, and how the universalist ideas of nonevangelical scholars affect missions.

This book can be read in several ways. It can be read from front to back, since there is a logical progression. Each chapter, however, can stand alone, so the reader can skip from chapter to chapter as interest demands. We hope this volume will provide a balance to other books critical of evangelical missions. We are convinced that the evangelical position, properly presented, is by no means weak and outmoded, as some of its detractors maintain.

We would like to thank Claire Sigountos and Greta Johnson for their typing, and Tom Fehr for his proofreading and help in assembling the suggestions for further reading.

Preface

Few questions have troubled the hearts and minds of Christians down through the centuries as greatly as the one addressed in this book. Our age is no exception. Could it really be otherwise? We human beings were created in God's image and that image is being gradually recreated in us by the Holy Spirit. The more we become like God the more we shall grieve over the sin and the lostness of our fellow humankind. God loves all the world, every human being—even Hitler and Saddam Hussein. Since God is also the sovereign and righteous Judge of all the universe, he may have to will human beings, whom he created and loves dearly, into eternal punishment for their sins. But, wonder of wonders, and hard as it may be for us to understand, he does not wish that any should perish. Remember how Jesus wept over Jerusalem? And in some way faintly analogous to our human experience, God grieves at the sin of those whom he created and loves. I have to ask myself, "How often have I wept over Chicago?"

When I was asked to write this preface, my first reaction was how greatly I was being honored by the request. The individuals writing these essays represent a remarkable group of thinking Christians chosen from among the ablest young scholars in the evangelical movement; a few "elder statesmen" have been thrown in for seasoning.

I am sorely tempted to dive into the discussion by interacting with every chapter, setting straight every crooked line and shoring up every slightest deviation from the pure truth as I see it. Those who read this preface will be relieved to learn that, in mercy (as well as in humility), I have strenuously resisted the temptation—although as always in my life, my resolution to resist temptation seems to wear thin at crucial moments.

Rather, I shall make a few general observations that may prove helpful to readers of this volume and make it more useful to them. With the earnest hope that it will not sound patronizing, I shall begin by saying that there is no real heresy in the volume. Bent exegesis, yes, as well as very careful and excellent exegesis. No one will agree with every position advocated here. Several authors may even hold to what some might consider heretical views. But they do not advance them in this volume.

That statement really demands careful definition of what we mean by heresy. Unfortunately, there is no unanimity as to what the term really refers to. The root meaning refers to something that is cut off. But cut off from what? We sometimes use the term for those who by their actions or doctrine cut themselves off from salvation. Of course, only God knows who has done that. But there are attitudes, lifestyles, and false doctrines that leave us no choice but to reckon that those who hold them fall outside the visible body of Christ. This is certainly a legitimate use of the word "heresy." But it is not the sense that I intend here. I refer, rather, to doctrines that evangelical Christians have generally held to be the clear, unequivocal, and essential teachings of Scripture. For example, no contributor advocates that all will be saved. Or that a person can be saved on grounds other than the sacrificial atonement of Jesus Christ or without faith in Christ (although some argue that it is possible to have faith in Christ without knowing the historical Jesus). And no contributor suggests that other religions represent valid, if less desirable, pathways to God.

Moreover, all argue that the final authority that should determine our doctrine is the teaching of Scripture. This is terribly important. We must never allow our doctrine to be controlled by our emotional or moral sensibilities. Many who write on this topic do so. They are ultimately guided by a superficial sentimentality (God is too good to condemn the heathen), or by a profound moral conviction (it does not seem just or fair). This is to proceed along a dangerous path. Our emotional life is as fallible as our intellectual life. Our minds are warped by sin and molded by pressures from those around us. Our finite intelligence simply cannot probe into the mind and plan of God. Because of this, we must be guided wholly by the written Word, the Bible, that God provides to shed light on our path.

Exegesis of Scripture is carried on by dedicated scholars who have earnestly sought to come to grips with what God has given us in his Word. The contributors to this volume do not always agree; and if some are right, others are clearly wrong. Nor are the chapters altogether free from appeals to sentiment, social outrage, and emotional repugnance to certain interpretations of Scripture. Yet all the authors declare, with evident sincerity, that in this delicate matter they are seeking the will of God as he has seen fit to reveal it in the Scriptures. And that is the way it should be.

The contributors avoid forming doctrine by drawing what seem to be "logical" conclusions from other doctrines. In one sense, this is necessary. If a new gospel contradicts the one revealed gospel, we must reject it (Gal. 1). Yet this is always dangerous. When it comes to the plans and purposes of God, we dare do no more than conclude that God will not flatly contradict his revealed character. And we must exercise extraordinary caution in judging what conflicts with the character of this infinite God.

Again this volume keeps to a minimum the false dichotomies that prejudice our conclusions. One of the worst prejudgments (often cited by liberal scholars) is questioned in the title of this book—*Through No Fault of Their Own?* No responsible Christian should argue on this basis. As several contributors have pointed out, Scripture is abundantly clear that all human beings are at fault—except the Savior. People are never condemned merely because they did or did not hear the saving message of the gospel. We are sinners who deserve God's punishment. According to the Bible, God would be a God of perfect love had he condemned all humans to eternal punishment. We have failed to live up to the light we have, whether that be the light of nature or the special light that lights every one who comes into the world (John 1:9).

Even the question "Is it fair?" is hardly appropriate. Christians know that the Judge of all the earth will assuredly do what is right (Gen. 18:25). But it is extraordinarily risky for us to speculate on what acts would be "fair" for God. Does that mean that God must treat all exactly alike? With the same amount of grace precisely measured out to each individual on earth? Is it fair, for example, that one person is born and reared in a Christian family with father and mother deeply solicitous for their child's spiritual welfare, whereas another is born on the streets of Chicago and reared, if we dare use the term, by an inner-city gang, or still another, born and reared in a fanatical Muslim home in Iran?

In Romans 9 Paul faces this problem in an even more acute form than it is raised in this book. How could a sovereign God, who controls history and works out all things for the good of those who love him, ever have raised up in history a Pharaoh and then condemned him forever? Paul's answer is twofold. He first reminds us that we are finite and no more capable of judging God's actions than a lump of clay is prepared to assess the motives of a human potter as he makes it into a vessel. Our only reasonable stance is humble, loyal, filial trust in the infinite wisdom of a holy and loving God.

But Paul also gives a second answer to reassure us that God does have good reasons for doing what he does. His decisions are not arbitrary. He is not a callous Allah who flings human subjects into history with careless indifference—"These are for hell, and I care not."

When we face imponderable issues about which we as human beings really can know nothing apart from revelation, our best response is to wait humbly upon our God for whatever wisdom he cares to provide. And that is just what troubles me! If there is anything lacking in the American evangelical church today, it is a deep sense of humility and awe as we finite creatures stand in the presence of the infinite and holy God. At worst, we seek a convenient God who will round out the comforts of our "good life"—all this and heaven too! At best, we look upon God as a buddy, our friendly companion, with whom we can share the joys of life. We need a lot more of the sense of awesome fear that gripped Moses as he stood before the burning bush, or of Isaiah who cried out in awe, "Holy, holy, holy is the LORD Almighty; the whole earth is full of his glory" (Isa. 6:3). Only then are we prepared to face the questions raised in this volume.

After I had finished outlining this preface, I sat in my study and pondered once again the chapters I had read. I asked myself, Is there anything that could have been added to help us as we approach the problems addressed in this volume?

Yes, there is. Or so, at least, it seems to me. We need a deep sense of the awfulness of sin. Not that any author for one moment would deny an evangelical theology of sin. I am confident that each one could pass any test you might give covering the biblical doctrine of the sinfulness of all human beings and our need for salvation wholly by the grace of God. But the awful ugliness and repulsiveness of sin did not seem to me to shine through with a crystal brilliance characteristic of the writings of Moses and Isaiah and Paul and John. Could it be that the church is facing this issue of the lostness of humankind in acute form today because as a people we have lost a biblical sense of the awfulness of sin?

P.S. Just in case you may think I am cravenly hiding behind a neutral preface, I, as a committed evangelical and as an amateur theologian, would like to indicate where I stand on the issue under discussion. God is not only a lot better than we are; he is also a lot smarter than we are. By contrast with his infinite mind, our minds are like lumps of clay. Therefore, it is utterly foolish to think that we can ferret out the details of what God has in his mind and plan—unless he chooses to reveal it to us. If we try to reach beyond what God has clearly revealed, we waste our time.

As I have already said, the fate of those who have never heard has been a troublesome issue throughout history. Yet Scripture has not given us enough information to resolve this problem. God does not want us to spend enormous amounts of time investigating things about which we can do absolutely nothing.

What God has revealed clearly and unequivocally is just this:

1. God is infinitely more concerned to be holy, just, good, and fair than we are. We can trust him to do what is right.
2. Sinners—all of us—can be forgiven and made fit for eternal fellowship with God in his great kingdom only through repentance from sin and personal faith in Jesus Christ.
3. While God does not want us to waste time speculating about the fate of those about whom we can do nothing, there is something we can do. And he will hold us responsible for doing it. We can and must, with all our ability and strength, faithfully bear witness by word and life to our next-door neighbor, and to all those whoever and wherever they may be whom we can reach with the gospel. *That* he has revealed, and to that command we must be obedient.

—Kenneth S. Kantzer

Contributors

Darrell L. Bock
Ph.D., University of Aberdeen
Associate Professor of New Testament Studies
Dallas Theological Seminary

David K. Clark
Ph.D., Northwestern University
Professor of Theology
Bethel Theological Seminary

Harvie M. Conn
Th.M., Westminster Theological Seminary
Professor of Missions
Westminster Theological Seminary

William V. Crockett
Ph.D., University of Glasgow
Professor of New Testament
Alliance Theological Seminary

John D. Ellenberger
D.Miss. (Cand.), Fuller Theological Seminary
Assistant Professor of Missiology and Anthropology
Alliance Theological Seminary

Millard J. Erickson
Ph.D., Northwestern University
Executive Vice President and Dean
Bethel Theological Seminary

Carl F. H. Henry
Ph.D., Boston University; Th.D., Northern Baptist Theological Seminary
Visiting Professor
Trinity Evangelical Divinity School

Kenneth S. Kantzer
Ph.D., Harvard University
Distinguished Professor of Biblical and Systematic Theology
Trinity Evangelical Divinity School

Scot McKnight
Ph.D., University of Nottingham
Assistant Professor of New Testament
Trinity Evangelical Divinity School

Douglas Moo
Ph.D., University of St. Andrews
Associate Professor of New Testament
Trinity Evangelical Divinity School

John N. Oswalt
Ph.D., Brandeis University
Professor of Old Testament and Semitic Languages
Asbury Theological Seminary

Timothy R. Phillips
Ph.D., Vanderbilt University
Assistant Professor of Historical and Systematic Theology
Wheaton College Graduate School

Clark H. Pinnock
Ph.D., Manchester University
Professor of Christian Interpretation
McMaster Divinity College

Frederick W. Schmidt
D.Phil., Oxford University
Assistant Professor of New Testament Studies
Messiah College

James G. Sigountos
Ph.D., University of Chicago
Associate Professor of New Testament and Patristics
Alliance Theological Seminary

Aída Besançon Spencer
Ph.D., Southern Baptist Theological Seminary
Associate Professor of New Testament
Gordon-Conwell Theological Seminary

Tite Tiénou
Ph.D., Fuller Theological Seminary
Professor of Theology and Missiology
Alliance Theological Seminary

Charles Van Engen
Ph.D., Free University of Amsterdam
Associate Professor of Theology and Mission and Latin American Studies
School of World Mission, Fuller Theological Seminary

Jerry L. Walls
Ph.D., University of Notre Dame
Associate Professor of Philosophy of Religion
Asbury Theological Seminary

Timothy D. Westergren
M.A., Alliance Theological Seminary
Pastor, Chicago Lawn Alliance Church

R. Bryan Widbin
Ph.D., Brandeis University
Associate Professor of Old Testament
Alliance Theological Seminary

Theological Questions

1

The State of the Question

Millard J. Erickson

In this volume we consider a topic of great current interest in Christian circles, both lay and academic. It concerns the fate of those who have never heard the gospel, and ultimately the issue of universalism (will everyone be saved?). In order to see the issues clearly, we need to note the development of beliefs constituting what may be referred to as the orthodox or traditional view of Christianity.

The Orthodox View

The following set of beliefs characterizes the traditional view of Christianity:

1. All humans are sinners, by nature and by choice, and are therefore guilty and under divine condemnation.
2. Salvation is only through Christ and his atoning work.
3. Belief is necessary to obtain the salvation achieved by Christ. Therefore, Christians and the church have a responsibility to tell unbelievers the good news about Jesus Christ.
4. Adherents of other religions, no matter how sincere their belief or how intense their religious activity, are spiritually lost apart from Christ.

5. Physical death brings to an end the opportunity to exercise saving faith and accept Jesus Christ. The decisions made in this life are irrevocably fixed at death.
6. At the great final judgment, all humans will be separated on the basis of their relationship to Christ during this life. Those who have believed in him will spend eternity in heaven, in everlasting joy and reward in God's presence. Those who have not accepted him will experience hell, a place of unending suffering, where they will be eternally separated from God.

With some variations, this set of beliefs has characterized orthodoxy down through the years. It was implicit—and at times explicit—in the early church's preaching. It was clear in Jesus' statement that "no one comes to the Father except through me" (John 14:6) and in Peter's message that "salvation is found in no one else, for there is no other name under heaven given to men by which we must be saved" (Acts 4:12). It is implied by passages such as 1 Corinthians 15:21–22, 1 Timothy 2:5, and Hebrews 9:12. There have been some major exceptions. For example, Origen (ca. 185–ca. 254) taught the doctrine of *apokatastasis* or restoration. He held that the future punishment will be limited in duration and will purify, so that all things will eventually be reconciled to God, in keeping with 2 Corinthians 5:18–19.[1] Over the years there have been numerous movements that have, in various ways, softened the traditional position. The twentieth century has seen a real acceleration away from the orthodox view toward a more universalistic position that, in one way or another, denies that the "heathen" are really lost. It will be the purpose of this chapter to examine the current condition of the question.

Factors Contributing to Universalistic Views

A number of factors have contributed to the development of universalistic views. In most cases, modification has resulted from a combination of two or more factors, but usually it is possible to identify one as the most distinctive feature of the adjusted conception.

Emotional. The idea of large numbers, perhaps even a majority, of the human race being separated from God and exposed to endless suffering is abhorrent to many sensitive Christians. The thought of endless suffering is bad enough, even if it involves only one person. When extended to large numbers of persons, it seems intolerable.

Anthropological. It was relatively easy to think of those who had never heard of Christ as being lost, when such people could be

1. Origen, *On First Principles* 1.6.2.

thought of as primitive, savage, and engaged in bizarre religious practices. That they had committed sins worthy of endless punishment did not seem greatly incongruous, if they practiced head-hunting or cannibalism. With the shrinking of our globe, however, and increased contact with persons from other nations and other religions, we have come to see that many people are sincere and ethical. That they should be condemned to such an awful fate simply because they have not heard of Christ is unacceptable to many Christians.

Theological. The traditional doctrine of the last things appears to conflict with other doctrines taught in Scripture. In particular, the love of God, as usually understood, seems hard to reconcile with the idea that large numbers of persons will be condemned to anguish with no hope of ever being delivered from such a state.

Philosophical. In a sense, this is an extension of the theological dimension. Analytic philosophers have seriously questioned whether the words used by theologians have any real meaning. If the idea of a "loving" God administering endless punishment does not call into question the meaning of divine love, what would? What does it mean to say God is "just" if he condemns multitudes who never had a chance to hear the name of Christ? What is the meaning of human responsibility if people are condemned for sins that they commit because they have inherited a sinful nature from Adam? If the theological challenge bears upon the truth of the concepts of the last things, then the philosophical challenge relates to the meaningfulness of those concepts.

Phenomenological. It has been widely assumed by Christians that the Christian religion is truly unique among world religions. Some students of world religions, however, find sufficient parallels within a number of other religions to cause them to wonder whether belief in such uniqueness can be maintained.

Ecclesiastical. The ecclesiastical argument has both a general point and a more specific point. The general point is that birthplace largely determines a person's religious beliefs. Thus, most Indians are Hindus, most Chinese are Buddhists, and most Arabs are Muslims. Even with respect to varieties of Christian belief, most Northern Europeans are Lutheran, most Southern Europeans are Catholic, and most residents of Utah are Mormons. The specific version of this is a practical argument. Christianity is not making much progress winning devotees of other world religions. Most of its converts are adherents of local religions rather than of major world religions. Indeed, some of these world religions are now beginning to evangelize, or proselytize, depending upon one's perspective, among Christians. Christianity, while growing, is not keeping pace with worldwide population growth. The world is becoming relatively less Christian all the time.

Exegetical. The study of several passages crucial for the traditional view has resulted in its modification. For example, the *textus classicus* for everlasting punishment has been Matthew 25:46, where "eternal punishment" parallels "eternal life." Some exegetes now say the result, not the process, of the punishment may be everlasting. It should be observed that in many cases, the motivation for renewed study of the passages has originated with one of these other considerations.

Varieties of Universalism

Let us now look briefly at several ways the traditional view is being modified. These are in effect varieties of universalism, and will give us the terminology of universalism with which to work.

The first view holds that there are many ways to be saved, or to obtain a proper relationship with God or with the supreme being of the universe. On this basis, not only those who consciously trust in Christ have salvation, but sincere adherents of Buddhism, Judaism, Hinduism, Islam, and other religions have alternative but equally valid routes to eternal life. In effect, the same God is being worshiped by these persons, whether they call him Yahweh, Brahma, or Allah. There is, in other words, a pluralism of religious truth. The role of Jesus Christ is not normative for all. It is not necessary to know Jesus or even necessary for people of other religions to be unwittingly reconciled to God through his saving work.

A second view says that Christianity is true and salvation is only through Christ, but more persons may actually be Christians than either they or others realize. This means that a person may trust in Christ without knowing his identity or the details of his life, or that the work of Christ is automatically effective in persons' lives, without their having to take action.

A third position says that conscious faith in Christ is required, but that all will indeed believe. One subclass of this view is optimistic about the success of the evangelistic and missionary endeavor, believing that the preaching of the gospel will meet with a universally affirmative response. Others hold that those who have not had a chance to believe during this life, or have had a chance but have not availed themselves of it, will be presented with the gospel in the life hereafter, and will then believe. A final subclass is the restorationist position, similar to that of Origen, which maintains that after a period of purging all will be fit to receive eternal life and will, of course, believe.

A final position is not really a species of universalism. It does not emphasize that all will be saved, but, rather, that none will be lost. It holds that all who survive will be saved. This view, commonly referred to as annihilationism, says that those who have not received eternal life will cease to exist, whether as a natural consequence of a nature that has no immortality, or because God will destroy them.

Twentieth-Century Developments

The twentieth century has been a period of greatly increased contact with other cultures, both directly through travel and immigration, and indirectly through new methods of communication, especially television. It has also been a period of rapidly accelerated sharing of theological scholarship.

Pluralism

The twentieth century has seen a growth in religious pluralism. One of the best-known early proponents of this approach was Wilfred Cantwell Smith. In recent years, probably the most outspoken advocate of pluralism has been John Hick. On a more popular level, the work of Paul F. Knitter, especially his book *No Other Name?*, has done much to draw attention to this movement.

It has not been lack of awareness of the traditional view that has resulted in these men coming to the positions they now hold. Hick underwent a conversion to orthodox or "born-again" Christianity and was involved in Inter-Varsity during his student days at the University of Edinburgh.[2] Knitter was a Roman Catholic missionary. For several reasons, however, they have come to the view that salvation, or at least a proper relationship with God, can be found within the several religions.

Hick's position can be summarized as follows:

1. Christianity is a minority religion and becoming more so. With only about one-fourth of the world's population Christian, it is also failing to keep pace with the population growth. In particular, it lacks success with adherents of other world religions.[3]
2. There is the problem of cultural relativity, although Hick does not use that term. He notes that the place where one is born strongly correlates with what one believes.[4] He therefore wonders about the justice and love of a God who would ordain that people be saved in a way that precludes the majority of people from such salvation.[5]

---

2. See John Hick, *God Has Many Names* (Philadelphia: Westminster, 1982), 13–19.

3. Ibid., 60–61; John Hick, *God and the Universe of Faiths: Essays in the Philosophy of Religion* (New York: St. Martin's, 1973), 138.

4. Hick, *God Has Many Names*, 61; Hick, *God and the Universe of Faiths*, 100, 132.

5. Hick, *God and the Universe of Faiths*, 122–23; Hick, *God Has Many Names*, 31.

3. The quality of religious faith and life in other religions indicates that Christianity does not have an exclusive claim to this. Measured by pragmatic standards, the religions are largely much the same.[6]

4. When analyzed phenomenologically, the same religious experiences are found in the several religions. Although the precise rituals, terminology, and songs may vary, they are more alike than had previously been thought and admitted.[7]

Knitter takes somewhat broader grounds for his arguments. His first consideration is philosophical. He assumes a "processive-relational" view of reality, in which everything is developing and becoming. This becoming is taking place through interrelating. The second starting point is sociology-psychology. As people move to a postconventional understanding of identity and morality, their values take on a more universalistic quality. This requires interacting with persons from other cultures. To be a good citizen of any nation requires being a good world citizen. Finally, Knitter works from a consideration of politics and economics. In a world in which geopolitics and worldwide economics have become realities, aggressive, egocentric activity by various religions cannot continue.[8]

These men, then, believe all religions make possible a proper relationship with God. It is, of course, possible to hold to pluralism without true universalism. Such a position would hold that one may be "saved" by any one of several religions, but that persons who are not religious at all are outside the scope of God's favor.

Universalistic Inclusivism

Universalistic inclusivism holds that salvation is through Christ, but the application of his work may be considerably broader than has been thought. Probably the sharpest reversal of thinking here can be seen in the twentieth-century Roman Catholic Church. The previous position of the church was that there not only was no salvation outside Christianity, but also no salvation outside the church. The church, through the sacraments, controlled and dispensed God's grace. A number of modifications of this strict view have taken place, however.

The Second Vatican Council broadened the understanding of the church and its membership. Thus, it spoke of degrees of membership

---

6. Hick, *God and the Universe of Faiths*, 130; cf. Eugene Hillman, *Many Faiths: A Catholic Approach to Religious Pluralism* (Maryknoll, N.Y.: Orbis, 1985), x.

7. Hick, *God Has Many Names*, 62–66.

8. Paul F. Knitter, *No Other Name? A Critical Survey of Christian Attitudes toward the World Religions* (Maryknoll, N.Y.: Orbis, 1985), 9–13.

in the church. Catholics are fully incorporated into the church. Other Christians, who at one time were considered heretics and schismatics and then later were "separated brethren," are seen as linked to the church. And other religious persons are understood as "related" to the church. Thus all may, in varying degrees, participate in the benefits that Christ accomplished for his church.[9]

A second aspect of this softened attitude is found in Karl Rahner's concept of the "anonymous Christian." Anonymous Christians are people who do not have an explicit, overt, or conscious Christian faith. So far as others know, or as they themselves know, they are not Christians. Yet they are actually Christians and participate in God's grace.[10]

There are Protestant versions of universalistic inclusivism as well. One is the idea of universally effective redemption, found in the later writings of Karl Barth, although he was careful to avoid acknowledging universalism. According to this view, Christ did indeed reconcile all persons to God through his death, so all do receive that benefit. The view takes such texts as Romans 5:18–19, 1 Corinthians 15:22, and 2 Corinthians 5:19 quite literally. All have actually been reconciled, but may not be aware of it; they therefore may not be experiencing fully the benefits of the death of Christ.[11] This is coupled with a view of election in which God has elected Christ, and, with him, all of humanity.[12] While interest in Barth's theology has declined in broader circles, a number of evangelicals have shown increased interest in him, so we may expect some heightened influence of this view in evangelical circles.[13]

One other development that falls in this general classification is the growing interest in what may be termed "implicit faith." This is the concept that through general or natural revelation some may come to faith in Christ without knowing the details of that faith, simply by casting themselves upon the mercy of God. Hints of this are found in Romans 1:19–20 and 2:14–16. While there have been evangelical theo-

---

9. "Dogmatic Constitution on the Church," in *The Documents of Vatican II*, ed. Walter M. Abbott (New York: Herder & Herder, 1966), 30–35, sects. 13–16.

10. Karl Rahner, *Theological Investigations* (Baltimore: Helicon, 1969), 4:390–98.

11. Karl Barth, *The Humanity of God* (Richmond: John Knox, 1960), 60–62.

12. Karl Barth, *Church Dogmatics*, trans. Geoffrey W. Bromiley (Edinburgh: T. & T. Clark, 1957), 2.2.145–81.

13. Bernard Ramm, *After Fundamentalism: The Future of Evangelical Theology* (New York: Harper & Row, 1983); Richard Quebedeaux, *The Worldly Evangelicals* (New York: Harper & Row, 1978), 152. Donald Bloesch shows great interest in Barth. In fact, there are more references to Barth in the first volume of his *Essentials of Evangelical Theology* than to any other theologian except Luther. Although Bloesch is close to Barth's view of election, he rejects the universalistic implications of Barth's view. See *Essentials of Evangelical Theology* (New York: Harper & Row, 1978), 1:166–69.

logians who have held this interpretation, they have generally maintained that relatively few would be saved through that means. This explains Paul's plea in Romans 10:14–17 for people to preach the gospel, while again seemingly alluding to others outside the covenant who may come to know God (vv. 18–21). There may be a growing sense of confidence in the extent of this general revelation becoming efficacious, although unless this were universally effective, we would not have true universalism.[14]

Universalistic Exclusivism

A third position, universalistic exclusivism, holds that all will come to God through conscious trust in Christ. It seems unlikely that many today would hold that the gospel is universally effective, since the declining percentage of Christians in the world is one reason for persons moving to the broader positions (such as inclusivism or pluralism). There are indications, however, of a growing interest in the idea of an opportunity for belief in Christ after this life. While this has often been referred to as the doctrine of a second chance, some are simply advocating that those who have not had a first chance to believe in this life will have such a chance after this life. Thus, although not universalism, this position has a universalizing tendency.

One evangelical who has recently declared himself in support of such a view is Clark H. Pinnock. Pinnock not only sees a potential for considerable efficacy in general revelation,[15] but he also believes that "the unevangelized are given an opportunity to encounter Jesus Christ as Savior after death if not before it."[16] This, he says, is required by logic. It is also supported by some biblical texts that refer to a proclamation of the gospel after death, notably 1 Peter 3:19–20 and 4:6.[17] This is not universalism and should not be stretched to become that, because there are simply too many biblical references to judgment and destruction of the wicked.[18] Yet this argument has a stronger universalist bent than the traditional view, because even some whom the enemy had thought were securely his are taken from him.

14. Bruce Demarest, *General Revelation: Historical Views and Contemporary Issues* (Grand Rapids: Zondervan, 1982), 253–62; James N. D. Anderson, *Christianity and World Religions: The Challenge of Pluralism* (Leicester: Inter-Varsity, 1984), chap. 5. On this topic, see the remarks of David K. Clark, "Is Special Revelation Necessary for Salvation?" in this volume (bibliography in n. 7 of Clark's chapter).

15. Clark Pinnock, "The Finality of Jesus Christ in a World of Religions," in *Christian Faith and Practice in the Modern World: Theology from an Evangelical Point of View,* ed. Mark A. Noll and David F. Wells (Grand Rapids: Eerdmans, 1988), 160–64.

16. Ibid., 165.

17. Ibid.; Clark Pinnock, "Review of *Jesus: The Death and Resurrection of God,* by Donald G. Dawe," in *TSF Bulletin* 10 (Mar.–Apr. 1987): 35.

18. Pinnock, "Finality of Jesus Christ," 167.

Annihilationism

There is a final option that seems to be growing in popularity among evangelicals. This is the idea that, even though not all persons will be saved, those who do not come to salvation will not experience endless, painful punishment. Their punishment is extinction, whether at death or at some point in the future, after a sufficient punishment.

Among evangelicals who espouse such a view are John Stott and Clark Pinnock.[19] Stott finds the concept of eternal, conscious torment emotionally intolerable, but as an evangelical cannot settle the issue on the basis of emotions.[20] There must rather be biblical and theological reasons, and he finds several.

1. The terminology of killing, destruction, and the like suggests termination, not perpetuation of existence.
2. The imagery of fire suggests destruction or consumption of persons, not endless suffering.
3. Justice seems to require that there be a finite duration to the punishment for finite sin, unless the impenitence continues throughout eternity. Otherwise, the "eye for an eye" principle would seem to be violated.
4. The eternal existence of rebellious, impenitent individuals conflicts with God's ultimate triumph over evil. The texts often used to support universalism teach God's complete and final victory over evil and the final submission of all things to the Lord (John 12:32; 1 Cor. 15:28; Eph. 1:10; Phil. 2:10–11; Col. 1:20).[21] Such victory suggests that all rebellion must be eliminated in order to restore cosmic harmony.

It appears that there will be growing controversy over this issue in evangelical circles, with much of the discussion centering upon the meaning of the biblical terms and concepts. Edward Fudge, for

---

19. John R. W. Stott, "Judgement and Hell," in David L. Edwards and John R. W. Stott *Evangelical Essentials: A Liberal-Evangelical Dialogue* (Downers Grove, Ill.: Inter-Varsity, 1988), 312–29; Clark Pinnock, "Fire, Then Nothing," *Christianity Today* 31/5 (20 Mar. 1987): 40–41. Interestingly, Pinnock's theology provides three possibilities for those who have not heard the gospel explicitly during their lifetime: efficacious general revelation, a hearing of the gospel after death, and extinction for those who still do not believe. Pinnock explicitly rejects pluralism ("Finality of Jesus Christ," 156–57) and more extreme extensions of the inclusivist position as posited by Rahner (or Rahner's interpreters? See "Finality of Jesus Christ," 164–65). Scot McKnight ("Eternal Consequences or Eternal Consciousness?") and Timothy R. Phillips ("Hell: A Christological Reflection") examine Stott's and Pinnock's views in some detail (both in this volume).

20. Stott, "Judgement and Hell," 314–15.

21. Stott, however, cannot accept universalism as a viable option.

example, has written a lengthy treatise on annihilationism, which concentrates largely upon the biblical terminology and imagery.[22] Some denominations, which in other respects are considered evangelical, hold to some form of annihilationism, and debate on this point broke out in the Consultation on Evangelical Affirmations in May 1989. There are varieties of annihilationism, some of them resting upon a view that humans do not possess the power of surviving death, unless such is specially granted to them. Pinnock, for example, believes that the traditional view depends upon an understanding of the human soul as immortal—an understanding that is Greek, not biblical, in origin.[23] He also sees this as a necessary bulwark against universalism. If the traditional view of hell as endless torment is the alternative to universalism, then "universalism will become practically irresistible in its appeal to sensitive Christians. . . . If the only options are everlasting torment and universalism, then I would expect large numbers of sensitive Christians to choose universalism."[24]

Related Theological Issues

Theology is organic. Its doctrines are interrelated. The stance taken on one doctrine definitely affects the construction of others. The discussion of the fate of those who have never heard will involve extensive treatment of a number of other important theological issues.

1. The nature of God. What really is the character of divine love and divine justice?
2. The nature of the human. Do human beings have a permanence or eternality, conferred upon them by God, so that they will live on eternally, regardless of whether they receive salvation?
3. General revelation. How much can be known about God from nature and human personality? Can it enable people to enter a saving relationship with God?
4. Sin. What is the nature, extent, and effect of original sin? Does it attach to each person from birth and result in condemnation, apart from any conscious personal sin by the individual? Does it sufficiently cloud the understanding to prevent sinners from knowing God adequately from general revelation?
5. Salvation. Is salvation a forensic justification based upon the work of Christ, which Hick believes to be the underlying issue

22. Edward William Fudge, *The Fire That Consumes* (Houston: Providential, 1982).
23. Pinnock, "Fire, Then Nothing," 40–41. See also Carl F. H. Henry, "Is It Fair?" in this volume.
24. Pinnock, "Fire, Then Nothing," 40.

in the exclusivist position? What is the nature of faith? Specifically, how much must be known and believed about Christ for one to exercise saving faith in him?

6. Christ. Is Jesus the unique and only incarnation of God?
7. Authority. What is the relative place of the biblical revelation and of emotional considerations in determining what doctrine will be held and taught?
8. Hermeneutics. If two concepts, both of which appear to be taught by Scripture, logically entail a third concept that seems to conflict with Scripture, how does one proceed? To what extent do the implications of ideas affect the validity of those ideas?
9. Presuppositions. What is the role of philosophical and other presuppositions underlying the interpretations of Scripture that have led to certain theological conceptions? For example, is the idea of the immortality of the soul a Greek imposition upon Scripture, and what contemporary presuppositions may determine the opposite view, such as functionalism, behaviorism, and materialism?
10. Worldview. What is the nature of reality, and of the relationship of space and time, matter and the immaterial, to one another and to eternity and infinity?
11. The church. To what extent is the ministry of the church affected by the conclusions drawn here, especially in the areas of missions and evangelism, as well as discipleship and counseling?

The fate of "those who have never heard" is an issue facing everyone, not merely theologians or missionaries in far-off places. This question, with its corollary ideas of universalism and annihilationism, touches most of the major doctrines of the Christian faith. Because evangelicalism has historically identified itself with the exclusivist position, a move away from such a stance would significantly alter its character. The wide-ranging discussions in the remainder of this book are, therefore, timely and important.

2

Is Special Revelation
Necessary for Salvation?

David K. Clark

In many Sunday evening youth group discussions and late-night
college dorm sessions, Christians have raised this question: "What
happens to those who haven't heard about Jesus Christ?" This
pressing objection to traditional Christianity revolves around a nonnegotiable evangelical claim: only by knowing Jesus Christ can one be
rightly related to God. But what about those who, purely by geographical or historical accident, have lived in cultures where not even one
person has heard about Jesus? Do they have any chance of a right relation to God? In this chapter we will examine not the exegetical aspects
of this question, but its logical structure.

Unpacking the Problem

The problem of assessing the fate of non-Christians arises at the
intersection of several claims:

1. God desires all persons to have an opportunity to experience
   salvation. (We assume that if God desires something, he does
   whatever he can to bring that thing about.)

2. If one is to experience salvation, it can only be by knowing Christ.
3. If one is to know Christ, it can only be by coming in contact with special revelation (for evangelicals, this generally means Christ himself or the Bible).[1]
4. God is powerful enough to see to it that everyone comes in contact with special revelation.
5. Not all persons in human history have had contact with special revelation.

Unless we accept the disputed idea of "middle knowledge,"[2] these five statements cannot all be true; at least one of them is false. Evangelicals consider (2) nonnegotiable although some liberals cast it aside, and they accept (4) although it is regularly doubted by process theologians. Given the evangelical view of special revelation, (5) is true. So while some undoubtedly live with the tension, those evangelicals who have resolved the dilemma must do so by denying (1) or (3). Either they claim that God does not desire to save all persons or they suggest that knowledge about God through modes of revelation other than Christ or the Bible can provide sufficient knowledge for the Holy Spirit to elicit saving faith.

The Context of the Question

In the current debate swirling around the claim that Christ is the only way to God, four distinct positions have been advocated. *Exclusivism* maintains the traditional ideal that only one religion enables contact with God. For Christians, this has historically meant the affirmation of position 2.

1. Some people might want to include other God-given experiences as legitimate modes of special revelation. Examples might include angelic visitations, impressions, dreams, visions, or other revelational experiences. We can allow for modifications in what counts as "special revelation." These do not alter the structure of my argument as long as we continue to hold that not all people have had contact with special revelation (point 5).
2. All five points could be true if God has "middle knowledge," i.e., if God knows infallibly what all people would freely do in every possible set of circumstances. If God knows this, he could anticipate all those who would freely accept Christ if only they received special revelation and then guarantee that those persons at least get special revelation. The others who would not have responded in faith would not receive special revelation; God knows that giving it to them would be pointless. In this case, points 1 to 5 could all be true. For a statement of this middle knowledge option, see William Craig, "'No Other Name': A Middle Knowledge Perspective on the Exclusivity of Salvation Through Christ," *Faith and Philosophy* 6 (Apr. 1989): 172–88. Middle knowledge has some assertive opponents; see Bruce Reichenbach, *Evil and a Good God* (New York: Fordham University Press, 1982), 14–16, 69–74; Robert Adams, "Middle Knowledge and the Problem of Evil," *American Philosophical Quarterly* 14 (Apr. 1977): 109–17.

Inclusivism holds that while only one religion is true, followers of other faiths who sincerely practice their own religion—even if they overtly reject the true one—can be saved because they are really covert followers of the one true faith. Although several prominent theologians hold this position, inclusivism is generally illustrated by Karl Rahner's "anonymous Christian" thesis. Simply put, Rahner tries to retain an exclusive claim about Christianity while acknowledging the possibility of salvation through other religions—even for those who overtly reject Christ.

Pluralism suggests that world religions are all culturally bound expressions of genuine contact with the divine. Potentially all faiths are equally "true," so sincere believers in any religion can be rightly related to the Ultimate. Pluralists are led by John Hick, who is being joined by a growing troop of followers.

Relativism argues that we simply have no way to decide matters of religious "truth" (if there even is such a thing). Contrary to the pluralists' opinions, relativism is in fact the alternative to exclusivism. Pluralists must reveal, usually at more general levels of thought, a commitment to claims they must embrace as exclusively true. For example, pluralists are exclusive in the debate between exclusivism and pluralism. They believe (exclusively) that exclusivism is wrong and pluralism is right. Again, in the dispute between irreligion and religion, they believe (exclusively) that the former is wrong and the latter is right. It is the relativists who believe in no exclusive truth and who occupy the farthest pole from exclusivism.[3]

In the context of these views, the question of special revelation and salvation is relevant only within exclusivism. Obviously, for pluralists and relativists, no one particular set of religious ideas could take priority over another as the vehicle of apprehending the divine. For them, the question is meaningless. Even in inclusivism, although it maintains a priority of one world faith over others, sincere followers of other religions can be saved. So inclusivism affirms emphatically that what evangelicals call natural revelation can suffice for salvation. Only within the conceptual framework of exclusivism does the problem of special revelation arise.

Another part of the context arises from differing views of special revelation. Revelation is the God-initiated act of self-unveiling. Special revelation has two connotations for evangelicals. It can mean the divine self-expression that is intended for a particular group of people (the elect) or a supernatural, miraculous sort. With either connotation, the

---

3. See David K. Clark and Norman L. Geisler, *Apologetics in the New Age: A Christian Critique of Pantheism* (Grand Rapids: Baker, 1990), 185–202.

critical issue for evangelicals is that revelation is conceived to be, at least in part, a source of information about God and his call to faith. Traditionally, Christians have believed that a mentally capable person cannot experience saving faith without this information. (Presumably, those mentally incapable of understanding the gospel—children and the severely retarded—are mercifully saved by God despite their ignorance.)

In contrast to special revelation stands general or natural revelation, a more unfocused and rudimentary form of God's self-unveiling. Those who emphasize that special revelation is intended only for the elect contrast it to general revelation, which is intended for all humans. Others choose to contrast special revelation with natural revelation, the self-unveiling that comes through nonmiraculous means like nature, conscience, or providence.

For Karl Barth and many of his existentially oriented theological relatives, however, special revelation has quite a different connotation. For them, it has no informational function. Special revelation is not at all a communication of information about God; it is communion with God himself. Barth vehemently rejects both natural theology and natural revelation. But many neo-orthodox thinkers who acknowledge with Emil Brunner the existence of natural revelation still deny the informational dimension of "propositional revelation" (that is, informational revelation in the form of cognitive statements). In neo-orthodoxy, special revelation is the experience of personal relationship with God, of a person-to-person, I-Thou "encounter."

If this view of revelation is correct, my title question must be answered affirmatively. Revelation is God coming to me, meeting me face to face, and hearing from me a response of faith. Revelation can be found only where this intimate, subjective, and personal response to God takes place. Is special revelation, that personal, one-on-one meeting with God, necessary for salvation? Of course it is. In a sense, it *is* salvation. Clearly, the question is not an issue for those who work within a neo-orthodox framework.

Liberal conceptions of revelation, on the other hand, imply a negative answer to the problem. Here revelation is generally conceived to be the insights of great religious geniuses. The very idea of a special revelation from God is diluted if not eliminated. An exclusive, historically based revelation is a scandal to the liberal mentality with its sometimes sentimental view of God's inclusive love and grace. Rather than basing theology on a conceptually meaningful special revelation to which only some persons have access, it is better, say liberals, to ground religion in a universal human experience of morality or reason. This move deliberately places the Buddha's or Muhammad's "revelations" in the same league, if not on a level playing field, with biblical revelation. Within these categories, special revelation has no prominent place. Is special revelation, the unique, authoritative divine self-disclosure in

Christ, necessary for salvation? Of course not; no such revelation exists. Clearly the question is not an issue for those with a liberal mind set. In sum, the question I am analyzing is meaningful only for those working with the traditional categories accepted by evangelicals.

The Traditional Reformed View

Since they assume a special revelation with an informational function, how have evangelicals answered our question? Under the influence of the Reformation, the tendency has been to reject point 1, that is, to deny that God desires all persons to have an opportunity to experience salvation. Although Calvin has a rich understanding of the light available to everyone through general revelation, he also argues that the nonelect are completely blinded to this light by finitude and sin.[4] What he gives with one hand, therefore, he removes with the other. A person without special revelation simply cannot be saved. This approach could be called the traditional Reformed view.

Obvious objections harass this position. Morally and biblically, it seems that God should want to save as many as possible. If God is able to give at least the opportunity for salvation to all (because he is powerful enough to do so), and special revelation is necessary to that goal, then a high priority for the divine plan through the ages should be, it seems, the dissemination of the information contained in that revelation. Yet God has not done this. The only reason could be that God has not really willed for all to be saved. In this position, point 1 is deemed false.

But what of the moral principle that persons should be condemned only for failing to do what they know is right and are able to do (or for doing what they know is wrong and are able to avoid)? The saying, *Ignorance is no excuse,* applies only in cases where a person *ought to know* the law and through culpable negligence does not. When the state patrol officer stops me for speeding, I cannot get off the hook by saying, "Gee, I didn't know the speed limit was 55 mph." I am responsible to know that; if I do not, I am guilty of negligence. When a person is innocently ignorant, however, we normally assume that ignorance *is* a valid excuse. Most people think it unjust to convict people on the basis of a law of which they were innocently ignorant.

The argument Paul makes in Romans 1:18–23 supports this line of thought. He does not argue, "Those who do not have the law of spe-

---

4. John Calvin, *Institutes of the Christian Religion,* ed. John T. McNeil, trans. Ford Lewis Battles (Philadelphia: Westminster, 1960), 1.4.4; 1.5.13–15. See also Charles Hodge, *Systematic Theology,* 3 vols. (Grand Rapids: Eerdmans, 1952), 2:646; William T. Shedd, *Dogmatic Theology,* 3 vols. (Nashville: Nelson, 1980), 1:67; Carl F. H. Henry, *God, Revelation and Authority,* 6 vols. (Waco, Tex.: Word, 1976), 2:86.

cial revelation are entirely ignorant of God's law. But that's too bad. Ignorance of the law is no excuse. They will be condemned anyway." Rather, his point is precisely that no one is ignorant of the law: "Those who do not have the law of special revelation know God's law through natural revelation. Ignorance is irrelevant here; no one is ignorant. They will be condemned for failing to live up to what they do know." In fact, anyone who believes that God saves all children too young to understand the Bible implicitly accepts this principle.

Those who solve the problem by denying point 1 generally respond by saying that the light of general revelation provides people with a knowledge of God sufficient to condemn them. This is exactly what Paul says in Romans 1:20: "So . . . [humans] are without excuse." But, it is argued, while general revelation is enough to damn humans because they are no longer innocently ignorant, it is not enough to save them.

This response sticks closely to what Paul concludes explicitly. All Paul really says about the effects of natural revelation in Romans 1:18–23 is that it renders rebellious humans without excuse before God. He is silent as to whether there exist humans who are not permanently rebellious, but who have responded positively by God's enabling grace to the glimmers of light they have seen in natural revelation.[5] General revelation might help people like these if there are any. Those who deny point 1 fill Paul's silence by assuming that all humans who have not received special revelation must be included in the category of permanently rebellious humans who are without excuse. Of course, others might fill Paul's silence by assuming that the category of those who are without excuse is not filled with absolutely all humans without special revelation, but by all those involved in "godlessness and wickedness . . . who suppress the truth by their wickedness" (v. 18).

If one admits with Calvin that our God of love does not desire some to be saved, a critical implication follows: if natural revelation can justly damn, but never save, then those who receive no special revelation are condemned for failing to do something they cannot do. God expects them to do the impossible (to exercise faith in Christ) and then condemns them eternally for failing to do it. This is described as "just" because those who are so condemned actively rebelled against God (it was all they *could* do) and were duly warned of the consequences of that rebellion (they were not innocently ignorant).

The claim that natural revelation renders one without excuse but cannot save is not required by Romans 1:18–23, although it is consistent with it. Romans 1:18–23 is also consistent with the claim that natural revelation fails to bring salvation to those who are rebellious

---

5. This issue is discussed in this volume in greater detail by Aída Besançon Spencer, "Romans 1: Finding God in Creation," esp. n. 32.

and wicked, but potentially leads to salvation for those who respond to it. Romans 1:18–23 is therefore circumstantial evidence for the traditional Reformed view. And those who find it demonstrative do so because they assume on some other ground that only those with special revelation can be saved. This is principle 3. And when this is assumed, point 1 must give way, and so logic forces Reformed theologians to deny that God wills or desires to save all. In this view, when Paul speaks of those who are condemned, yet without excuse, he includes every person who has received no special revelation.

The Universalist Alternative

One way to evade these problems is to deny point 5, which says that not all persons have had contact with special revelation. You could logically hold (1), which affirms God's desire to save all, and (3), which says that special revelation of Christ is necessary to salvation, if you deny (5), that is, if you believe that God gives special revelation to all humans either in this life or the next. Many universalists take this approach. Barth implies a view something like this with his claim that all are elect in Christ, the Elected One, although he pleads the Fifth Amendment on the question of universalism.[6] What could be more logical than Reformed universalism: God both sovereignly elects all who are saved and sovereignly elects all to be saved?

Holding that God gives special revelation to all, however, does not entail that one is a universalist. God could give special revelation to all, and yet some might reject its saving message and be justly cast out of God's presence. All that is required here, to blunt the basic objection about God's justice, is simply that each person have an opportunity (whether through natural or special revelation) to respond to God's promptings. God need not save everyone to be just, but the moral principle of distributive justice (that is, justice as fairness) does seem to require that each one have a genuine opportunity to be saved (if any at all are given this chance). As attractive as universalism is, however, it flies in the face of too much biblical evidence to be a viable option for evangelicals.

The Implicit-Faith View

Some evangelicals have solved this dilemma by denying point 3, which asserts that the only way to know Jesus Christ is to come into contact with special revelation. They believe that information sufficient for salvation can be found outside special revelation. This position could be called the implicit-faith view.

---

6. Karl Barth, *The Humanity of God* (Richmond, Va.: John Knox, 1960), 61–62.

In this approach, people in a culture that has no contact with Christ or the Bible see through nature that a God exists and through conscience that they are out of touch with him. Although they know nothing of Christ specifically, God prompts them to cast themselves into his hands for safekeeping. They are saved just as any other people are saved: through God's gracious action on behalf of those who are moved by God to call on divine mercy for rescue. They are saved *objectively* on the basis of Christ's work of atonement; they are saved *subjectively* in that God elicits a faith response to the glimmer of light in natural revelation. It is true both that it is only through Jesus Christ they are saved (that is, [2] is true) and that they have no conceptual knowledge about Christ (that is, [3] is false).

Clarifying an ambiguity in (2) and (3) will help. Both use the phrase *knowing Christ*. People must know, that is, have a personal relation to God in Christ, if they are to be saved. But they do not need to *know about* (that is, have their own mental awareness of) Christ if they are to be saved. They are in right personal relation to God only because of the necessary objective reality of the cross, but their own intellectual grasp of the historical event by which they benefit is nil. Since they do not *know about* Christ, their faith in Christ is real, but implicit. In fact, these people may differ only a little from sincere but theologically ignorant Christians whose comprehension of the meaning and details of the atonement is nil. Despite their intellectual deficiencies, they are marvelously saved by God's grace.

The implicit-faith view differs from relativism and pluralism in that it maintains exclusivistically the necessity of Christ's objective work. It differs from inclusivism—and this is critical—in that it does not claim that a person who has heard of Christ and who overtly rejects him is a believer. The principle of being saved through natural revelation applies only to those who have not heard of Christ. Upon hearing about him, those who have implicit faith in Christ immediately proclaim, "This is the one we have been following all along." When those who implicitly follow Jesus Christ actually hear about him, they respond immediately and positively. If they do not, this suggests that real faith has not yet taken root in their lives.

Several evangelicals have taken this kind of view. Augustus H. Strong, who thought Socrates might have been saved, advocated this position, as have Millard Erickson and Clark Pinnock. James I. Packer thinks it possible.[7] C. S. Lewis maintains that, "the truth is God has not told us what His arrangements about the other people are. We do

7. Augustus H. Strong, *Systematic Theology: A Compendium*, 3 vols. (Old Tappan, N.J.: Revell, 1907), 3:842–44; Millard J. Erickson, "Hope for Those Who Haven't Heard? Yes, But . . .," *Evangelical Missions Quarterly* 11 (Apr. 1975): 122–26; Clark Pinnock, "The

know that no man can be saved except through Christ; we do not know that only those who know Him can be saved through Him."[8] His words suggest the implicit-faith view although they are cryptic enough to be compatible with inclusivism. It is too much to read a specific theory from his novel, *The Last Battle,* where Aslan, the Christ symbol, claims for himself all who sincerely worshiped the false God, Tash.[9]

How many persons will find Christ through natural revelation? Will it be dozens or billions? Among those who hold the implicit-faith view, some see the cup as half-empty, some as half-full. Pinnock says, "I do not know how many, but I hope for multitudes,"[10] and Lewis would probably agree. Strong says that "the number is so small as in no degree to weaken the claims of the missionary enterprise upon us."[11] Erickson and Packer are even more skeptical than Strong. The point is, however, that some can potentially be saved, based on the atonement of Jesus Christ, through the information content of natural revelation. This view solves the dilemma by denying, not God's willingness to save all, but the necessity of gaining the informational content for salvation from special revelation.

A Major Objection

Evangelicals can find plenty of objections to the implicit-faith view. A critical objection is that this view dilutes the urgency of the call to missionary service. Why challenge all obstacles to present the gospel about Christ to those who otherwise would not hear if that message is not necessary for salvation? Strong's claim represents one immediate response: so few are saved in this way as to make the theoretical possibility of salvation without special revelation practically irrelevant.

But consider the assumption on which this objection stands. It assumes that the missionary mandate applies to me only in cases where my neighbor has *no other means* of gaining the information necessary to salvation. It assumes that *if* my neighbors (either across the street or across the sea) can possibly know about Christ in some way other than by my telling them, then I am not responsible to tell them about Christ. But that is patently false. My neighbors have lots of ways to hear. The Johnsons, the Rabinowitzes, the Roses, and the Beckers

---

Finality of Jesus Christ in a World of Religions," in *Christian Faith and Practice in the Modern World: Theology from an Evangelical Point of View,* ed. Mark A. Noll and David F. Wells (Grand Rapids: Eerdmans, 1988), 152–68; James I. Packer, "'Good Pagans' and God's Kingdom," *Christianity Today* 30/1 (17 Jan. 1986): 22–25.

8. C. S. Lewis, *Mere Christianity* (New York: Macmillan, 1960), 65.

9. C. S. Lewis, *The Last Battle* (New York: Macmillan, 1956), 164–65.

10. Pinnock, "Finality of Jesus Christ," 164.

11. Strong, *Systematic Theology,* 3:843.

can all see D. James Kennedy on television, attend a Billy Graham meeting, receive a tract from Campus Crusade for Christ, hear James Dobson on the radio, or see God in nature and their own consciences. These facts in no way absolve me of responsibility for telling them about Christ in a winsome, appropriate manner. Similarly, that my neighbors across the sea might see God in nature or hear him in conscience in no way absolves me of my responsibilities toward them.

The Real Issue

The real issue between the traditional Reformed view and the implicit-faith view revolves around broader theological commitments. These commitments run on two continuums: one between God's transcendence and immanence and the other between human sinfulness and godlikeness. For those accustomed to Reformed modes of thinking, the need to maximize the distance between God and human beings leads to stressing the transcendence and sinfulness poles, a depreciation of general revelation, and a skittishness about any human involvement in the process of salvation. These emphases spin a web of beliefs that inevitably lead to a denial of point 1.

The downside in this web of beliefs involves trying to answer several thorny problems. How could God create human beings whom he presumably loves and then use them *only* to display the divine glory through their damnation? Does it make sense to say that God gives the damned enough light through general revelation to render them without excuse (and so to bring it about such that it is their fault they are damned) when the light of general revelation is not sufficient for them to be anything but damned, and when the God who can give them special revelation will not lift a finger on their behalf? These are weighty questions, and commitment to this web of beliefs greatly complicates the apologetic task. These problems are difficult to resolve. Indeed many simply dodge them by appealing to mystery. At the same time, certain notions of the sovereignty, greatness, and majesty of God are in some sense enhanced by this mode of thought, and this advantage appears to some to be great enough to make the apologetic difficulties it raises worth shouldering.

For those attracted to the implicit-faith view, these apologetic burdens are too heavy to bear. They believe it is better to admit a richer sense of the godlikeness of the human person (because of the image of God) and a fuller understanding of the immanence of God through his action in the world. (These can be affirmed while retaining a robust respect for sin and the total inability of humans to save themselves.) By acknowledging that God desires to save all and provides everyone with an opportunity to be saved, this view frees Christian evangelists from crossing the hurdles implicit in the traditional

Reformed view. In this way, it could actually contribute to evangelistic fervor in that the message being shared is more reasonable.

The drawback of this network of beliefs, however, must be faced squarely. Those who feel drawn to the traditional Reformed view fear too much emphasis on human godlikeness and divine immanence. These themes threaten to place God and human beings on the same plane. Closing the gap between the divine and human carries the risks of both a reduction in the sense of God's sovereign majesty and an increase in the human participation in salvation. Now it is by no means logically necessary, as even Packer admits,[12] that the implicit-faith view compromises God's absolute sovereignty and the totally gracious character of salvation. Yet it is surely true that the strength of the traditional Reformed view lies in its stout defense of these ideas.

It goes beyond the purpose of this chapter to argue fully for either of these views. My purpose has been to lay out the logical relations between them. One could wonder why the Scripture says relatively little about the subject. It is due, no doubt, to the fact that for those reading Scripture, the possibility of their being saved without Scripture is a moot point. Biblical authors were not much interested in debating a speculative point.

Some evangelical authors have opted for the traditional Reformed view and others for the implicit-faith view. It is the broader theological stance a person chooses that determines this decision. To affirm both (1) and (3), to believe both that God desires all to be saved and that special revelation is necessary for salvation, puts several fundamental theological principles (namely, the omnipotence of God and the finality of Christ's work) under siege. To protect these, we are forced to give up either (1) or (3). But my responsibility to participate in God's great plan of evangelism is logically independent of my choice between these two options. Either way, I am to make disciples as I go into all the world.

12. Packer, "'Good Pagans' and God's Kingdom," 25.

3

Hell: A Christological Reflection

Timothy R. Phillips

B illions have had no opportunity to hear the gospel. Traditionally, Christians have taught that the destiny of these unfortunate people is eternal punishment in hell. It is no surprise, therefore, that within the history of theology three alternatives to the classical doctrine of hell have developed: revisionist eschatology, universalism, and annihilationism. This chapter first establishes the theological significance of hell by showing that each option subverts the definitive work of Christ, and then develops the classical notion of hell.

Revisionist Eschatology

For much of the contemporary theological world, it is not hell, but a personal life after death that is anachronistic. The outcome of the Enlightenment's insistence that the secular establishes the parameters for interpreting revelation is revisionist Christianity. Even Jesus' bodily resurrection is abandoned: "It is no longer necessary for Christians to concern themselves with old myths purporting to give special *gnōsis* in regard to life beyond the grave."[1] As a result, these theologians under-

---

1. Gordon D. Kaufman, *Systematic Theology: A Historicist Perspective* (New York: Scribner, 1968), 471, 468.

stand heaven and hell as a mythological expression of first-century faith, not God's revelation.

For the evangelical, however, the structures of history cannot confine Christ's kingly work. God, who ought to be reigning as King over an obedient creation, incarnated himself in Jesus Christ to reverse the fall and its tragic consequences. Jesus demonstrated in his own person that kingdom realities had invaded history and changed its destiny (Matt. 12:28–29). Christ "disarmed the powers and authorities" (Col. 2:15); Jesus now reigns as Lord, awaiting the consummation. At that time, Christ will bring these eschatological realities to completion. All enemies will be conquered; all humanity will be raised to answer to Christ, the final Judge (Matt. 25:31–46; John 5:24–29; 1 Cor. 15:20-28; Eph. 1:22). Life after death is indeed a reality because Christ's kingly work has established this future.

Universalism

Universalism's vision of salvation for all has proved attractive in our pluralistic and humanistic age. It generally builds on two assumptions.[2] First, God's infinite love is necessarily and eternally directed to all. Anything less, it is argued, is not the love of Christ. Second, free finite agents cannot eternally resist God's infinite power of reconciling love. Admittedly, not everyone gains a loving communion with God during this life and some must pass through purgatory, where they are slowly transformed through remedial punishments into the image of Christ. The New Testament authors, claims the universalist, display the same confidence in God's omnipotent love when they envision all creation being reconciled (Col. 1:20) "so that God may be all in all" (1 Cor. 15:28).

But the universalist argument is one-sided, undercutting Jesus' prophetic work as the revelation of God. For the same Jesus who seeks out social outcasts also warns of retributive punishments: "When the Son of Man comes in his glory, . . . he will say to those on his left, 'Depart from me, you who are cursed, into the eternal fire prepared for the devil and his angels. . . .' Then they will go away to eternal punishment" (Matt. 25:31, 41, 46). Does this represent a necessary and eternal love? Universalists often respond that Jesus' statements reflect his cultural context, not his creative genius; or that these are conditional statements intended to deter, not teach. But such disclaimers

---

2. Modern defenses of universalism include Friedrich Schleiermacher, *The Christian Faith*, ed. Hugh R. Mackintosh and J. S. Stewart (Edinburgh: T. & T. Clark, 1928), §163; John Hick, *Death and Eternal Life* (London: Macmillan, 1976); John A. T. Robinson, *In the End, God* (London: James Clarke, 1950).

make Jesus either ignorant of God's moral character or guilty of intentionally misleading his hearers. Moreover, concessions of this sort assume that modern insights determine the legitimacy of Christ's statements.

Why is universalism unable to accept the totality of Christ's prophetic work? The answer lies in its reconception of God's love. Certainly, God is love. But Christ's revelation of the nature of God's love diverges from the universalist portrayal in three ways. First, universalists assume that the Godhead *must* have a saving love toward the world. But when Jesus boldly proclaimed the presence of the kingdom of God, he was not providing insight into an immanent law of history. He was announcing God's unique supernatural intervention in him alone (John 14:6). The particularity of this act, in fact, illustrates the freeness of God's salvific work and thus the reality of grace.[3]

Second, universalism's hypothesis of a future purgation assumes that God's universal love is eternal. But Jesus' sharp contrast between this age and the next, when the final judgment for the deeds of this life occurs, hardly permits this. The *offer* of God's saving love is not eternal, but limited to this life. That is why Jesus stresses the urgency of the present (Matt. 25:13; Mark 13:32–37). To take as axiomatic God's eternal pursuit of the sinner, once again, subverts the finality of Christ's revelation.

Finally, universalism's contention that God's love for us is necessary and eternal assumes that humanity is the highest intrinsic good, even for God. God must endlessly pursue reconciliation with every hostile human, it is argued, in order to be good himself! Similarly, only remedial punishment, not retribution, can be just; for only the former advances the good of humanity. But is the goodness and love of the biblical God perfected by the creature? Isn't this attempt to subvert God into humankind's servant precisely what Jesus assails? God alone is King, insists Jesus. "No one is good—except God alone." For that reason Jesus demands that humanity be God's obedient servant (Matt. 6:24; Mark 10:18; Luke 17:7–10).[4]

Because God's goodness is self-grounded, anything contrary to his

---

3. The uniqueness of God's act undergirds the distinction between general and special revelation. See Louis Berkhof, *Introduction to Systematic Theology* (Grand Rapids: Eerdmans, 1932; repr., Grand Rapids: Baker, 1979), 116–43. In addition, grace "epitomizes the *freeness* of God's saving action on our behalf" (Lewis B. Smedes, "Grace," in *International Standard Bible Encyclopedia*, ed. Geoffrey W. Bromiley, rev. ed. [Grand Rapids: Eerdmans, 1982], 2:549).

4. Leonhard Goppelt, *Theology of the New Testament* (Grand Rapids: Eerdmans, 1981), 1:77–86. Much of this argument is derived from Joseph Dabney Bettis, "A Critique of the Doctrine of Universal Salvation," *Religious Studies* 6 (Dec. 1970): 329–44, an important critique of universalism.

will is evil. Wrath and retribution, then, become reasonable expressions of his goodness. They bring about a forced submission to God's will, an obedience that ought to have been there in the first place. Retribution establishes that rebellion will never dethrone God's goodness. Consequently, passages that portray a time of "reconciliation," when "God is all in all," do not imply the conversion of hostile powers, but that God has finally and forcibly subdued all rebellion.[5]

Annihilationism

Recently annihilationism has begun making inroads among evangelicals. Key evangelical leaders, such as Clark Pinnock, John Stott, and Philip Hughes, claim that all humanity will be raised for the final judgment, whereupon the reprobate will be punished and then consumed.[6]

The annihilationist argues that the biblical language associated with the reprobate's final state implies the termination of life: "It would seem strange . . . if people who are said to suffer destruction are in fact not destroyed; and . . . it is difficult to imagine a perpetually inconclusive process of perishing."[7] But the assumption that *apollymi* and its cognates mean "annihilation" when referring to the future judgment is problematic. These Greek terms have a range of meaning. Jesus uses them in describing the "lost" coins or son (Luke 15), the "ruined" or "useless" wineskins (Matt. 9:17), and human death (Matt. 10:28). They never denote annihilation, even when referring to physical death. For Jesus cautions that those who can kill the body cannot kill the soul.

5. Peter T. O'Brien, *Colossians, Philemon*, Word Biblical Commentary 44 (Waco, Tex.: Word, 1982), 56–57.

6. For bibliography on Stott and Pinnock, see Millard J. Erickson, "The State of the Question," nn. 15 and 19 in this volume; Hughes' views are in Philip Edgcumbe Hughes, *The True Image: The Origin and Destiny of Man in Christ* (Grand Rapids: Eerdmans, 1989), 398–407. See also Harold E. Guillebaud, *The Righteous Judge: A Study of the Biblical Doctrine of Everlasting Punishment* (Taunton, England: Goodman, 1964). Those leaning toward this view include John W. Wenham, *The Goodness of God* (Downers Grove, Ill.: Inter-Varsity, 1974), 34–41; Stephen H. Travis, *I Believe in the Second Coming of Jesus* (Grand Rapids: Eerdmans, 1982), 198; Peter Toon, *Heaven and Hell: A Biblical and Theological Overview* (Nashville: Nelson, 1986), 200–201. In addition, "Evangelical Affirmations '89," which was convened by Trinity Evangelical Divinity School in May 1989, recognized annihilationism as an evangelical option. The resulting document, *Evangelical Affirmations*, repudiates universalism but not annihilationism: "We affirm that only through the work of Christ can any person be saved and be resurrected to live with God forever. Unbelievers will be separated eternally from God. Concern for evangelism should not be compromised by any illusion that all will be finally saved (universalism)" (Kenneth S. Kantzer and Carl F. H. Henry, eds., *Evangelical Affirmations* [Grand Rapids: Zondervan, 1990], 36).

7. David L. Edwards and John R. W. Stott, *Evangelical Essentials: A Liberal-Evangelical Dialogue* (Downers Grove, Ill.: Inter-Varsity, 1988), 316.

Why should the meaning suddenly shift to denote "annihilation" in the context of the future perdition?[8]

Jesus' description of the reprobates' punishment as "eternal" (Matt. 25:46), employing the adjective *aiōnios* (which usually denotes an everlasting duration), is often highlighted as the key exegetical argument against annihilationism. But some have countered that

> when the adjective . . . is used in Greek with nouns of *action* it has reference to the *result* of the action, not the process. Thus the phrase "everlasting punishment" is comparable to . . . "everlasting salvation." . . . No one supposes that we are . . . being saved forever. We were . . . saved once and for all by Christ with eternal results.

Similarly, "eternal punishment," it is argued, does not denote an eternal process of punishing but a punishment that occurs once and for all with eternal results.[9]

But this exegetical argument is weak. Certainly *aiōnios* can denote the result of an action: "everlasting salvation" (*aiōnios sōtēria*) refers to Christ's work delivering us from Satan and God's wrath, an event that properly occurs once and for all. But does this phrase refer *only* to this once-and-for-all event, and thus preclude a continuous action? Does eternal salvation, to use the example cited, denote only a punctiliar reality? If so, the blessed in heaven could claim that they are no longer being saved by Christ—in any sense of the term! But is that implication not at odds with Scripture's description of believers as existing only "in Christ" (2 Cor. 5:17; Col. 2:6–7)?[10] The annihilationist has conveniently ignored other meanings of *sōtēria*, such as the act of sustaining and preserving life, which cannot be confined to the punctiliar. So *aiōnios sōtēria* refers to Christ's eternal (*aiōnios*) salvation of the blessed, an action that is everlasting as well as final. Since the verb *punishing* also cannot be confined to the punctiliar, everlasting punish-

---

8. The parallelism underlying Jesus' contrast between the two eternal destinies of "life" and "destruction" in John 3:16, 10:28, and Matt. 7:13–14 sheds light upon Christ's intent. Certainly Christ is not contrasting survival and extinction, for "life" is more than simple existence. Rather, Christ is contrasting two qualitatively different types of existence, one involving a loving communion with God and another lacking it (a state of "ruin").

9. Basil F. C. Atkinson, *Life and Immortality* (Taunton, England: Goodman, 1962), 101; Edward W. Fudge, *The Fire That Consumes* (Houston: Providential, 1982), 37–50, 194–96. Even sympathetic scholars acknowledge the weakness of this argument. See Stephen H. Travis, *Christian Hope and the Future* (Downers Grove, Ill.: Inter-Varsity, 1980), 133–36; John W. Wenham, *The Enigma of Evil* (Grand Rapids: Zondervan, 1985), 34–41.

10. Herman Ridderbos, *Paul: An Outline of His Theology* (Grand Rapids: Eerdmans, 1975), 57ff., 376ff., 556ff.

ment should likewise be interpreted as referring to an action that is both everlasting and final.[11]

These and other linguistic arguments must ultimately confront Jesus' view of hell. Jesus teaches that "whoever rejects the Son will not see life, for God's wrath remains on him" (John 3:36). As long as God's wrath abides on them, the damned must exist. Jesus' picture of hell as a place where "*their* worm *does not die,* and the fire is not quenched" (Mark 9:48), suggests that this worm belongs to them as their due and that this manifestation of God's wrath is unending.[12] Stott's retort that the worm and fire exist "until presumably their work of destruction is done" is alien to the text.[13] And this brings us to a fundamental objection. If Jesus had actually taught annihilationism, why is there not one saying in the Gospels that declares this?[14]

Given these exegetical difficulties, the annihilationist typically appeals to God's justice. While acknowledging God's retributive judgment, the annihilationist insists that this punishment must be commensurate with the evil deed. As Stott says: "Would there not . . . be a serious disproportion between sins consciously committed in time and torment consciously experienced throughout eternity?" Further, why must the wicked be kept in existence simply to suffer? An everlasting torment is vindictive, the annihilationist charges, and thus incompatible with the love of God.[15]

What is the extent of punishment due the sinner? This is annihilationism's central challenge. Christ's priestly work of atonement reveals God's love toward humanity as well as his unalterable requirement of retribution for sin. At the cross God in Christ became our substitute to bear the punishment for our sins. "He did this to demonstrate his justice," said Paul, "so as to be just and the one who justifies those who have faith in Jesus" (Rom. 3:25–26; compare 2 Cor. 5:21; 1 Pet. 2:24).[16]

11. In addition, Rev. 20:10 describes hell in terms of "everlasting torment." This construction cannot be construed as simply denoting a once-and-for-all act of torment. Even Fudge admits this text is problematic for his position ("The Final End of the Wicked," *Journal of the Evangelical Theological Society* 27 [1984]: 332).

12. Edward J. Young, *The Book of Isaiah* (Grand Rapids: Eerdmans, 1972), 3:536–37. James Orr, *Christian View of God and the World* (Edinburgh: Elliot, 1893), 341–43.

13. Edwards and Stott, *Evangelical Essentials,* 317.

14. This is significant since annihilationism was one of the many eschatological options during Jesus' time. See Roy A. Stewart, *Rabbinic Theology* (Edinburgh: Oliver & Boyd, 1961), 160; Emil Schürer, *The History of the Jewish People in the Age of Jesus Christ,* rev. and ed. Geza Vermes, Fergus Millar, and Matthew Black (Edinburgh: T. & T. Clark, 1979), 2:545.

15. Edwards and Stott, *Evangelical Essentials,* 318–19.

16. For the best exegetical defense of retribution, propitiation, and an objective substitutionary atonement, concepts which undergird my argument, see Leon Morris, *The Apostolic Preaching of the Cross* (Grand Rapids: Eerdmans, 1956).

Moreover, the cross reveals the specific penalty required for sin. If Christ was simply a human, albeit the perfect person, his substitutionary work would suggest that the penalty is simply a finite loss. Suffering a finite penalty, such as annihilation, is consistent with that scenario. But Christ was not simply a human. Only the God-man could establish this reconciliation. God himself was present at the cross. For Jesus' cry, "My God, My God, why have you forsaken me?" (Matt. 27:46), is that of the Judge, the "Lord of glory" (1 Cor. 2:8) himself, accepting the punishment due us. Jesus' priestly work therefore establishes that the penalty for sin against the infinite must be infinite. Similarly God's punishment of the damned will be infinite, of everlasting duration.[17]

Jesus' priestly work proves that sin must be punished and that the penalty for sin is God's infinite wrath. Anything less disparages the cost of our salvation.

The Classical View of Hell

Every alternative to hell calls into question Christ's work. Nothing less than the person and work of Jesus Christ is at stake in the doctrine of hell. But what is the nature of hell? The popular imagery of a little red demon waving a pitchfork obscures hell's essential features. The christological parameters established above will now be used to develop a proper understanding of hell.

Sheol, where the dead in the Old Testament take up their abode, contained the seeds for the idea of hell. God's progressive revelation led to the idea of a place of final retributive punishment called Gehenna. This term, derived from the Hebrew *gê-hinnōm*, originally referred to the Valley of Hinnom south of Jerusalem. The infamy associated with this location—the place where human sacrifices were offered to the pagan god Molech, the refuse dump for Jerusalem, and finally as a prophesied place of God's judgment—made it an appropriate symbol for God's eschatological wrath. These connections, which Jesus and the New Testament writers refined, characterize hell as a place of everlasting, irreversible, retributive punishment.[18]

---

17. It is no accident that, historically, annihilationism has gone hand in hand with a denial of Jesus' deity. For example, among Protestants the Socinians aggressively advocated annihilationism.

18. See 2 Kings 16:3; 21:6; 2 Chron. 28:3; 33:6; Jer. 7:32; 19:6. Hans Bietenhard, "Hell," in *The New International Dictionary of New Testament Theology*, ed. Colin Brown, 3 vols. (Grand Rapids: Zondervan, 1975–78), 2:205–10; "γέεννα" and "ᾅδνς" in *Theological Dictionary of the New Testament*, ed. Gerhard Kittel and Gerhard Friedrich, trans. Geoffrey W. Bromiley, 10 vols. (Grand Rapids: Eerdmans, 1964–76), 1:657–58, 146–49.

Retribution for Sin

Retribution, the essential theological principle underlying the reality of hell, is fundamental to the biblical concept of God.[19] Retribution refers to God, the supreme Judge, punishing those who have rebelled against his rule (Isa. 3:11; Matt. 25:31–46). This is not a capricious but a retrospective act that is directed toward past sinful deeds (Matt. 25:31–46; 2 Cor. 5:10; Rev. 20:12). God inflicts this punishment, not to rehabilitate the sinner, but to rectify and reestablish his good and righteous rule (Rom. 2:5–11; 12:19). Retribution means that sinners pay the penalty solely because they owe it. In addition, God's judgment cannot be confined to the inevitable process of cause and effect in a moral universe; these penalties and ills are not simply intrinsic to the sinful deed. Rather, retribution is God's personal wrath that inflicts an extrinsic punishment upon sinners.[20]

Irretrievable Bondage

Retribution is not simply a threat. Christ's work as King confirms there will be a final judgment. At that time God's gracious offer of salvation will cease, and the wicked will be subdued, judged, and permanently confined to Gehenna.

Scripture's portrayal of Gehenna as a real place is unmistakable. The imagery of a "furnace," a "lake," and a "prison" *into* which the damned are thrown cannot be easily dismissed.[21] At the very least these terms emphasize that Gehenna refers to a continuing objective reality, not merely a single act of destruction, such as annihilation.

Moreover, Christ's kingly work assures us, through the doctrine of hell, that evil will no longer harm God's people. Scripture consequently describes hell as a place of bondage, separated by an unbridgeable chasm from heaven—"nor can anyone cross over from there" (Luke 16:26).[22] Christian philosopher Peter T. Geach has even proposed a

19. Important works on retribution include Morris, *Apostolic Preaching of the Cross;* and Stephen H. Travis, *Christ and the Judgement of God: Divine Retribution in the New Testament* (London: Marshall Pickering, 1986).

20. Because God inflicts punishment through natural phenomena, such as plagues (Exod. 7–11), earthquakes (Isa. 26:5), and famine (Ezek. 5:8–17), these penalties cannot be construed as simply the natural result of sin. Furthermore, Paul's use of *orgē*, which denotes an emotion or feeling in the Godhead, shows that wrath is not an impersonal process of causation in a moral universe, but God's own personal act (Rom. 1:18–32).

21. Furnace is used in Matt. 13:42, 50; lake in Rev. 19:20; 20:10, 14–15; prison in Matt. 5:25–26; 13:40–42, 49–50; 18:32–35; 2 Pet. 2:4–9; Jude 5–7.

22. While the parable of Lazarus and the rich man occurs in Hades, not Gehenna, and the details of parables cannot be pressed, Jesus is certainly teaching here that an impassable gulf exists between hell and heaven. This spatial chasm should have stalled those fanciful speculations in Christian literature that the blessed rejoice in seeing the damned being tortured. For examples and discussion, see Jonathan Edwards, *The Works*

temporal chasm between heaven and hell. At the last judgment, he speculates, history itself will be split into two different futures so that the damned have no contemporary time relation with the blessed. Each future will exclude the other possibility so that "the damned will know that there is no conceivable restitution for them. Time cannot run backwards to bring them back before Judgment Day." Whatever one may think of this view, Jesus' use of the phrase *everlasting (aiōnios) punishment* denotes the irretrievable finality of hell.[23]

The Penalties of Hell

Christ's priestly work reveals that the penalty for sin is God's infinite wrath. According to the classic theological rationale, the gravity of sin is defined by its object, God, the only infinite Being. And "sin being an infinite evil, deserves an infinite punishment." Thus an everlasting punishment is just.[24]

But what are the penalties of hell? While Christianity has consistently affirmed that hell's penalties are spiritual and physical, debate arises over the specific nature of these penalties. Proponents of the classic view of hell fall along a continuum between two poles. At one end hell's punishments are conceived merely as loss, which the scholastics termed *poena damni* (the pain of loss). Torment or *poena damni et sensus* (the pain of loss and sense) lies at the opposite pole.

Loss as the Penalty of Hell. Hell as loss has been popularized by C. S. Lewis, Stewart Salmond, and Edward Pusey.[25] The underlying premise is that the reprobate have pridefully rejected everything foreign to them, even God, and as a result cannot be converted. The only just punishment for these individuals is to remain what they are. The penalty of hell is a self-sentence of isolation, an exclusion from God and others. Since this is self-chosen, the damned actually enjoy this horrible freedom; indeed "the doors of hell are locked on the *inside*."[26] In this view, God does not impose external penal conditions on the damned.

---

of Jonathan Edwards (repr., Edinburgh: Banner of Truth Trust, 1974), 2:87; and Julius Müller, *The Christian Doctrine of Sin,* trans. William Urwick (Edinburgh: T. & T. Clark, 1868), 1:239.

23. Peter Geach, *Providence and Evil* (Cambridge: Cambridge University Press, 1977), 145. Geach's theory is problematic because he denies a spatial chasm between heaven and hell. The meaning of *aiōnios* is discussed in more detail by Scot McKnight, "Eternal Consequences or Eternal Consciousness?" in this volume.

24. Edwards, *Works,* 2:83. This is a commonplace in Christian theology. See Thomas Aquinas, *Summa theologiae* suppl. 99.1; *Summa contra Gentiles* 3.140–46.

25. C. S. Lewis, *The Problem of Pain* (New York: Macmillan, 1962), 118–28; Stewart Salmond, *The Christian Doctrine of Immortality* (Edinburgh: T. & T. Clark, 1903), 526–29; Edward B. Pusey, *What Is of Faith as to Everlasting Punishment?* (Oxford: James Parker, 1880), 23.

26. Lewis, *Problem of Pain,* 127.

Rather, the penalties of hell are limited to the intrinsic consequences of sin, primarily the loss of a reconciled relationship with God. This is a just sentence, proponents argue, because it is self-chosen.

The New Testament, however, depicts God as actively subduing and punishing the reprobate in hell. Lewis responds that Scripture speaks of hell as both "a sentence inflicted by a tribunal" and the sinner's own preference for "darkness to light," and that both concepts in the long run are the same. But how can they be the same? Self-isolation is not equivalent to an externally imposed imprisonment; only in the latter must the individual acknowledge the superior authority. More to the point, does Christ really reign as King in this view? Is rebellion "pacified"? Is God ever "all in all"? Lewis's answer that in creating beings with free will God "submits to the possibility of such a defeat," simply begs the question.[27] If the damned are "successful rebels to the end," God never truly reigns as King.

Torment as the Penalty of Hell. The classic view of hell maintains that spiritual and physical punishments have penalties of loss and suffering. Scripture and Christ's own work solidly support this view.

The punishments of hell involve spiritual loss—a total exclusion from God's loving presence. This is reflected in Christ's statement: "Depart from me, you who are cursed" (Matt. 25:41). Biblical phrases such as *outer darkness, destruction,* and even *death* suggest the forfeiture of that state for which we were created, a "life" of communion with God. This "second death" is a "worthless" and ruined existence, as the refuse heap of Gehenna connotes (Matt. 8:12; 22:13; 25:30; Luke 9:25; John 3:16–18; 2 Thess. 1:9; Jude 12; Rev. 21:8).

Jesus' portrayal of hell as "weeping and gnashing of teeth" denotes the conscious spiritual suffering of the damned (Matt. 8:12; Rom. 2:9; Rev. 20:10). The "undying worm" (Mark 9:48) has traditionally been interpreted as the soul's internal torment. Similarly, fire is a graphic symbol of intense pain (Matt. 25:41). This torment has several sources. Certainly God's searing holiness will make the damned aware of his wrath (Rom. 2:5–9; Jude 15; Rev. 14:9–11). And having seen the happiness and joy of the blessed on judgment day, the damned will covet and grieve for those goods (Luke 16:19–31). Since the reprobate know they are locked into an existence with no possible alternative, as the images of "dungeons" and "everlasting chains" suggest, their grief intensifies (2 Pet. 2:4; Jude 6). Yet the damned regret only the consequences of their sin, not the sin itself.

Hell also involves physical loss, separation from the physical comforts of heaven. Since Christ declares that the reprobate are now experiencing, at least in part, God's wrath, there are parallels between sin's

---

27. Ibid., 122–23, 127.

physical effects in this life and the next (John 3:36). Thus the body will not obey the soul, but will find itself bound by fleshly and carnal things. So Scripture describes the reprobate as "brute beasts, creatures of instinct" (2 Pet. 2:12–22) and like "wild waves of the sea, foaming up their shame" (Jude 10, 13; Rev. 22:15).

Hell does not consist in simply the deprivation of goods, but also physical suffering, for the damned "will be paid back with harm for the harm they have done" (2 Pet. 2:13). The pictures of "gnashing teeth," "beatings," and "fire" refer to this physical affliction (Matt. 13:42; Mark 9:48–49; Luke 12:47).

The speculations within this tradition on hell's fires are not as weighty as the attention or even the ridicule they have received. Certainly most theologians until the Reformation affirmed a natural fire. Besides reflecting the church's battle with the gnostics' denial of the resurrected body, this thesis was linked to their contention that the biblical notion of retributive punishment includes the penalties of loss and sense. As long as those points were not in dispute, Augustine, for instance, was open to a metaphorical interpretation of "fire."[28] Taking up that suggestion, many Protestants discounted a physical fire, concluding that this imagery broadly denoted torment. Since Christ experienced the punishment and wrath due us, and physical fires were apparently not a part of his torment, a natural fire is indeed problematic.[29]

A more decisive controversy involves the appropriateness of this punishment. How can everlasting torment be construed as the just penalty for a finite offense? As explained above, Jesus declares and shows that the penalty for sin against God is infinite. Eliminating hell's torments trivializes Christ's prophetic and priestly work. In addition, it depreciates his kingly office. For Christ's kingly administration of the cosmos will change at the last judgment. Creation, as we now experience it, profits from common grace. God is patient; he does not immediately inflict sinners with their just due, even though they pervert and ravage creation, contemptuous even of God himself. But his mercy ceases with the final judgment. No longer will God call the reprobate to salvation. No longer will the Spirit elicit aspirations for higher values. The reprobate will be petrified in their wickedness. With

28. Augustine, *City of God* 21.9.
29. John Calvin, *Institutes of the Christian Religion,* ed. John T. McNeil, trans. Ford Lewis Battles (Philadelphia: Westminster, 1960), 3.25.12; Francis Turretin, *Institutio theologiae elencticae* 20.7; William Ames, *The Marrow of Theology* 1.16.22. The key arguments against a physical or natural fire are (1) these "hell-fires" were prepared for incorporeal beings, Satan and his angels, so these fires are probably not the same as physical fire; and (2) a physical fire is unlikely, since it would conflict with the description of hell's darkness.

the consummated kingdom, creation will serve God, executing his good and righteous will. When the damned "try to use the inanimate creatures (as they now do, defiling and plundering the Earth . . . for their wicked purposes) they will find that Nature at last manifestly obeys her Master and not them—and so the ordinary course of Nature will continually frustrate, enrage, and torment them."[30] In effect, the reprobate, formerly at the summit of created beings, are placed in subjection to all other created things so that God's order is preserved. This torment of the reprobate is not capricious, but the consequence of their own acts. And since the reprobate are no longer successful rebels, God finally reigns as King over an entirely obedient creation![31]

Jesus: The Only Way

Christ's own warnings regarding the finality and horror of hell are deeply disturbing to evangelicals. The only way for sinners to extricate themselves from final judgment is through personal faith in Jesus Christ. Yet billions have never had the chance to hear the gospel. What is their future? In view of the horrible reality of hell as a place of retributive, irreversible torment, can we still affirm that Christ is the only way?

Consistent with the overwhelming data of Scripture, we must be pessimistic about those who have never heard. Yet, we sense that Christ's cosmic work of reconciliation is not exhausted by the meager results we now see (Col. 1:20). This has prompted some to demand a future probation. But that strategy is wrong. How could we be so brazen, even contemptuous, as to impose our demands on our Lord and Savior?

Moreover, Jesus' response to a lost world was to humble himself, take the nature of a servant to suffer for our sake, and boldly preach the good news of the kingdom. We as his disciples should reflect Jesus' self-sacrificial love, and selflessly expend our lives by participating in his plan of reconciliation (2 Cor. 5:18–21). Proposals that subvert the necessity of missions, or even its motivation, cannot reflect Christ's love for the lost.[32]

---

30. Geach, *Providence and Evil*, 146. For a similar view, see Calvin, *Institutes of the Christian Religion*, 3.25.12.

31. An interesting suggestion arising from Leckie's analysis of Thomas Aquinas is that the reprobate have lost their ethical existence. Thus their wickedness is no longer morally evil, but more on the order of natural evil (see Joseph H. Leckie, *The World to Come and Final Destiny* [Edinburgh: T. & T. Clark, 1922], 199ff.). But Ames' caution is helpful at this point: "Concerning . . . the manner of torture and the nature of the attendant circumstances, the Scripture has said nothing definite, because it is not necessary for us to know" (Ames, *Marrow of Theology* 1.16.16).

32. On this, see the chapter by John D. Ellenberger, "Is Hell a Proper Motivation for Missions?" in this volume.

The quandaries we sense must be left to Christ. He alone is the final Judge who determines the fate of the lost. In fact, it is only because we personally know God himself in Jesus Christ that we can trust him and totally commit this decision to him. For we know that no sentence will be pronounced except by God himself, who has endured our condition and suffered to save every person.[33]

33. The answer James Orr gave at the beginning of this century targets the central issue: "A strong distinction ought to be drawn between things which Scripture expressly teaches, and those things on which it simply gives no light. . . . There is room here for a wise Agnosticism" (*Christian View of God and the World,* 338).

Will God Change His Mind?
Eternal Hell and the Ninevites

Jerry L. Walls

The doctrine of eternal hell has been accepted by most orthodox Christians largely because it seems to be taught clearly in the Bible. We are informed in Scripture that Christ unambiguously taught that some persons will not receive God's salvation and those persons will consequently suffer eternal damnation. Thus, any hope of universal salvation seems to be cut off by what God has revealed to us in straightforward terms.

Yet, is it not possible that God might change his mind? Even if God revealed to us categorically that some will be lost (because of their rejection of salvation), is it not open to God to reverse his decision on this matter? Could it be possible that God will, in the end, save not only those who have never heard the gospel, but literally everyone? After all, in several passages of Scripture, God is depicted as changing his mind.

One of the more memorable is in the Book of Jonah, where God commands the prophet to tell the Ninevites that their city will be overthrown in forty days. Despite the apparent unconditional nature of the pronouncement, the Ninevites seek God's mercy and are spared the threatened judgment. On the face of it, it looks as if God has changed his mind.

This incident has puzzled many thoughtful persons, and has been extensively debated by theologians. It has been suggested that perhaps God will not make good on his threat of eternal hell, just as he did not make good on his threat to the Ninevites. Maybe God will change his mind about eternal hell just as he did about the fate of the ancient city.

This raises the question of exactly what God might change his mind about. Might God give those in hell a second chance to repent and be saved? Or might he decide to annihilate the damned rather than keep them alive forever? Both these suggestions assume that those in hell would want to escape it and that one's fate is sealed at death. Some, however, have argued that the damned actually prefer hell to heaven and would not repent even if given the chance.[1] If hell is thought of like this, God's change of mind might involve something like a decision to override the freedom of the damned, and somehow make them willing to repent.

For the purpose of this chapter, it does not matter what God's change of mind is thought to be about. I am primarily concerned with the more basic question of whether a change of mind can be intelligibly attributed to God, and, if so, in what sense.

Changing One's Mind

Let us begin to probe this issue more carefully by asking just what it means to change one's mind. When do people change their minds, and why do they do so? Do they have full control over their minds, so that they can change their minds at any time and about anything they so desire? Is a change of mind the result of an active decision, or are people passive when their minds change? That is, do people find that their minds have simply changed, without any deliberate choice in the matter?

The answers to these questions will vary, I think, with different instances of mind change. In some cases it seems clear that change of mind is due to an active decision. Consider this example. A man is shopping for a new car and sees several he likes. All of these cars are attractive to him, have similar features, and are in the same price range. Finally, he thinks he has made up his mind and tells his children that he will buy the red Chevrolet. The next morning, however, he announces that he has changed his mind and will purchase the

---

1. This is the picture of hell C. S. Lewis gives in *The Great Divorce* (New York: Macmillan, 1946). Of course, Lewis questions whether hell is a place of torment; it might be a place of relative pleasures; see *The Problem of Pain* (New York: Macmillan, 1962), 126.

blue Ford. But then he changes his mind yet again and finally settles on a green Chrysler.

In a case like this it is evident that the change of mind is actively produced since the choice was largely an arbitrary one. All the cars were satisfactory so far as the man was concerned and he could well have chosen any one of them. That is why he changed his mind several times before coming to a final decision.

Now consider a second example. An ethicist who believes abortion is right undertakes a study of the medical and physiological aspects of the issue. In the course of the research, she learns several significant facts that she had not previously known. She begins to see the picture in a different light and, in the end, she says she has changed her mind on abortion.

In this case, the change of mind seems to be more passive than active. Indeed, it would be more accurate to say the ethicist *had* a change of mind than to say she *changed* her mind. She did not choose to come to believe abortion is wrong, but just found herself believing this at some point in her investigation. The change of mind here is not arbitrary, as in the previous example. The ethicist does not simply choose to believe abortion is right one day and then decide the next day it is not.

Think now of a third example. A father promises to buy his son a car for his eighteenth birthday. Before his birthday arrives, however, the son is arrested and convicted for driving under the influence of alcohol. In response to this the father says he has changed his mind and will not buy the car as promised. In this case it is arguable that the change of mind is only apparent rather than real. For perhaps the father's promise was implicitly a conditional one. That is, he promised to buy his son a car on the assumption that his son was sufficiently mature and responsible to own a car and properly use it. But without this assumption, his promise was no longer in force. So in an important sense the father did not change his mind at all about buying the car. All along he planned to buy the car *if* his son proved himself responsible. His change of mind concerned only his belief that his son was sufficiently mature to own a car. After the arrest, he no longer believed his son possessed the necessary maturity.

Now then, with these examples before us, let us come back to the questions I raised at the beginning of this section. People typically change their minds, or have a change of mind, when confronted by information or evidence that causes or inclines them to believe differently about some matter than they had before. Such a change of mind is essentially passive in nature. Change of mind may involve, of course, action as well as belief. So people whose minds have changed may also act differently than they had intended.

But not all changes of mind are due to the influence of new information or insight. Sometimes people change their minds at will when facing a choice between equally viable alternatives. In such cases, they seem to have control over their minds, at least to a large extent, and they have to "make up their minds" which way to go.

Sometimes when people change their minds in such a case, particularly if they do so frequently, it is due to fickleness. That is, they lack the character to make a decision and stick with it.

Did God Change His Mind Regarding the Ninevites?

Before applying this discussion to the issue of eternal hell, let us come back to the case of Jonah and the Ninevites. There are several ways of construing this incident, and each of them raises different questions and has different implications for our conception of God.

One possibility is that God knew all along that the Ninevites would repent and that he would not overthrow their city. This follows if God has infallible knowledge of all future events, including the choices of free agents. On this interpretation, God's change of mind is only apparent rather than real. Many traditional theologians have preferred this interpretation despite the fact that it raises at least one awkward question: Why did God send his prophet to predict an event that he knew would not occur? Does this not make God a deceiver? As we shall see, these theologians are not without a solution to this difficulty.

One of the primary reasons traditional theologians have favored this interpretation is because of their conviction that a literal change of mind cannot be attributed to God. Calvin, for instance, gives the following explanation of what Scripture means when it speaks of God's "repentance":

> Surely its meaning is like that of all other modes of speaking that describe God for us in human terms. For because our weakness does not attain to his exalted state, the description of him that is given to us must be accommodated to our capacity so that we may understand it. Now the mode of accommodation is for him to represent himself to us not as he is in himself, but as he seems to us.[2]

Calvin interprets God's unfulfilled threat to the Ninevites in the same vein. Although the declaration of judgment seemed unconditional, it is clear from the outcome that it contained a "tacit condition."[3] Indeed, the very fact that God sent his prophet indicates that

2. John Calvin, *Institutes of the Christian Religion,* ed. John T. McNeil, trans. Ford Lewis Battles (Philadelphia: Westminster, 1960), 1.17.13.
3. Ibid., 1.17.14.

the threat was a conditional one. Otherwise, God would simply have destroyed them without warning. Jonathan Edwards takes this same view, pointing out that the Ninevites must have understood the prophecy as conditional or they would not have turned to fasting and repentance in the hope that they might avoid judgment.[4]

According to this view, then, God neither changed his mind nor proclaimed what he knew to be untrue. He intended all along to forgive the Ninevites, and his message of warning to them was his means of moving them to repentance.

It is worth noting that Augustine suggests a different interpretation of God's prediction concerning Nineveh. There is a sense, he points out, in which the city was overthrown, although it was not in the manner Jonah expected. "For sinners are destroyed in two ways—either, like the Sodomites, the men themselves are punished for their sins, or, like the Ninevites, the men's sins are destroyed by repentance. God's prediction, therefore, was fulfilled—the wicked Nineveh was overthrown, and a good Nineveh built up."[5] Whatever the merits of this suggestion, Augustine also denies that God literally changes his mind. What God proclaims is true and his purpose does not waver, although humans may misunderstand that purpose.

A second possibility is that God did not know whether the Ninevites would repent, but his pardon of them did not involve a real change of mind. According to this view, God's intentions are fixed, but are, as Thomas Morris puts it, "indexed to, or conditional upon, contingencies in the created universe." Morris elaborates the point:

> As many biblical scholars have pointed out, and as the prophet Jonah discovered to his chagrin, divine warnings, announcements of God's intentions to punish, often, if not always express conditional intentions. Why can't it always and immemorially have been the case that God intends to do A if B arises, or C if D comes about? This would be fully compatible with an informed reading of those passages which seem to portray God as changing his mind in response to human activity as situations develop.[6]

So this view is like the first one in holding that God's threat to the Ninevites was conditional. Unlike the first view, however, God did not

---

4. Jonathan Edwards, *The Works of Jonathan Edwards* (Leeds: Edward Baines, 1811), 7:520.

5. Augustine, *The City of God*, trans. Marcus Dods, in *A Select Library of Nicene and Post-Nicene Fathers of the Christian Church*, ed. Philip Schaff and Henry Wace, 1st series, vol. 2 (repr., Grand Rapids: Eerdmans, 1977), 21.24.

6. Thomas V. Morris, "Properties, Modalities, and God," *Philosophical Review* 93 (1984): 47.

know the Ninevites would repent. But this is not to say that God did not expect the Ninevites to repent and, therefore, turned out to be mistaken when they did. Rather, God held no belief one way or the other about whether they would in fact repent. So his mind did not change in any way when things turned out the way they did.

There are, however, ways of interpreting the story that allow for a real change of mind on God's part. One of these is suggested by Richard Swinburne, who mentions Jonah in a discussion of divine omniscience. According to Swinburne, God knows everything that it is possible to know, but the future actions of free persons are not knowable in principle. So not even God can know with certainty what actions free persons will perform. Since he knows all the circumstances surrounding human behavior, he can "predict human behavior correctly most of the time, but always with the possibility that men may falsify those predictions."[7] Swinburne goes on to defend his view of omniscience by citing some biblical examples:

> Typically in the Old Testament God has certain plans for men and at their intercession changes them. Consider Abraham's intercession for Sodom (Gen. 18), or the intercession of Moses for the children of Israel (Exod. 32). Or God may change his plans because men change their behavior (the book of Jonah tells how God spared Nineveh because it repented).[8]

This interpretation of the incident differs from the previous one because Swinburne apparently thinks God was actually planning to destroy Nineveh and did not anticipate its repentance. God had an actual change of mind in the sense that some new facts emerged that he did not expect, and he changed his plan of action accordingly.

Other interpretations of this incident are possible, but there is no need to mention them here. Let us now turn to the doctrine of eternal hell and the suggestion that this doctrine may not be true because God might change his mind about it.

Will God Change His Mind about Hell?

In view of the discussion up to this point, I think we can readily see there are a number of problems with the proposal that God might change his mind. As we have seen, sometimes a change of mind is arbitrary. It is hard to see how this sort of mind change could be ascribed to God, particularly with respect to something like eternal hell. For Christians have usually believed there is nothing arbitrary

---

7. Richard Swinburne, *The Coherence of Theism* (Oxford: Clarendon, 1977), 176.
8. Ibid., 177.

about the punishment of eternal hell. Rather, it is the appropriate end for those who refuse salvation and persist in sin. There is no reason, then, to think God might simply change his mind about hell in the way people might change their minds about which car to buy or what to order in a restaurant.

More typically, however, change of mind is not arbitrary; it results from new information or insight acquired by the one whose mind is changed. This kind of change of mind does not fare much better when applied to God. Indeed, it is ruled out logically if God knows everything and never gains new information or insight. Moreover, if God knows everything, he knows his own future actions. It would be incoherent to say God changed his mind about a certain action if he infallibly knew all along what he would do.

The implications for the doctrine of eternal hell are clear. If God knows some persons will persist in rejecting salvation and if he knows he will neither annihilate them nor override their will, then there is no coherent sense in the thought that he might change his mind about eternal hell.

But even if one does not believe God knows the *actual* future choices of free persons, including his own, there are still problems in ascribing a literal change of mind to him. For surely God knows all *possible* actions anyone might perform, all situations that might arise, and all courses the history of the world might take. If so, he could never be taken by surprise. Furthermore, it is surely reasonable to believe, as Morris suggests, that God knows how he would respond to any situation that might arise. Surely God never has to improvise and he never wavers or vacillates about what he should do.

Thus, if God has decided that repentance must be prior to death and if some have not so repented or will not so repent, then there is no reason to think such persons can be saved. For God would not make such a decision without a good reason, and if there is such a reason he would not act against it. On the other hand, if there is no such reason, and persons may repent after death, then there may be hope that all will be saved. But this is not because God might change his mind. Rather, it would be that God intended from the beginning that all would be saved *if* all eventually repented. God would be prepared for the possibility that all would repent, as well as the possibility that some would not, and he would know how he would respond to either situation.

Naturally, in order to hope that all will be saved, we must assume that God has not revealed that some will be eternally damned.[9] Those

9. The problem for universalists is that the New Testament clearly states that some will decisively reject God, and therefore be eternally lost. The New Testament evidence

passages of Scripture that seem to teach that some will suffer eternal damnation must be interpreted differently than they have been by most traditional theologians.[10] The obvious move in this regard is to interpret those passages as tacitly conditional threats, much like God's threat to overthrow Nineveh.

For this move to be legitimate, however, there must be some good reason to believe that the scriptural pronouncements about hell are indeed conditional warnings rather than absolute declarations that some will be lost. If there is nothing in Scripture to indicate that the threats about hell are conditional warnings, the problem persists about God's truthfulness if it turns out that all are saved. This problem is particularly acute if God has absolute foreknowledge of all future events, including free choices. That is to say, God's truthfulness is greatly compromised if he infallibly knows that all will be saved, but his revelation in Scripture leads us to believe some will surely be lost.[11]

Some have attempted to circumvent this problem by suggesting that God has a good reason for leading us to believe some will be damned, even though none actually will be. God has done this, it has been argued, in order to restrain us from sin and lead us to repentance.[12] In the same vein, it might be proposed that God uses the prospect of eternal hell to motivate us to evangelize the world.[13]

While this notion has at least some plausibility, it also has some serious problems. Besides raising questions about God's truthfulness, there is the further matter that God seems to have been found out in his designs. Jonathan Edwards rejects this thought as blasphemous:

> Though God *intended* men should believe it to be certain, that sinners are liable to an eternal punishment; yet they suppose, that they have been so cunning as to find out that it is not certain: and so that God had not laid his design so deep, but that such cunning men as they can discern the cheat, and defeat the design: because they have found out, that there is no necessary connection between the threatening of eternal punishment, and the execution of that threatening.[14]

is discussed in this volume by Aída Besançon Spencer, "Romans 1: Finding God in Creation"; Douglas Moo, "Romans 2: Saved Apart from the Gospel?"; Scot McKnight, "Eternal Consequences or Eternal Consciousness?"; and William V. Crockett, "Will God Save Everyone?"

10. For a good defense of the view that Scripture gives plenty of reason to hope for universal salvation, see Hans Urs von Balthasar, *Dare We Hope "That All Men Be Saved"?* trans. David Kipp and Lothar Krauth (San Francisco: Ignatius, 1988).

11. See Edwards' argument of this point (*Works*, 7:517–18).

12. See William V. Crockett, "Will God Save Everyone in the End?" n. 15 this volume, for discussion of this topic.

13. For an analysis of this argument, see the chapter in this volume by John D. Ellenberger, "Is Hell a Proper Motivation for Missions?"

14. Edwards, *Works*, 7:519.

While this criticism has a good deal of force, I do not think it is decisive. For it could be that God did not intend all persons to believe in eternal hell, but perhaps, say, only the spiritually immature, who require such motivation. Others, then, could discern that there is no necessary connection between the threat of eternal punishment, and the execution of such punishment, without defeating God's designs.

Still, I think Edwards' argument is essentially correct and we should not hold that God has misled us, for whatever lofty reason. We should not look for a hidden agenda in God's word to us, but should accept at face value what is clearly revealed.

So I conclude that the notion that God might change his mind about eternal hell is dubious at best, if not downright incoherent. There is no reason to hope that all, including those who have never heard, will be saved on this basis.

Part

2

Biblical Exegesis

5

Salvation for People Outside Israel's Covenant?

R. Bryan Widbin

Sometimes when Christians read the Old Testament they get the impression that God was relatively unconcerned with the vast nations that surrounded Israel. It is easy to assume from a surface reading that God was active only in ancient Israel. Does this mean no individual outside the chosen people knew the true God? To answer this, we must discuss God's dealings with Israel and her neighbors.

The record of Israel's interaction with the nations around her reads like a "Who's Who" of the ancient Near East. Because Israel was situated in the mainstream of international travel and commerce, there was always a lively interchange with all sorts of people. In addition to contacts within her own Canaanite milieu, Israel had impressive links to the megacultures of Egypt and Mesopotamia, among others. One can imagine that this influenced the way Israel viewed herself in relation to the rest of the world.

It is not surprising, then, that the traditions of Israel recorded in the Bible reach back beyond her ethnic ancestors to the beginnings of humankind and its creation in the image of God. The early narratives of Genesis assume that God made all humans equal in dignity and worthy of his eternal care. The wisdom literature of the Bible assumes these universal realities as well, that God is involved in the lives of all people simply because they *are* people.

Despite these ideals, Israel was not always open to her "brothers" outside her borders. Her willingness to interact with other peoples ebbed and flowed as her political and economic circumstances changed. But even in the best of times, Israel was slow to open herself to outside influence. For Israel, every contact with the nations potentially compromised her unique relationship with Yahweh, her God—ironically the same God through whom she was related to all peoples in creation. So there was an inescapable tension in Israel that was grounded in her theology. She had to grapple with the reality that while she was related to all the nations through creation, nevertheless, God called her to be separate from them. Israel was to be "in the world, but not of the world," and to live accordingly.

In this chapter, I will lay out the ideas that gave rise to Israel's tension: (1) Israel is uniquely God's people, (2) Israel is to be a light to the nations, (3) God involves himself with some outside Israel. Israel tried to hold these ideas together in a creative dialogue. In contrast, modern scholars attempt to resolve the tension, usually by choosing one of these alternatives at the expense of the others.[1] But efforts like these, as Israel herself often found, proceed at great peril to the whole picture. Both ancient questions about Israel and modern questions about those who have never heard can be answered more satisfactorily if we do as Israel did and leave all three ideas together.

Israel Alone—God's Unique Nation

While acknowledging the common origins of humanity, the Old Testament depicts Israel as unique among the nations. Interestingly, such a sense of uniqueness was not an isolated phenomenon. The contemporary literatures of Mesopotamia, Egypt, and Anatolia express similar beliefs about the national identities of their peoples. What is remarkable, however, is the basis for the biblical claim.

Unlike her neighbors, the distinctiveness of Israel had nothing to do with *her* achievements, whether political, cultural, or religious.

---

1. Examples of the thoroughly exclusivist or universalist interpretations of the data may be located, respectively, in Harry M. Orlinsky, "Nationalism-Universalism and Internationalism in Ancient Israel," in *Translating and Understanding the Old Testament: Essays in Honor of Herbert Gordon May*, ed. Harry T. Frank and William L. Reed (Nashville: Abingdon, 1970), 206–36; and Moshe Greenberg, "Mankind, Israel and the Nations in Hebraic Heritage," in *No Man Is Alien*, ed. J. Robert Nelson (Leiden: Brill, 1971), 15–40.

What distinguished Israel from other nations was her conviction that she owed her entire history—not just the beginning—to the gracious initiative of Yahweh on her behalf. She held to the then radical belief that she was not a self-made nation, but rather existed only by the grace of Yahweh. In acknowledging this she found a positive relationship with the Creator of heaven and earth, an experience he had intended for all his creatures. For Israel, theologically speaking, election and redemption were nearly the whole ball game, and this demanded a priority in her consciousness and praise (Deut. 26:5–11).

In effect, Israel differed from all other nations in acknowledging what the others would not. Her identity was located in Yahweh's effort, not in her own. She belonged exclusively to the gracious God of creation who would not permit himself to be extended into or confused with any other deity (Deut. 6:4). It is not surprising, then, that the primeval history (Gen. 1–11) and the history of the patriarchs and matriarchs (Gen. 12–50) reflect significant barriers that divide Israel's experience with God from that of other nations.

The initial narratives of the Bible make clear that, early on, history had progressed in a fragmented fashion. The designs of humankind had resulted in distinctions that separated people from one another and from God. Even God's covenant with Noah's family (Gen. 9:1–17), which guaranteed existence to all creation, could not prevent the spread of these ill-conceived divisions in the human family. God's initiative and commitment to all remained firm, but the people chose to ignore him and seek success through their own efforts. In the end, a barrier arose between God and the entire earth (Gen. 11:1). The Babel story, then, parodies the original unity of creation by showing that all creation resisted worshiping its Creator (Gen. 11:1–9).

The fact that the author of Genesis intentionally puts the Babel episode at the conclusion of the primeval history cycle, out of natural sequence, is an important detail.[2] Placed here, the episode provides an unhappy ending to the story of God's up-and-down dealings with humanity before Israel. Babel deprives the reader of all optimism that the human race will eventually turn to the Creator on its own. Alienation and judgment have spread to all peoples on earth.

How remarkable that the call of Abram comes as an order by Yahweh to get out of the world and its commitments (Gen. 12:1–9)! But after Babel this is the only kind of call that makes sense. Nothing else will do in the context of a world in rebellion. All prospects for

---

2. Note that Gen. 10 assumes the diversity of languages, a concomitant of the geographical division of nations on the earth (vv. 5, 20, 31). Yet it is the Babel episode in Gen. 11 (in flashback?) that *actually accounts for* language diversity and the spread of humanity (vv. 7–9).

blessing hinge on Abram's recognition that a barrier exists between himself and the world.

It is interesting that the entire Abrahamic cycle of stories is framed around the patriarch's separation from Mesopotamia, the larger setting of the event at Babel. Having left this land with his family many years before, we find Abraham faced with a serious dilemma near the end of his life (Gen. 24:1–9). Will his son Isaac have to go to Mesopotamia in order to get a suitable bride? Abraham does not equivocate in his response. He insists that his son be prevented at all costs (even his marital prospects!) from setting foot on Mesopotamian soil. Again, as at Moriah (Gen. 22:1–19), Abraham is willing to sacrifice even the promise of blessing through descendants (Gen. 12:2) in order to maintain the distinctive calling of his people.

The identity of Abraham, and in him that of Israel as a whole, is clear.[3] He and they regarded themselves as distinct from the nations in their commitment to Yahweh. From Israel's perspective, it was in her calling alone that Yahweh would work to achieve his purposes for the world.[4]

Evidence of Israel's distinctiveness is by no means limited to her ancestral traditions. This line of thought dominates entire books of the Old Testament, such as Deuteronomy, where the barriers erected in the narratives of Genesis are extended into virtually every conceivable aspect of life.

But perhaps the best reflection of Israel's calling is found in Old Testament legal texts that display her ritual system. Recent study of the whole matter of ritual has revealed its importance for understanding societies and their essential values.[5] M. Wilson notes that "men express in ritual what moves them most, and since the form of expression is conventionalized and obligatory, it is the values of the group

---

3. One may observe that the life of Abraham mirrors the experiences of Israel. Note, e.g., the broad strokes of movement from Mesopotamia (Gen. 11:27–12:4) to Canaan (12:5-9); to temporary residence in Egypt, where conflict brings plagues on Pharaoh and his dynasty (12:17); to an agreement in the central hill country (13:1–13); to a battle for control of Canaan (14:1–16); and, finally, to contact with Salem (Jerusalem?) (14:14–20).

4. With few exceptions (discussed below), all attempts at relationship with other national groups in these materials are compromised by a consciousness of distinctiveness on the part of Israel's ancestors (Gen. 12:10–20; compare Exod. 1–12; 20:1–17, esp. vv. 10–11; 26:1–33; and, most notably, 34:1–31, where issues of land, covenant, and circumcision come into play), or the refusal of others to acknowledge Yahweh and his involvement with this people (Gen. 14:21–24; Exod. 5:1ff.; Deut. 25:17–18). These factors highlight the barrier that exists between Israel and others.

5. Bernhard Lang, ed., *Anthropological Approaches to the Old Testament* (Philadelphia: Fortress, 1985); also see the discussion in Gordon J. Wenham, *Numbers: An Introduction and Commentary,* Tyndale Old Testament Commentaries (Downers Grove, Ill.: Inter-Varsity, 1981), 25–39.

that are revealed."[6] Ritual identifies fundamental categories that are believed to exist in the world and preserves them in the symbols and behavior of the community. It brings into full view a picture of life as it is. Those who participate in the system commit themselves to this reality and so are joined to the community.

Reality for Israel was her covenant relationship with Yahweh. The covenant imitated creation—relationship with the Creator, other humans, and the world God had made. It exemplified the primal order and harmony of the world established according to the will of God.

In Israel's ritual system the covenant functioned as a standard that divided the world into two spheres. Whatever conformed to the original order of God's creation, and therefore appeared to be in relationship with him, was "clean." Whatever distorted the picture of creation or appeared out of relation with the Creator was "unclean."[7] There was no middle ground, and no doubt where Israel stood. Her relationship with God demanded a moral and ritual distinctiveness ("holiness," Lev. 11:44–45; 19:2). As for the nations, they were an obvious picture of chaos. Their religious priorities and lack of concern for justice in society were considered symptoms of the confusion that reigns far from God. Outside "the camp" of Israel was the wilderness, the place of nothingness and death. This was the abode of the nations.

Ritual helped preserve for Israel a sense of her unique identity. She believed that her relationship with Yahweh separated her from the other nations of the world (Lev. 20:26). If this was true, then it was natural to assume that a barrier existed between the nations and a life-giving relationship with Yahweh as well.

Israel—A Light to the Nations

So far we have seen an exclusive picture of God's involvement in the world. What has been sketched in broad terms is the belief that Yahweh, the only authentic God in existence, had begun a work of grace solely in the nation of Israel. He did this by separating her from a rebellious world turned in on itself. Whatever else might be said, this concept was a priority for Israel. One might say that it was the basic understanding under which she operated.

Nevertheless, there is a strange irony in this portrait. The very belief that cut Israel off from the nations at the same time opened up the possibility of interaction with these nations. As remarkable as it seems,

---

6. M. Wilson, *American Anthropologist* 56 (1954): 241; quoted in Wenham, *Numbers*, 26.

7. For an interpretation of various elements of Israel's ritual in accordance with this view of the world, see Mary Douglas, *Purity and Danger* (London: Routledge & Kegan Paul, 1966); Douglas Davies, "An Interpretation of Sacrifice in Leviticus," *Zeitschrift für die alttestamentliche Wissenschaft* 89 (1977): 387–99.

Israel's conviction about her common origin with the nations was as fundamental as her belief in the exclusiveness of Yahweh.

Israel believed that Yahweh alone created and sustained the universe,[8] and because of this she acknowledged that Yahweh controlled all nations, not just Israel. From time to time, Israelite prophets dusted off this neglected belief and stressed that Yahweh cared about the destinies of all peoples (Amos 9:7). And if as Master of the universe Yahweh holds exclusive rights to judge all nations, including Israel (Amos 1:3–2:16), then the possibility of divine mercy is open to all who repent.

So what of Israel's conviction about her separation from the nations? Might this be an aberration or at best an exaggeration of her self-awareness? It is true that at times Israel's exclusiveness got in the way of Yahweh's purposes (e.g., the case of Jonah). Still, Israel's calling to separation cannot merely be set aside. For, as it turns out, it is the key to her legitimate involvement with the nations around her.

We must remember that Israel saw the world in categorical terms. She stood opposed to the nations who were far from God; she was divided from them in her history, worship, and destiny. There is not the slightest hint she thought the nations were worshiping Yahweh under other names (Judg. 10:6). So, we might ask, how could the nations find their way to God in their state of rebellion? The answer is, of course, through Israel herself—a mediator who was "in the world, but not of the world." Israel's exclusive relationship with Yahweh was the ideal for all creation. And so long as Israel maintained this relationship, she could bear witness to the nations around her, demonstrating that blessings come when a nation acknowledges the gracious Creator.

This unique role for Israel is forecast in her ancestral history. Abram is found among the nations that dispersed after Babel (Gen. 11:10–32). And yet literary patterns cast a special light on this man among the nations.[9] He will be another Noah, singled out of the chaos of universal judgment to be the catalyst in the redemption of a world sorely in

8. This view rejects the position, originally expressed by Gerhard von Rad, that creation was largely an ancillary theme to redemption in ancient Israel and developed only to full conception at the time of the exile. See "The Theological Problem of the Old Testament Doctrine of Creation," in *The Problem of the Hexateuch and Other Essays,* trans. E. W. Trueman Dicken (New York: McGraw-Hill, 1966), 131–43. In the ancient Near Eastern religious context, it is difficult to imagine Israel conceiving of Yahweh as a Redeemer-God in isolation from cosmic conceptions. For a study of the merging of these concepts in the theology of Jeremiah, see Helga Weippert, *Schöpfer des Himmels und der Erde,* Stuttgarter Bibelstudien 102 (Stuttgart: Katholisches Bibelwerk, 1981).

9. The genealogical notices (Gen. 5:32; 11:10–26) link Adam, Noah, and Abram, each ten generations apart. This literary pattern identifies these individuals as single representatives and bearers of the potential for blessing of human life in history. See Michael Fishbane, *Text and Texture: Close Readings of Selected Biblical Texts* (New York: Schocken, 1979), 30–31, 39.

need of it (Gen. 12:1–3). God will bless him with many descendants. But his blessing will become a blessing for "all peoples on earth."

We are given few details as to how this will come about. But perhaps we can discern how Israel thought she would become a blessing by examining her treatment of outsiders. She was not closed to all Gentiles, but rather opened herself to outsiders who acknowledged her existence and, thus, her God. The Old Testament is filled with such people, for example, the "mixed company" (Exod. 12:38) that joined Israel at the exodus, or the resident aliens who ratified the covenant and lived a protected existence within the confines of the "holy" land (Lev. 19:10; Deut. 16:11–15; 29:10 [Heb. v. 9]; Ruth; 1 Kings 8:41–43).

In addition, the Old Testament contains dramatic stories of outsiders "blessing" Israel's God, recognizing him as the only true God (e.g., Rahab in Josh. 2:8–11; Naaman in 2 Kings 5:15). These occasions highlight the inevitable tension that existed between Israel's exclusive identity and her role as informant to other peoples. The tension is best seen in the conflicts individual converts to Yahweh experienced. Rahab's testimony compelled her to deceive her own people in order to protect the Israelite spies (Josh. 2:2–7). Naaman, a participant in the royal Assyrian cult, perceived the conflict immediately. His position and cultic obligations compromised his new commitment (2 Kings 5:17–18). The prophet Elisha could offer no solution to his dilemma (5:19). If one acknowledges the barriers that divided Israel and the nations, these matters are, in fact, irresolvable.[10]

The vision of universal blessing expands when we reach the prophets to include the nations of the world.[11] This prophetic theme contains tantalizing allusions to the debacle at Babel. The prophets imagined a day when all people would use the same language to worship truly the one and only Yahweh (Isa. 45:23; Zeph. 3:9). The people of Israel would play a distinctive role in this, of course. They might even have had a notion that this language of praise would be their own (Isa. 19:18).

Although Israel was a highly exclusive nation, she was to play a role far beyond her own religion and culture. The reputation of Yahweh throughout the world was tied to her existence in history. Naturally, the way she bore witness to Yahweh changed with her political status. But whether she was an independent nation with a continual influx of foreigners or a landless people in exile, her unique "mission" was to reflect the incomparable power and mercy of Yahweh. Ideally, others

10. For a penetrating discussion of this event, see Gerhard von Rad, *God at Work in Israel*, trans. John H. Marks (Nashville: Abingdon, 1980), 47–57.

11. See John N. Oswalt, "The Mission of Israel to the Nations" (in this volume), for a survey of the prophetic conception of Israel's witness to the nations.

would come to acknowledge him through contact with, or at least awareness of, the nation of Israel. She was to be the lighthouse that guided the nations into the port of Yahweh.

Salvation Outside the Covenant Community

We might now assume that the picture is complete. The nature of Israel's identity and the role it implied seem to rule out any other divine activity among the peoples of the world. But this is not the case.

A third conviction stands in the Old Testament alongside Israel's commitment to her unique identity among the nations and her role as catalyst in world redemption. This conviction is anchored in Israel's fundamental belief that Yahweh is the sovereign God and the Creator of *all* humanity. As Lord of the universe, Yahweh reserves the right to choose his involvements (Exod. 3:12–14; 33:19).[12] He stands ultimately beyond all human manipulation and will respond in mercy to anyone who humbly seeks him.[13]

The Old Testament never hides the fact that some outside Israel recognize their dependence on the God of creation. When encountered by Israelites, such people have already responded to God by acknowledging him as Creator and Lord. They have arrived at their decision apart from any contact with Israel. Called "God-fearers," they are "blameless and upright" (Job 1:8), conscious of a standard of morality that will not exploit the weak and vulnerable (Gen. 20:11; Exod. 1:17; 18:21; Deut. 25:18). They are people who resist manipulating situations for self-interest, precisely the opposite of what the nations did at Babel. Most important, their fear of God parallels that of the ideal Israelite (see Gen. 22:12; Lev. 19:14, 32; Pss. 15:4; 22:23 [Heb. v. 24]; 61:5 [Heb. v. 6]; 66:16)! "To fear God," says Phyllis Trible, "is to worship God . . . and the worship of God abolishes all idolatries."[14]

When one thinks of God-fearers, inevitably Melchizedek and Jethro come to mind (Gen. 14:18–20; Exod. 18:1–27). These individuals share a number of characteristics.[15] But what cannot be missed is that both recognize divine activity in Israel and issue praise in the name of

12. For this interpretation of the enigmatic ʾ*ehyeh* ʾ *ăšer* ʾ*ehyeh* ("I am who I am"), see Samuel Terrien, *The Elusive Presence: Toward a New Biblical Theology* (San Francisco: Harper & Row, 1978), 113–19.

13. This third conviction does not set aside Israel's belief that she was unique among the nations in her experience and acknowledgment of Yahweh. This was her testimony and the key to community solidarity in the covenant.

14. Phyllis Trible, *Genesis 22: The Sacrifice of Sarah*, Gross Memorial Lecture 1989 (Valparaiso, Ind.: Valparaiso University Press, 1990), 8.

15. For example, both are priests of foreign nations that come into conflict with Israel during her formative period. Both appear at times of Israel's deliverance to give independent testimony to God's gracious activity. Both are contrasted with nations who

Israel's God. A remarkable act from foreign priests whose nations subsequently become enemies of Israel!

The enigmatic Melchizedek, priest-king of Salem, encounters Abram after his victory over a Mesopotamian raiding party in Canaan (Gen. 14). Whatever else might be said about the significance of this meeting,[16] the reader is immediately struck by two points: (1) Abram and Melchizedek show respect and appreciation for one another, and (2) they know and worship God by the same name, El Elyon.[17] These are startling facts! As far as we know, these men had no previous contact with one another. Abram lived on the fringe of Canaanite society with a different cultural orientation than that of the city-states (Gen. 13). Are we not to assume that Abram and Melchizedek came by their knowledge of El Elyon independently, perhaps through their distinct revelations of God?

Jethro, the Midianite father-in-law of Moses, is even more remarkable.[18] Not only is this Gentile credited with organizing the Israelite judiciary (Exod. 18:13–25), but his words of praise upon hearing of the exodus from Egypt identify him as a worshiper of Yahweh (18:10–11)! How did this Gentile discover the covenant name of God? The language of his confession at Sinai ("Now I know . . .") suggests a deepening of his faith rather than a conversion from paganism (compare 1 Kings 17:24; Ps. 135:5).[19]

In the final analysis, it is virtually impossible to deny that Israel believed Yahweh was active in the world independent of her covenant.

---

do not fear God but intend to profit from Israel. Both remain part of their "heathen" nations after the event.

16. See Claus Westermann, *Genesis 12–26: A Commentary*, trans. John J. Scullion (Minneapolis: Augsburg, 1985), 184–85, for the extensive bibliography on Melchizedek.

17. Compare 14:19–20 with 14:22 and 33:20. For the use of this title in Israelite hymnic tradition, see Pss. 115:15; 121:2; 124:8; 134:3. There is good reason to believe that the patriarchs knew their God as El, but need not have drawn this name from Canaanite contexts, as is often supposed (compare the plain sense of Exod. 6:1–3). Later the name *Yahweh* could have been inserted in certain contexts (e.g., Gen. 14:22) to identify the older name with the new one. See Gordon Wenham, "The Religion of the Patriarchs," in *Essays on the Patriarchal Narratives*, ed. Alan R. Millard and Donald J. Wiseman (Winona Lake, Ind.: Eisenbrauns, 1983), 161–95 (esp. 190).

18. It is interesting that in aggadic materials (that is, talmudic and rabbinic interpretation of the nonlegal passages in the Old Testament), Jethro is portrayed alternately as a Gentile convert to the Mosaic religion and as an idolater who opposed it. These portraits alleviate the tension created by an independent Yahwist who assists Israel in forming its judicial system. For citations, see Aaron Rothkoff, "Jethro," in *Encyclopedia Judaica* (Jerusalem: Keter, 1971), 10:19–20.

19. This observation has always troubled scholars. One may assume, of course, that Jethro had become a Yahwist through the testimony of Moses in the wilderness. Some have even preferred that it was the other way around. Hence, the elaborate "Kenite Hypothesis," which supposes that Moses learned of the name *Yahweh* from Jethro dur-

Admittedly, problems do arise when one tries to integrate this with her unique sense of identity and role. But it is important to note that Israel herself was not unduly bothered by any conflict here. If anything, she was embarrassed by her failure to recognize God-fearing Gentiles in her acquaintance (Gen. 20:1–18, esp. v. 11). And there is never a hint that Israel saw "the fear of God" among the nations as something less than a redemptive experience. She accepted it on both practical and theological grounds. Israel's exclusive calling was to be a testimony to the nations. What happened apart from that was Yahweh's business.

But Israel did reject, it seems, the notion of entire God-fearing nations. At least, she had no evidence they existed. The God-fearing Gentiles of the Old Testament are presented frequently as individuals who stand against the tide of their own people. It is for individual Gentiles that Abraham looks to stave off the destruction of Sodom and Gomorrah (Gen. 18:16–33). It is individual Gentiles who, according to the prophet Ezekiel, are insufficient to save an entire nation in rebellion (Ezek. 14:13–20).[20] From Israel's perspective, only a righteous nation could be a blessing to the nations of the earth (Gen. 12:1–3).

Yet, how did individual God-fearers come to faith outside the witness of Israel? As one might imagine, trying to investigate this phenomenon in literature oriented to the nation of Israel is not an easy matter. The Old Testament treats the "God-fearers," by and large, as an anomaly. No explanations are offered for how they came to acknowledge the transcendent God in a rebellious and idolatrous world. For the writers these matters were best left in God's hands.

Still, there are a number of significant facts to consider. Melchizedek and Jethro knew the names of God that, according to the Bible, were communicated to Israel through special revelation. The reader will hardly imagine that Gentiles acquired these names simply by observing the wonders of nature. In the cases of Melchizedek and Jethro, at least, we cannot rule out an independent revelation of God. Perhaps even the religious traditions of the Canaanites and Midianites contributed as two foreign priests sought the true God apart from their religions.

---

ing his stay in the wilderness. See, among others, Harold H. Rowley, *From Joseph to Joshua,* Schweich Lectures 1948 (Oxford: Oxford University Press for the British Academy, 1950), 149–55. These theories, as do all attempts to make the religions of Jethro and Moses dependent on one another, fail for lack of evidence.

20. In my estimation, the prophet employs here the names of venerable, righteous Gentiles (Noah, Danʾel, and Job) to indicate the universal truth of his point. This perspective assumes that Danʾel is the figure referred to in the Ugaritic epic of *Aqht,* and not the biblical Daniel. See Ezek. 28:3, where Ezekiel appeals to the standard set by Danʾel before the ruler of Tyre, a Phoenician (Canaanite) city. See John C. L. Gibson, *Canaanite Myths and Legends,* 2d ed. (Edinburgh: T. & T. Clark, 1978), 103–22.

Israel's view of herself and the world was conditioned by her understanding of God and his work of grace in her. The knowledge of Yahweh was the goal of all creation. And Yahweh himself had achieved that goal in Israel by separating her from the rest of the nations steeped in idolatry and immorality. The barrier between Israel and other peoples was as real as the boundaries of her nation.

So what of the fate of the surrounding nations? And what about those in Israel who followed the course of other civilizations against the will of God? Oracles of doom against the nations and the wicked in the community fill the Old Testament. Those who set themselves against the people and purposes of God find only devastation in this life. Their doom, as we discover in apocalyptic literature (e.g., Dan. 7), is not limited to this present world, but continues into eternity.

In the midst of this rebellion, Israel lived in Yahweh's land. She was part of the family of humankind, situated geographically, politically, and morally in the very center of it (Ezek. 5:5–17). Her God-given identity implied a function on behalf of humanity. Ideally, she would draw all peoples to God through the testimony of his mercy and power in her.

But was Israel God's only means of reaching the nations? The examples of Melchizedek, Jethro, and others[21] suggest that some individuals find salvation in Yahweh apart from Israel's influence. The realization that Yahweh was at work outside her was only further evidence of the truth she knew. The one and only Yahweh sought the ultimate redemption of all the peoples of the earth.

21. Other God-fearers such as Abimelech (Gen. 20) and Job could also be considered.

6

The Mission of Israel
to the Nations

John N. Oswalt

The Old Testament teaches that Israel had an obligation to bear witness to her neighbors. Few would deny that statement today. But there is less agreement as to the nature of that witness. Lately, many have argued that Israel had no sense that hers was the only way to God. Naturally, if this were so, Christian missionaries should question whether converting people from other religions is a proper goal.[1] This chapter will survey the prophetic books, where a majority of references to the nations occur, and will define more clearly the nature of Israel's mission to the nations. The prophetic writings will be studied in chronological order as far as can be determined. This will permit a synchronic view of the data, providing an opportunity to observe any chronological developments that may

---

1. See, e.g., Richard H. Drummond, *Toward a New Age in Christian Theology* (Maryknoll, N.Y.: Orbis, 1985), 14; and John Hick, *God Has Many Names* (Philadelphia: Westminster, 1982), 57. For a classic statement of the opposing point of view, see Harold H. Rowley, *The Missionary Message of the Old Testament* (London: Carey Kingsgate, 1944), esp. 45.

have taken place. In cases where dating is disputed, as for Joel and Isaiah, some effort will be made to see how the concepts fit with the different proposed dates.

Joel

Joel may be the earliest extant prophetic writing or one of the latest, depending on which reasoning seems more conclusive. Older commentators dated it to around 835 B.C., during the infancy of Joash, while almost all recent commentators place it during the postexilic period.[2] Whatever date one assigns to the book, it has some explicit things to say about the nations, particularly in chapter 3 [Heb. chap. 4]. The tone is resolutely negative. The nations that have ruthlessly pillaged Judah will be defeated by God and barred from the Holy City. They (represented by Edom and Egypt) will be desolate (3:19 [Heb. 4:19]), while God's people (Judah and Jerusalem) will be abundant (3:18 [Heb. 4:18]).

In contrast to this grim picture is the clear possibility that the promise in Joel 2 is intended to have universal aspects. Without question the preceding setting is specific to the Jews (note the terms *children of Zion* [AV], *you,* and *my people* throughout vv. 23–27). Nevertheless *kol bāśār* ("all flesh"; 2:28 [Heb. 3:1]) is clearly universal in its application elsewhere (Gen. 6:12, 13, 17; Num. 18:15; Isa. 49:26, "Then all mankind will know that I, the LORD, am your Savior"). While the references to *your* sons and daughters and *your* old and young men could be said to limit the scope of the idea, the undefined menservants and maidservants of verse 29 [Heb. 3:2] seem to broaden it again, as does "everyone who calls" (*kōl ʾ ăšer yiqrāʿ*) in verse 32 [Heb. 3:5].[3]

Thus, the specific references to the nations in Joel focus strictly upon the judgment they deserve because they mistreated God's people. Yet, alongside God's judgment is the saving outflow of his Spirit, which would indeed be available through Israel to all persons. How these ideas might bear upon the date of the book will be considered later.

---

2. Some of the older commentators supporting an earlier date for Joel are Robert Jamieson, Andrew R. Fausset, and David Brown, *Jeremiah–Malachi* (repr., Grand Rapids: Eerdmans, 1948); Carl F. Keil, *The Twelve Minor Prophets,* trans. James Martin, 2 vols. (repr., Grand Rapids: Eerdmans, 1975); and Theodore Laetsch, *Bible Commentary on the Minor Prophets* (St. Louis: Concordia, 1956). Two recent commentators arguing for a later date for Joel are Leslie C. Allen, *The Books of Joel, Obadiah, Jonah, and Micah,* New International Commentary on the Old Testament (Grand Rapids: Eerdmans, 1976); and Hans Walther Wolff, *Joel and Amos,* trans. Waldemar Janzen, S. Dean McBride, Jr., and Charles A. Muenchow, Hermeneia (Philadelphia: Fortress, 1977).

3. For a good treatment of this universal aspect, see Keil, *Twelve Minor Prophets,* 1:212–18. For a recent statement of the opposing point of view, see Allen, *Joel,* 96–105.

Hosea and Amos

In both Hosea and Amos, the picture is much different. Here the focus is almost wholly upon the present or the near future. Furthermore, the center of attention is the failure of Israel to maintain its covenant obligations to God and the resultant curse that is about to fall upon the nation. Israel and Judah alike have forfeited their favored status and come under judgment as just two more of the nations (Amos 1–2; compare Isa. 21). The upshot of this is that the nations to whom the Israelites have turned instead of God (Hos. 7:8–11) will be used by God to punish his own (Hos. 9:3–6; Amos 6:14; 9:9).

Given this emphasis upon Israel's present sin, it is not too surprising if there is no extended reference to her mission among the nations. Nonetheless, there are still tantalizing single references in each of the books. In each case they appear in the final section of the book, which describes the restored nation's glorious future. Hosea 14:6–7 [Heb. vv. 7–8] describes restored Israel as a beautiful tree under whose shade people will again rest. While this may be merely one component of the imagery of restoration, it may also be a statement of Israel's continuing function.

In Amos 9:11–12 the Septuagint has the fallen tent of David being restored "so that the remnant of men and the nations "that bear my name may seek the Lord" (NIV margin). The Masoretic Text is more enigmatic and may be the harder reading; it has "that they may possess the remnant of Edom and all the nations that bear my name." Nevertheless, even that reading, with its "nations that bear my name," suggests that the possession involved is not merely the disinheriting of former oppressors (as in Obad. 18–21). Somehow Israel's glorious future involves a wider focus than mere nationalism.

Jonah

The wider view hinted at in Hosea and Amos is of course at the heart of the message of Jonah. The book's implication that Israelites have an obligation to bear God's word even to their enemies is so well known that it needs little further comment here. However, there is one point that needs to be made in this context. Precisely in the time of Amos and Hosea, with their narrow emphasis upon Israel's sin and the punishment that is to fall upon them from Assyria, an Israelite prophet is sent to Assyria with a word from God.[4] It is as though God is calling on Israel to look beyond the present situation and see the

4. Allen's commentary on Jonah is a moderate statement of this conclusion. See Keil, *Twelve Minor Prophets*, 1:380–89, for the classic statement in defense of the book's authenticity.

larger implications of their relationship to God. That relationship is not one of privilege, but of responsibility.

Micah and Isaiah

The apparent dichotomy between Israel's privilege and her responsibility seems to be bridged in Micah and, to a greater extent, in Isaiah. On the one hand, as in Amos and Hosea, there is great attention given to the present disastrous condition of the nation and the destruction of the Holy City that those conditions will engender. It is because of corrupt political and religious leaders (Mic. 3:11) that this disaster will occur (Mic. 4:11–12). Yet, in direct juxtaposition to this diatribe against those who have failed in their mission of revealing God in Israel comes the famous depiction of the mountain of the Lord (4:1–5) that clearly sets forth Israel's mission to the nations. Ruined Zion will become the highest mountain of all and all the nations will come to it to learn the law of God. The statement seems to serve two purposes in its present setting. On the one hand, in the light of this future universal role of revelation, the present failures of the leaders in the national context are the more despicable. On the other hand, this passage makes it plain that, despite the failures of Israel and Judah, God's intentions for them were such that they could not, and would not, be abandoned.[5]

Isaiah's use of the same image is instructive. Arguments over which prophet originated it have so far been inconclusive.[6] However the question is answered, Isaiah uses the imagery to good effect. At the head of chapter 2, it stands in stark contrast to both chapter 1 and to 2:5–4:1, the next section. The contrast is so stark we are brought up sharply by it. How can the harlot city of 1:21 be the fountainhead of law and word in 2:3? To a significant extent this question and its answer set the agenda for the rest of the book: How can rebel Israel become servant Israel for the purpose of revealing God's glory to the world?

But we must return to Micah for a moment. Some might say that any concept of mission in 4:1–5 is negated by the conclusion of Micah 4 (and all of chap. 5) where the daughter of Zion is invited to thresh the nations and give whatever is left as an offering to God (4:11–13).

---

5. Mic. 4:5 should not be seen as a sign of indifference on Micah's part. There is every reason to take it as a statement of current fact. In spite of the present adherence of the surrounding nations to idols, if Israel would be faithful to her God, the day would come when all nations would recognize Israel's God alone.

6. If one of the prophets originated the idea it seems likely to have been Micah. The image in Mic. 4 follows naturally from 3:12, but seems to break in abruptly after Isa. 1:31. See John N. Oswalt, *The Book of Isaiah, Chapters 1–39*, New International Commentary on the Old Testament (Grand Rapids: Eerdmans, 1986), 112–19.

Surely this expression, corresponding to that of Joel, conveys Israel's normative attitude toward the nations—not obligation, but domination—and 4:1–5 must be read in that light. Thus the flowing of the nations to Jerusalem would be as slaves.[7]

There is no need, however, to force either of these ideas into subordination. They are coordinate. Israel can be both blessing and curse—as indeed can God. To those who come in submission and acceptance he offers a blessed parent-child relationship. But to those who insist on taking his gifts by force, he shows nothing but implacable hostility. Thus, it is not at all inconsistent that Zion should be at the same time a source of life and a source of death to the nations.[8] This same collocation of ideas appears even more starkly in Isaiah 14. Verse 1 tells us that foreigners will unite with the house of Jacob while verse 2 says Israel will enslave the oppressors. These ideas are not polar opposites, but complementary. It is as God destroys the nations that persist in oppressing his people that the nations are moved to seek his mercy and grace.

None of the other prophets matches Isaiah for his full-orbed treatment of this subject. From chapter 2 until chapter 66, in which we are told that all humankind will worship God (v. 23), the nations are never far from Isaiah's view. In fact, a good case can be made that chapter 6 is in its present position in the book in order to show that just as the man of unclean lips was made able to declare the glory of God to his nation, so the people of unclean lips (as described in chapters 1–5) could be made able to declare that glory to the nations (66:18–20).[9]

When the book is seen in this way chapters 7–39 are a discussion of Israel's need to recognize the glory of God. The great irony of these chapters is that instead of trusting God and thus representing him to the nations, Israel becomes enamored with the glory of the nations and turns her back on God. The burden of the section, then, is to show the folly of such a move. Against this backdrop four allusions to mission are noteworthy. The first of these occurs at the end of the description of the messianic kingdom in chapter 11. The earth will be so full of the knowledge of the Lord that violence and destruction will cease (11:9). While it may be argued with some force that the passage

---

7. For this point of view, see Delbert R. Hillers, *Micah,* Hermeneia (Philadelphia: Fortress, 1984), 49–53.

8. See Gen. 12:3 for this thought. D. W. Van Winkle reaches this same conclusion (that it is not a case of either-or, but both-and) in his "Relationship of the Nations to Yahweh and to Israel in Isaiah 40–55," *Vetus Testamentum* 35 (1985): 446–58. Nor is this a new position. It was already espoused by Gustav F. Oehler in his *Theologie des Alten Testaments* (Stuttgart: Steinkopf, 1882), 804–11.

9. See Oswalt, *Isaiah,* 55ff.

is descriptive and not prescriptive, it is still a witness to what the prophet expected to be the outcome of Israel's experience.

The second allusion appears in chapter 19 at the end of the oracle against Egypt. Verse 24 states that a day will come when, as a result of God's healing, Egypt and Assyria will join with Israel to become a blessing "on the earth." Whether this is an allusion to Genesis 12:3 is unclear, but the same concept is certainly at work: God's blessing must be shared.

The third allusion to a mission of Israel among the nations is found in chapter 25. Chapter 24 summarizes the oracles against the nations (chaps. 13–23), and speaks of their total destruction. Chapter 25 then says that, because this destruction will be a manifestation of God's absolute faithfulness to his own, all peoples will come to "this mountain" (Zion) to worship God. There he will prepare a feast for "all peoples" (v. 6), in the context of which he will destroy death for all the nations (v. 7).[10]

The common thread in all three of these passages is the idea that it is by means of Israel that God will show himself to the nations. There is a sense in which Israel is passive in all this. It is as the nations observe how God treats his people, and as his qualities are manifested by his people, that the nations are drawn to him. Thus the question must be raised whether Israel has a responsibility to the nations or merely to God. Probably the prophet was not thinking in either/or categories, as 12:4 would indicate. There Israel is commanded to active witness: "Make known among the nations what he has done, and proclaim that his name is exalted."

The final allusion to Israel's mission to the nations in chapters 7–39 appears in chapter 39, where Hezekiah's failure to give glory to God before the visiting Babylonians is directly linked to the coming exile in Babylon. More than is superficially apparent, this linkage leads directly into chapters 40–66. It is not merely the mention of Babylon nor even the allusion to the coming exile that makes this chapter such a bridge. Rather, it is this whole aspect of witness. Hezekiah, and by extension the whole nation, had failed to be a vehicle for demonstrating God's glory to the nations. Thus, the exile results, but not merely as a punishment; it also becomes the vehicle whereby Israel's mission can be fulfilled.

---

10. Chaps. 24–27 have sometimes been referred to as the "Little Apocalypse" since they speak in rather universalistic terms about God's triumph over the nations. Whether this is a correct identification of the material is open to question because many of the characteristic features of apocalyptic are not found. See Oswalt, *Isaiah*, 440–41; and Oswalt, "Recent Studies in Old Testament Eschatology and Apocalyptic," *Journal of the Evangelical Theological Society* 24 (1981): 289–302.

This idea of representing God before the nations is crucial in chapters 40–48 and again in chapters 56–66. In chapters 40–48 God expresses his unmerited favor to the exiles by telling them that not only has he not forsaken them, but he will use them to demonstrate his Godhead against the Babylonian idols. (For this same idea in slightly different words, see Ezek. 36:22–36.) Israel's deliverance, a brand-new thing, will demonstrate that their God is indeed God of the whole world. In a series of ringing affirmations God insists that Israel will be the means of the nations recognizing their folly and turning to him (41:20; 42:10–13; 44:23; 45:1–6, 14, 22–25).

Again, Israel's role here is primarily passive. It is as God delivers them, demonstrating both his own incomparable power and the impotence of the idols that the nations will come to recognize that God alone is God, the "Holy One." This is not to say there is no active role for Israel to play. We need only to think of chapter 39 to see the counterpoise. But it is to remind ourselves that any witness to the nations is predicated solely on the salvific activity of God on his people's behalf.

The identity of the Servant of the Lord in chapters 42–53 is of course a matter of continuing controversy.[11] But it must suffice here to point out that not only is the Servant a covenant for the people (ʿām—surely Israel), he is also a light to the nations (42:6) and filled with the Spirit of God to bring justice to the nations (42:1; see also 49:6; 51:4–5). These descriptions are so like those used in unquestionably messianic passages elsewhere in the book (especially 11:1–6) that we can only conclude the Servant referred to here is the Messiah. Thus, Israel's Anointed One has an expected worldwide ministry and through him Israel does as well.[12]

The ministry of Israel to the world takes on a more active focus in chapters 56–66. Here the parochial narrowness that seems to have characterized Israel through much of its history is challenged. Genealogical and cultic correctness are shown to be of no value unless they are accompanied by heartfelt obedience. In this respect an obedient foreigner is much more pleasing to God than a disobedient purebred Jew (56:6). Nor is this merely an abstract example. God says he will bring the foreigners into his very temple so that it may be "a house of prayer for all nations" (56:7). God will not allow the Jews to turn in on themselves, congratulating themselves upon their good fortune in election or in escaping from Babylon. No, they have a mission

---

11. For further discussion see Oswalt, *Isaiah,* 49–52.

12. For the purposes of this chapter it is important to note that even if we were to agree with medieval Jewish exegesis and conclude that the Servant is always Israel, the import for our topic would be unchanged: Israel has a mission to the wider world.

to perform, and God will endow them with his Spirit for its performance (59:21).

This mission is made explicit in chapter 60 with its promise that the nations and their kings will come to the light that will dawn upon Israel (60:1–3). To be sure, one aspect of this promised coming is servitude (60:10–14), but this is not the total picture, for there is also the sense that the nations will come to Zion out of recognition of what wondrous things Israel's God has done for her (61:9; 62:2). Again, the key concept is witness. Israel is not necessarily commissioned to convert the nations, but she is to make the Lord known everywhere (64:2 [Heb. v. 1]). This idea is stated in no uncertain terms in the final chapter of the book, where we are told that God will send survivors from the Jews to the nations to declare his glory so that all flesh shall come to worship before him (66:19–23).

Thus, the book ends on the note first introduced in chapter 2. God's ultimate purpose is that the nations should know and worship him, and Israel is the instrument by which that purpose will be accomplished. Nor is this a late concept, as the reechoing of chapter 2 makes plain. Since that passage is duplicated in Micah, which is securely dated to the last half of the eighth century B.C., we can confidently argue that the concept is endemic to the classical prophets from the earliest days of the movement.

Jeremiah

When we turn to Jeremiah we find a situation much like that of Hosea and Amos a century and a half earlier. Jeremiah, like them, is largely absorbed with the present tragic situation in his country and consequently gives little attention to any larger mission. His focus is upon the imminent destruction coming upon Jerusalem, which has defiled itself with the false gods of the foreign nations. Nevertheless, even here we find the picture of what was intended to be, and would yet be, the case: all the nations will gather to Jerusalem, to God's presence (3:17).

But from this promise it is a long thirteen chapters before another isolated word comes, "O LORD . . . to you the nations will come from the ends of the earth and say, 'Our fathers possessed nothing but false gods'" (16:19). And from here it is seventeen more chapters until we hear that "this city will bring me renown, joy, praise, and honor before all nations on earth" (33:9). Yet, although these words are few and far between in the book, their import is quite clear and perfectly consistent with what has been seen elsewhere: Jerusalem's restoration will not be an end in itself. Rather, it will be for the sake of a worldwide witness.

Ezekiel

A similar situation prevails in Ezekiel 1–33, which centers on the coming destruction of Jerusalem. Apart from the negative statement that the name of God will be profaned among the nations because of Judah (22:16), everything concerns the present sinful condition and the resulting hastening desolation.

The situation changes after chapter 33, when Ezekiel begins to speak of the restoration. The point is especially clear in chapters 36–37 where God speaks of the need to vindicate his holiness before the nations that had been led by Israel's defeat to doubt him (36:23, 35–36; 37:28). As in Isaiah 41–45, this witness is primarily passive. God shows the nations that he alone is God by delivering and purifying Israel. Still, Israel's role is crucial. Without her willing participation, God's purpose will not be realized.

It should also be pointed out that, as in most of the other prophets, God will vindicate his holiness in another way. He will use Israel to destroy the nations that persist in their enmity toward him. Gog is one of those that will discover God's sovereignty in this way (38:16, 23).[13]

Zephaniah, Zechariah, and Daniel

Among the remaining prophets, Zephaniah is typical of what has been observed thus far: comments about the mission of Israel are not frequent and they are surely not accorded primary status. Nevertheless, they are unmistakably clear, as in 3:9, where the peoples are given a pure speech so that they may call on the Lord's name. This is God's work, not Israel's, but it is accomplished within the context of Israel's life and faith.

In Zechariah, four important statements appear, each of which underlines a key point. Zechariah 2:11 [Heb. v. 15] speaks of the nations joining themselves to the Lord because of his blessings on Israel and his judgment on them. Zechariah 8:13 alludes to Genesis 12:3 and speaks of Israel, which had been a synonym for curse in the ancient world, becoming a vehicle of blessing. It will be such a blessing that the nations will come to Jerusalem to experience the favor of God, as Israel has (8:20–23). Finally, in 14:16–19 we are told that following the last battle, when all the enemy nations have been defeated, they shall all come up to Jerusalem to worship the King, the Lord of Hosts.

Interestingly, there are no explicit statements about Israel's mission

13. See Walther Zimmerli, *Ezekiel*, 2 vols., trans. Ronald E. Clements and James D. Martin, Hermeneia (Philadelphia: Fortress, 1979–83), 2:299–304, for a discussion of the range of interpretation of this figure. At the least it represents the forces of a world hostile to God's kingship.

in the Book of Daniel. But what we do find in the first seven chapters is a remarkable illustration of the nature and effect of that mission. As Daniel and his friends live out their devotion and obedience to God, the mightiest kings of the age are forced to recognize and in some cases submit to the God of Israel. This is a parable of what Israel's calling is about. To be sure, it is God's work that accomplishes the result; in many cases Daniel and his friends are mere vehicles for God's demonstration. On the other hand, they are eager, active participants in what God is doing. Moreover, again and again it is the very quality of their lives, as they confront the nations and their gods, that provides the catalyst for the divine demonstration. Thus, we are able to see in action exactly what the other prophets have in mind when they speak of Israel and the nations.

Israel and the Nations

What shall we say, then, about the prophetic conception of Israel's mission to the nations? First of all, there is little development in the concept. If we take Micah and Zechariah, two books whose dates are generally agreed upon as being early and late, respectively, we see little difference in the idea itself. Nor does the handling of this concept in Joel give any real help in assigning a date to that book. What Joel says about the nations is no less probable in 835 B.C. than it is in 435 B.C. If it be urged that the emphasis on the destruction of the nations is more like Zechariah, it must be pointed out that the treatment in both books is not unlike the oracle of Nahum against Assyria. If Joel is to be dated in the fifth century B.C., it must be on grounds other than this.

By the same token, it is not possible to date Isaiah 40–66 using its concept of Israel's mission. As noted above, the statements found in the last chapters of Isaiah are largely identical to those in Micah 4. Thus, I would argue that at least for the four-hundred-year period of classical prophecy this concept was relatively stable.

But what exactly was the concept? Can we now synthesize the various statements into one overall outline? Yes, the basic uniformity makes that possible. First, it can be stated with complete confidence that Israel did see itself as having a worldwide ministry. Nor is this merely, as some might suggest, an invitation to the world to become spectators to what God is doing on Israel's behalf. Much less is it limited to the nations becoming the servants of a victorious Israel. To be sure, these elements can be found at various points in the prophetic writings, but they do not in any sense exhaust what is being said. Rather, it is said again and again that the nations will come to Jerusalem in order to become full participants with Israel in worship and service to the Lord.

Second, it can be stated that Israel's function is that of witness as opposed to proselytizer. It is true that Israel is called upon at various points to go to the nations to declare the glory of God and his wondrous works. It is never stated, however, that the purpose of this declaration is to create converts. Israel, by its life and words, is to demonstrate what God is like and what he is doing. Beyond this, it is God who will do the drawing and the bringing of the nations to himself. In this context it is important to note the many times when no movement from Judah or Jerusalem is indicated at all. If Israel will simply be the Israel of God, the nations will be drawn to him.

Third, at the same time there is no sense in which Israel's God is depicted as being merely one among many to which the nations may eventually come. They must either bow in submission to him or be destroyed. It is as God demonstrates through Israel that he is incomparable, both in mercy and in power, that the nations will abandon their false religions and come to him. Thus, although it is true that Israel is not instructed to convert the world, neither is their calling merely to make a contribution to world theology. Their witness is normative.

Fourth is the universal nature of the promise. "All" nations, "all" people, and "all" flesh are some of the terms used to describe the scope of the involvement. There is no limitation on the impact that Israel's witness is to have. Since the Lord is sole God of creation, it makes sense that the truth should indeed be for all people.

Finally, we may observe that, fundamental as this witness is, it is not the dominant motif in the prophetic writings. Thus, it is not justifiable to say that worldwide salvation is what the prophetic writings are about. To be sure, the prophets clearly saw this as the end of history, toward which all things were leading. But their chief concern was more immediate than that. That concern was to call Israel to present obedience to her covenant Lord and to demonstrate what consequences could be expected if she would, or would not, obey. It is in the midst of doing this that the issue of mission arises. Why is God concerned about Israel's obedience or disobedience? Merely because it is a breach of covenant? Hardly. God is concerned because it is through Israel that the world is to come to know him. It is through Israel that the nations will come to recognize the vanity of their idolatrous religions and will come humbly to Jerusalem, submitting themselves to Israel's incomparable God, the only Savior.

7

Jesus and the Salvation of the Gentiles

Frederick W. Schmidt

How important is Jesus' attitude toward people of other faiths for the formation of our own attitudes? Put differently, must we hold the same beliefs about other religions as Jesus did? Among scholars who have addressed the problem of religious pluralism, the answer varies depending upon the approach each takes to the theological enterprise.

For some, the views of Jesus are irrelevant. Gordon Kaufman, John Hick, and Tom Driver argue that by definition religious claims are relative. The sayings of Jesus are no exception—all three conclude that they are as relative as any theological assertion we might make today.[1] Thus, Jesus' views cannot and should not be treated as normative, as if they were a fixed and unchanging standard.

---

1. Gordon D. Kaufman, "Religious Diversity, Historical Consciousness, and Christian Theology," and John Hick, "The Non-absoluteness of Christianity," both in *The Myth of Christian Uniqueness: Toward a Pluralistic Theology of Religions,* ed. John Hick and Paul F. Knitter (Maryknoll, N.Y.: Orbis, 1987), 5–8, 16–18; Tom F. Driver, *Christ in a Changing World: Toward an Ethical Christology* (New York: Crossroad, 1981), 66–74.

On the other hand, others such as Paul Knitter, John Cobb, and Bernard Lee argue that the views of Jesus indeed remain normative, even though they acknowledge that religious claims are relative.[2] Accordingly, each relies to one degree or another on the teaching of Jesus to support his views of religious pluralism.

These six scholars advocate "unitive pluralism," the notion that each religion must maintain its own uniqueness, but refine its identity by accepting its dependence upon other faiths.[3] Even though all six writers come to similar conclusions, they represent two significant approaches to the teaching of Jesus.

This chapter does not address those who deny that the teaching of Jesus has normative value. For these scholars, it might be *nice* to appeal to Jesus to support their position, but it is hardly *necessary*. Ultimately, the findings outlined here are little more than a matter of historical curiosity to them. Instead, this chapter addresses adherents of the second approach, who take the teaching of Jesus seriously and treat it as normative.

Pluralists who appeal to Jesus' teaching do so in two ways. Their approaches differ in the way they see Jesus relating to the Judaism of his day. One group is convinced that by recapturing the Jewishness of Jesus, they can discover the rationale for unitive pluralism. The other group arrives at the same conclusion, but believes that the teaching of Jesus transcended the Judaism of his day. But what did Jesus historically say, and are either of these views faithful to his teaching?[4]

Recapturing the Jewishness of Jesus

Some theologians contend that the Jewishness of Jesus provides the basis for unitive pluralism. This is particularly the case with Paul Knitter. Because Jesus proclaimed the kingdom *of God*, says Knitter, his theology was God-centered, and hence provides the necessary point of contact between our faith and the faith of others. The teaching of Jesus enables us to appreciate and learn from other religious traditions.[5]

2. Paul F. Knitter, *No Other Name? A Critical Survey of Christian Attitudes toward the World Religions* (Maryknoll, N.Y.: Orbis, 1985), 173–75; John B. Cobb, Jr., *Christ in a Pluralistic Age* (Philadelphia: Westminster, 1975), 97–110; Bernard J. Lee, *The Galilean Jewishness of Jesus: Retrieving the Jewish Origins of Christianity* (New York: Paulist, 1988), 1:69–71.

3. Knitter, *No Other Name?* 9. For more information on unitive pluralism and Paul Knitter, see in this volume Timothy D. Westergren, "Do All Roads Lead to Heaven?"

4. Given the brevity of this chapter, it is impractical to promise a "fresh" approach to the synoptic tradition. Instead, I will draw upon established scholarship on the issue. Due to the thorny issues regarding the historical character of John's Gospel, I will confine myself to the synoptic Gospels.

5. Knitter, *No Other Name?* 166–67, 173–75.

Significantly, Jesus did not place himself or the church at the center of his message. He placed God at the center. And if the views of Jesus were theocentric, then so should ours be. In other words, argues Knitter, we have lost and need to recapture the Jewishness of Jesus. The only obstacle in our way is the wooden, literalistic, Christ-centered approach of the New Testament.[6]

Knitter, in fact, drives the wedge so deeply between Jesus and Judaism (on the one hand) and nascent Christianity (on the other) that he appears to suggest that Jesus was immune from the effects of what he describes as the "classicist culture" that shaped the early church. At the heart of classicist culture are two interrelated convictions: (1) reality is "fixed and unchanging," and (2) it can have only one, normative, cultural expression.[7] Because the church accepted the prevailing classicist culture, according to Knitter, its message is exclusivistic and incapable of the kind of mutual appreciation and dependence necessary today among the world's religions. But the Jesus of Judaism did not share this outlook and its limitations. For Knitter, therefore, recapturing the Jewishness of Jesus is essential if Christians are to engage in meaningful interfaith dialogue.[8]

An Evaluation of Unitive Pluralism

Knitter's position is flawed by a series of incredible anachronisms. First, he radically separates the nascent church from first-century Judaism—an impossible task. The earliest "Jesus movement" was not "Christianity" at all. Indeed, much of the New Testament represents the attempts of a sect *within* Judaism to explain its relationship *to* Judaism.[9] This was to remain the case in some parts of the world until after the Bar Kochba revolt of 132. And in those areas, the worldview assumed by most "Christians" was largely "Jewish" in character.[10] To argue, then, that Jesus' teaching was immediately perverted by the church is based upon a dubious distinction between the church and its parent faith.

Second, Judaism—no less than nascent Christianity—was clearly

---

6. Ibid., 180, 182–84. This is not to suggest that Knitter believes the whole of New Testament Christology is equally "exclusivistic" or "normative." He singles out John and Hebrews, among others.

7. Ibid., 31–32, 183.

8. Ibid., 184, 186.

9. John Koenig, *Jews and Christians in Dialogue: New Testament Foundations* (Philadelphia: Westminster, 1979), 9–12.

10. Lawrence H. Schiffman, "At the Crossroads: Tannaitic Perspectives on the Jewish-Christian Schism," in *Jewish and Christian Self-Definition*, vol. 2: *Aspects of Judaism in the Graeco-Roman Period*, ed. E. P. Sanders, Albert I. Baumgarten, and Alan Mendelson (Philadelphia: Fortress, 1981), 155–56.

100   **Biblical Exegesis**

particularistic. First-century Jews maintained they were God's chosen people and, as such, believed they had a responsibility to the wider world.[11] The efforts of Jews to proselytize among Gentiles grows out of a sense of calling. Their zeal to win converts underscores the uniqueness of Israel's role and its message. Citing the words of Amos 3:2, Ephraim Urbach observes:

> The election of Israel is conceived as a prophetic calling involving the whole people. Israel is chosen as a messenger, as a servant of God who is to guard religion for all peoples and to radiate its truth to all nations. The existence of monotheism is bound up with the continued existence of the community of Israel, and Israel's future is predicated on the future of religion. The stronger the stress placed by the prophets upon universalism, the greater is their emphasis upon the special position of Israel.[12]

Judaism's particularistic outlook can also be seen in its tendencies toward sectarianism. Foreign domination and the turmoil that marked the Second Temple period led more than one group to claim that it was the "true" Israel or, at the very least, the remnant "nucleus" of a future, more faithful nation. Among those groups, for example, were the Essenes.[13] Retreating into the desert, they awaited God's deliverance, not only from the "pagans" of other nations, but from the "quislings" who had betrayed their own faith. Just how serious this matter was to them can be seen in the *Manual of Discipline*, found among the Dead Sea Scrolls. There we find the blessings and the curses that await humanity—blessings on those who join the community, but curses on those who oppose the elect: "May He deliver you up for torture at the hands of vengeful Avengers! May He visit you with destruction by the hands of Wreakers of Revenge! Be cursed without mercy because of the darkness of your deeds!"[14] Clearly, a worldview that prompted groups to make such judgments presupposes an unvarnished exclusivism.

11. This idea is an outgrowth of the prophetic tradition. See John N. Oswalt, "The Mission of Israel to the Nations," in this volume.

12. Ephraim Urbach, "Self-Isolation or Self-Affirmation in Judaism in the First Three Centuries: Theory and Practice," in *Jewish and Christian Self-Definition*, vol. 2: *Aspects of Judaism in the Graeco-Roman Period,* ed. E. P. Sanders, Albert I. Baumgarten, and Alan Mendelson (Philadelphia: Fortress, 1981), 273.

13. Joseph Blenkinsopp, "Interpretation and the Tendency to Sectarianism: An Aspect of Second Temple History," in *Jewish and Christian Self-Definition*, vol. 2: *Aspects of Judaism in the Graeco-Roman Period,* ed. E. P. Sanders, Albert I. Baumgarten, and Alan Mendelson (Philadelphia: Fortress, 1981), 25.

14. Geza Vermes, *Jesus the Jew: A Historian's Reading of the Gospels* (London: Fontana/Collins, 1973), 46.

These two problems underline the difficulty with Knitter's position, and others could be provided. The response of Palestinian Jews to the perceived idolatry of outsiders and the later, competing claims of church and synagogue also underscore the particularistic character of early Judaism.[15] Even the supposed movement of Judaism toward "the detribalization of deity" (to which Bernard Lee refers) was probably less an expression of emerging universalism, than it was a means of bolstering its own sense of election in the face of historical evidence to the contrary.[16]

The Polemics of Particularism

Admittedly, this particularism is seen most clearly in Jewish polemics against Gentiles, the intensity of which varied, depending upon the circumstances. As such, Judaism developed its position in a haphazard and uneven way; and the position that it developed can be described as having had a functional character.[17] Nonetheless, it is still particularism. To paraphrase Dr. Seuss's Horton the Elephant, "They said what they meant and they meant what they said."[18]

If we argue otherwise, anything said in time of crisis has a functional character only and can never reflect the abiding worldview of those who make such statements. Yet, exclusive language almost always develops in the context of polemics with other religions or in times of crisis.[19] To argue that such statements have no more than a functional role for those who utter them suggests that such statements rarely, if ever, represent the considered views of those who make them.

More important, early Judaism did more than just talk about exclusivism. Their statements were accompanied by actions that showed their exclusivism was more than empty rhetoric. It is difficult to know

15. On the former, see Jonathan Goldstein, "Jewish Acceptance and Rejection of Hellenism," in *Jewish and Christian Self-Definition*, vol. 2: *Aspects of Judaism in the Graeco-Roman Period*, ed. E. P. Sanders, Albert I. Baumgarten, and Alan Mendelson (Philadelphia: Fortress, 1981), 84–87; and Peter Haas, "The Maccabean Struggle to Define Judaism," in *New Perspectives on Ancient Judaism*, ed. Jacob Neusner et al. (Washington, D.C.: University Press of America, 1987), 1:49–65. On the latter, see Ephraim E. Urbach, *The Sages: Their Concepts and Beliefs*, trans. Israel Abrahams (Cambridge: Harvard University Press, 1987), 646–48.

16. Lee, *Galilean Jewishness of Jesus*, 69; William C. Placher, *A History of Christian Theology: An Introduction* (Philadelphia: Westminster, 1983), 23–25.

17. See Knitter, *No Other Name?* 184–86, on the nature of "confessional language" in the church. A critique of Knitter's position is provided by Westergren, "Do All Roads Lead to Heaven?"

18. Dr. Seuss [Theodore Geisel], *Horton Hatches the Egg* (New York: Random, 1968).

19. R. A. Markus, "The Problem of Self-Definition: From Sect to Church," in *Jewish and Christian Self-Definition*, vol. 1: *The Shaping of Christianity in the Second and Third Centuries*, ed. E. P. Sanders (Philadelphia: Fortress, 1980), 3.

what would pass as evidence of doctrinaire exclusivism if the evidence provided by early Judaism does not.

In the modern context, some might argue that ancient Judaism allowed its fear of syncretism to overrun more important considerations. Others might argue that the modern situation demands a new perspective. But this is hardly the same as arguing that the God-centeredness of early Judaism implied a willingness to believe all religions were equally valid.

So, both the early church and the Judaism of Jesus' day were exclusivist, each in its own way. This fact casts serious doubt on Knitter's entire enterprise. To recapture the Jewishness of Jesus is simply to recapture another brand of particularism, and will not further Knitter's case for unitive pluralism.[20]

If for a moment, however, we give Knitter the benefit of the doubt and assume his presentation is a matter of emphasis (and not a failure to deal with historical facts), then a different set of issues arises: Why look to Jesus or Judaism at all when rethinking the relationship between religious faiths? Can either really provide us with needed insight into the current challenges we face, if both are as deeply indebted to what Knitter believes is an outmoded way of viewing reality? Has Knitter isolated the few strands of both religions that continue to be of value, or has he simply failed to pursue the logic of his own position with sufficient rigor? Given the manifest weakness of his analysis, the last of these suggestions is closest to the truth.

Transcending the Jewishness of Jesus

Of course, another way of reading the evidence is to suggest that Jesus opposed the exclusivism of early Judaism and that his teaching directly challenged that perspective. Jesus, then, should not be identified with the narrow-minded Judaism of his day—he transcended it and therein lies the key to unitive pluralism. Relying upon Rudolf Bultmann and Norman Perrin, this is precisely the point made by John Cobb. Quoting Perrin, Cobb writes:

> The Jews thought "in terms of three groups of 'sinners': Jews who could turn to their heavenly father in penitence and hope; *Gentile sinners for whom hope was dubious,* most Jews regarding them as beyond the pale of God's mercy; and Jews who had made themselves as Gentiles, for whom penitence was, if not impossible, certainly almost insurmountably difficult." . . . Jesus so understood the claim of God for obedience that all pretense to righteousness was undercut. Repentance was a necessity for everyone.[21]

20. See Knitter, *No Other Name?* 31.
21. Cobb, *Christ in a Pluralistic Age,* 104 (emphasis added).

Much in this brief quotation is debatable. Limitations of space, however, force me to pursue only one question: Did Jesus break with the particularism of his day? Put another way, Did he remove the boundaries between Jew and Gentile as Bultmann, Perrin, and Cobb suggest?

Evidence from the synoptic tradition suggests that he did not. These questions are difficult because they are bound up in the thorny issues of the synoptic tradition.[22] But on any serious reading of the Gospels, there is little evidence that Jesus even addressed that question, let alone radically broke with the prevailing particularism of his day.

First, much of the evidence for Cobb's position is ambiguous. Parabolic references to the highways and byways, in which the king has his servants search for wedding guests, might refer to Gentiles. But the image need not have this meaning, nor is it likely in the context of Jesus' ministry that it did. Instead, it probably refers to the "publicans and sinners" with whom Jesus is so frequently associated in the synoptic tradition.[23] Similarly, the dogs and swine of Matthew 7:6 could refer to more than one thing or group of people, not just Gentiles.[24] Equally, it may be a general reference to the necessity of recognizing people for what they are.[25] Indeed, in its Matthean setting, the verse probably refers to admitting the "undisciplined" into the church, and not to Gentiles at all.[26]

Other texts in the synoptic Gospels, for example, Mark 13:10 and Matthew 10:18, suggest that Jesus envisioned a mission to Gentiles. But it is ironic that critical scholars like Cobb would cite such sayings as evidence for the historical Jesus when critical scholarship generally doubts that Jesus even said them. Scholars such as Ferdinand Hahn state that on linguistic and historical grounds both sayings are the creations of the early church or the Evangelists.[27]

By contrast, the synoptic traditions widely seen as authentic sug-

---

22. The criteria New Testament scholars employ to determine the authenticity of passages are currently under scrutiny. New criteria are being offered as an addendum to those already in use. In other cases, scholars have offered their approach as a substitute for existing criteria. And still others argue that it is impossible to rely on the sayings material found in the Gospels at all. See, e.g., John Dominic Crossan, "Materials and Methods in Historical Jesus Research," *Forum* 4 (1988): 3–24; and E. P. Sanders, *Jesus and Judaism* (London: SCM, 1985), 13–18.

23. See Joachim Jeremias, *Jesus' Promise to the Nations* (Philadelphia: Fortress, 1982), 24.

24. Because the saying is isolated and proverbial in character, it is impossible to be dogmatic about its meaning.

25. Jeremias, *Jesus' Promise to the Nations,* 20 n. 8; contra Vermes, *Jesus the Jew,* 49.

26. See Robert H. Gundry, *Matthew: A Commentary on His Literary and Theological Art* (Grand Rapids: Eerdmans, 1982), 123–24.

27. Ferdinand Hahn, *Mission in the New Testament,* Studies in Biblical Theology 47 (Naperville, Ill.: Allenson, 1965), 118–20, 126.

gest the opposite. Passages such as Matthew 15:24, 26, Mark 7:27, and (perhaps) Matthew 10:5–6 indicate that Jesus limited his message to Jews and may have instructed his disciples to do the same.[28] Indeed, the sayings reflect such a negative attitude toward Gentiles that Geza Vermes suggests that Jesus was (like his contemporaries) xenophobic.[29]

Vermes' explanation is not the only one possible, but, for whatever reason, it appears that Jesus did limit his ministry to Jews. And evidence from the New Testament, as well as the behavior of the primitive church, confirms this conclusion. Why would there have been so much debate in the infant church about whether to admit the Gentiles, and under what conditions, if Jesus had left unambiguous instruction on a Gentile mission?

John Riches has argued that Jesus sought to counter the Jewish expectation that all Gentiles would perish at God's hands. Against this, E. P. Sanders rightly observes:

> Had that been the uniform expectation, and had Jesus consciously "transformed" it, the early disciples would probably have had a clearer view about what to do about the mission to the Gentiles. They seem to reflect what is more likely to have been the common Jewish view: in the last days the Gentiles can be admitted to the kingdom on some condition or other.[30]

In other words, there is no evidence that Jesus transcended the particularism of his contemporaries or tore down the barriers between Jew and Gentile.

All the evidence, then, suggests that Jesus shared the expectations of other Jews. Like them he probably foresaw an eschatological in-gathering of Gentiles. As well, the early church, which grew out of Jesus and the Judaism of his day, was similarly particularist. So neither recapturing the Jewishness of Jesus nor arguing that he transcended his Judaism will support the case for unitive pluralism. In that respect, Knitter, Cobb, and others would be better advised to follow the lead of those like Hick, whose case does not depend on the teachings of Jesus.

Because the Evangelists never tell us what Jesus taught about other religions, we must be cautious in our conclusions. We must beware of forcing ancient texts to answer modern questions. Jesus taught about

28. Among others, see Jeremias, *Jesus' Promise to the Nations,* 26–29.
29. Vermes, *Jesus the Jew,* 49.
30. Sanders, *Jesus and Judaism,* 221.

many things in his ministry, but in the synoptic Gospels he never addresses the fate of those who will have no opportunity to hear his name. Thus, neither unitive pluralists nor their opponents can settle their dispute from the synoptic tradition. The question must be decided on other biblical and theological grounds, such as those discussed in the following chapters.

8

Acts 4:12—No Other Name under Heaven

Clark H. Pinnock

"Salvation is found in no one else, for there is no other name under heaven given to men by which we must be saved." These are words of Peter addressed to the Jewish leaders as recorded in Acts 4:12. This bold declaration to the Jewish authorities has been regularly taken in the history of doctrine and biblical interpretation to justify a strictly exclusivist stance with regard to the possibility of salvation for non-Christians. Because, according to the text, salvation comes through faith in Jesus' name alone, many have assumed that God's grace is not at work, and hope of eternal life is not a possibility apart from explicit faith in the name of Jesus by persons in this earthly life.[1] This reading of the text is something I wish to challenge. I will argue that Peter's state-

1. This strict paradigm is associated with a narrow interpretation of the ancient axiom "outside the church, no salvation," a formula that goes back to the earliest Greek fathers. See Hans Küng, *The Church* (New York: Sheed & Ward, 1967), 313–19. S. Mark Heim refers to this strict form of exclusivity by the term *imperial particularity* in *Is Christ the Only Way?* (Valley Forge, Pa.: Judson, 1985), 125–27. Paul F. Knitter refers to it as the conservative-evangelical model in *No Other Name?* (Maryknoll, N.Y.: Orbis, 1985),

ment does not necessarily have these dire implications because the text has been misinterpreted in a number of unfortunate ways.[2]

Let us inquire, then, into the meaning and significance of this striking statement by Peter. It will help achieve clarity if we ask what issues the text addresses and what issues it does not address, what is plainly taught in Acts 4:12 and what is not.[3]

What Acts 4:12 Teaches

Acts 4:12 makes three definite assertions, plainly and strongly. First, Peter insists that Jesus has introduced the long awaited messianic salvation into history (see the citation of Ps. 118:22 in v. 11). Through his ministry and work, Jesus has fulfilled and actualized what the Old Testament prophets had promised would come and what the whole world had been waiting for. Now, at last, the herald announced by the prophet Isaiah (40:9) has arrived, bringing good news to Zion and declaring, "Here is your God!" Clearly, then, Acts 4:12 makes a strong claim about the incomparability of Jesus and the salvation he brings. This is the moment of fulfilment, the advent of the kingdom of God, and salvation in the fullest sense now being available to faith. Truly blessed are the eyes and ears that see and hear these things.[4]

Second, Peter identifies the nature of salvation as holistic as well as messianic. In the circumstances of the Acts narrative, it clearly includes physical healing as well as a new relationship with God (vv. 7, 9). A cripple had been marvelously healed in the name of Jesus and had come to saving faith. Salvation, then, in Acts 4:12 is something

---

chap. 5. Evangelicals who have expressed themselves along these lines in print (a majority) include John Gerstner, Carl F. H. Henry, Harold Lindsell, Bruce Demarest, Robert H. Gundry, Millard J. Erickson, Jack Cottrell, Robert Morey, Harry Buis, Dick Dowsett, Robert C. Sproul, Lorraine Boettner, and Ajith Fernando.

2. For a more lenient approach to this whole area of concern, see my article "Toward an Evangelical Theology of Religions," *Journal of the Evangelical Theological Society* 33 (1990): 359–68; and a forthcoming book on the subject that I am now preparing. Evangelicals who pursue a more inclusive approach (a minority) include Charles Kraft, C. S. Lewis, James N. D. Anderson, John Sanders, Bruce Reichenbach, Stuart Hackett, Dale Moody, Neal Punt, John Stott, and Don Richardson.

3. I have to admit that the commentaries on Acts are on the whole disappointing. Perhaps this is because Acts is a long book to comment on and is viewed more as a historical than a theological tract. For whatever reasons the commentators do not face up to what Acts 4:12 means theologically for the canonical context. Whether Bruce or Haenchen, Longenecker or Conzelmann, they read the text as proof of the exclusivist paradigm.

4. F. F. Bruce comments ably on this text in his two commentaries on Acts. The idea of a new era of salvation opening up for humanity through Jesus is, of course, fundamental to all the New Testament witnesses, including especially Jesus himself. See, for example, Donald A. Hagner, *The Jewish Reclamation of Jesus* (Grand Rapids: Zondervan, 1984).

that restores bodies as well as souls. There is power to save and to heal in Jesus' name just as there was in the Galilean ministry of Jesus. Salvation here focuses on the power to make the lame man walk (3:12, 16). The Spirit who anointed Jesus has been poured out on the apostles.[5]

It is important to pause and note that salvation in Acts 4:12 is more than vertical justification, more than deliverance from the final judgment and hell-fire. Evangelicals frequently forget or ignore that fact, perhaps in their opposition to the social gospel. Peter tells us that physical healing is part of biblical salvation.[6] There is more than a touch of irony here, I think, when one considers that those who quote the text to support the exclusivist paradigm seldom in my experience acknowledge physical healing as part of salvation. They appear to be using the text to prove something it does not really say, while at the same time ignoring what it plainly does say.

Third, Peter is adamant that the messianic and holistic salvation he refers to is available only through faith in the name of Jesus. ("In the name" is a semitic expression meaning "by the authority of.")[7] Clearly there is an exclusive element here, a claim to uniqueness and finality. There is simply no other name with the kind of power to save that the name of Jesus has. Salvation in its fullness, then, is available to humankind only because God in the person of his Son Jesus provided it.[8]

What Acts 4:12 Does Not Teach

It seems, however, that in their zeal to magnify the finality of Jesus and the unique work that he accomplished for the salvation of the human race, exclusivists have distorted Peter's meaning. They have used his words to support ideas that lie beyond the scope of his intended teaching. They force the text to address questions that are conceptually related in our thinking, but not actually contained in

5. Michael Green delineates the broad meaning of the concept in his book *The Meaning of Salvation* (London: Hodder & Stoughton, 1965). His definition can handle the breadth of the usage implied in Acts 4:12.

6. Millard Erickson, generally a fine theologian, is disappointing when he defines salvation in a narrow way (*Christian Theology* [Grand Rapids: Baker, 1983], chap. 43). He also takes pains to deny that there is healing in the atonement (chap. 39) and to dampen expectations of ministries of healing in the modern church (chap. 41). He is far from Luke's mentality.

7. Such issues of interpretation are covered by Irene W. Foulkes, "Two Semantic Problems in the Translation of Acts 4:5–20," *Bible Translator* 29 (1978): 121–25.

8. One can see that Knitter is skeptical about this when he entitles his book, *No Other Name?* On the other hand, Lesslie Newbigin is not skeptical. See *The Gospel in a Pluralist Society* (Geneva: WCC, 1989), chap. 13.

Peter's remarks and their context. Surely this is not proper. Our respect
for the authority of the Bible means that we not only observe what
the text tells us but also respect its silences. Biblical authority means
heeding the positive teaching of the Bible and not reading our ideas
into it—however precious our opinions are to us. I am sure that Acts
4:12 is often taken to settle questions it does not address. I invite my
readers to consider such a possibility.

The first such question is the eschatological fate of unevangelized
people, whether they lived before or after Christ. Although this is a
question that weighs heavily on our minds, Acts 4:12 does not say
anything about it. The text speaks forcefully about the incomparable
power of Jesus' name to save (and heal) those who hear and respond
to the good news, but it does not comment on the fate of the heathen.
Although it is a question of great importance to us, it is not one on
which Acts 4:12 renders a judgment, either positive or negative. It is
not Peter's concern in Acts 4:12 to limit the possibilities of eschatological salvation for people; his concern is to make a ringing affirmation
of the incomparable saving power for life today, which is available to
everyone who trusts in Jesus. I realize that it is easy to assume Acts
4:12 gives a negative answer to the question on our minds (Can anyone who has not heard the name of Jesus participate in the eschatological kingdom of God?), but in actuality I hope the reader can see
that it says nothing at all about that. It is wrong to force Peter to say
what he declines to say.

Second, Peter's declaration does not render a judgment, positive or
negative, on another question that interests us a great deal: the status
of other religions and the role they play in God's providence or plan
of redemption. Now I grant that Peter judges the religion of Judaism,
in confrontation with the preaching of Jesus as Messiah in Acts 3–4, to
be an inadequate vehicle of God's endtime salvation (the same would
hold true, a fortiori, of any other religion in this situation). But Peter
does not say what would hold for Judaism or any other religion in the
situation where Christ has not yet been named, where the contest has
not been joined. Later passages in Acts (10:35; 14:17; 17:23) seem to
come closer to addressing that issue, but I would admit that even they
do not speak to it directly and decisively.[9] Certainly Acts 4:12 does not
address or answer this question.[10]

9. A contrary view may be found in the next chapter, Darrell L. Bock, "Athenians
Who Have Never Heard," n. 8.
10. Karl Rahner is surely right (apart from other aspects of his theory) to make a distinction between religions in the pre-Christian situation and those same religions when
the word of the gospel is preached. This judgment is based on the assumption that God
is just and loving. See Karl Rahner, "Christianity and the Non-Christian Religions," in
Theological Investigations (London: Darton, Longman & Todd, 1966), 5:115–34.

Let us remember too that Peter, when he says there is salvation in no other name, would be intending not only such names as Buddha and Krishna but also names of Old Testament worthies like Moses and David as well. His point is that no other name has ever had in it the power to do what can be done in Jesus' name only. Only Jesus can bring messianic salvation, even to the point of raising the cripple. Peter is magnifying the name of Jesus and the messianic salvation he has brought. A new era has opened up, the last days have begun. Thus we should not see him as denying that there have been and are lesser instances of saving power at work in the world where Jesus' name is unknown. Peter is magnifying a mighty act of God bringing in the kingdom, not discussing comparative religions. We should not generalize his remarks so far beyond the context of Acts 3–4.[11]

No Exegesis Without Presuppositions

It is time to step back and face up to the hermeneutical problem. Why is it that people read into texts such as Acts 4:12 meanings that are not there? First, it is due to reader interest. Readers cannot be completely objective when they read texts that tackle issues vitally important to them. They have an interest in the outcome of their interpretation. We do not see reality as it is but through the filters of our interests. Thus, we all come to a text like Acts 4:12 from somewhere, always with presuppositions, and that fact influences the results of our interpretation. Second, more specifically, we read texts such as Acts 4:12 in the context of a larger understanding of what the Bible says and what Christianity is. One could call that larger framework of interpretation a global pattern or root metaphor, and it definitely affects our exegesis. That presuppositional framework can easily become fused with the text and skew its meaning. In this case, I believe many are reading Acts 4:12 within the matrix of a hardline system that magnifies God's severity above God's kindness, while others are viewing things with a greater emphasis on God's compassion and justice. So this verse gets caught up into a vortex of competing frameworks and gets unfairly manipulated.[12]

---

11. Two scholars who see this plainly are John A. T. Robinson, *Truth Is Two-Eyed* (Philadelphia: Westminster, 1979), 105–6; and Kenneth Cracknell, *Towards a New Relationship: Christians and People of Other Faiths* (London: Epworth, 1986), 107–8. The fact that they both lean too far in the pluralist direction in their overall thinking for my liking does not change the fact that they have many insights.

12. I associate the hardline framework with Augustine and the more generous scheme with the Greek fathers of the church, such as Irenaeus. See Richard Swinburne, *Responsibility and Atonement* (Oxford: Clarendon, 1989), 2–3. Richard Rice refers to the influence of root metaphors in the context of this debate; see "Divine Foreknowledge

Acts 4:12 has special significance for the strictly exclusivist position, the view that restricts eschatological salvation to the number of confessing Christians. Given such a framework, there is the natural impetus to give the verse an interpretation it does not actually require. Like another favorite verse, John 14:6, Peter's words are seized upon opportunistically to bolster the paradigm that they hold on other wider grounds. The global paradigm influences people to manipulate the text and force it to say what it does not actually say.[13]

As one who interprets Acts 4:12 in a more lenient and less restrictive way, I likewise cannot claim to be free of bias in my exegesis. I, too, have a reader interest that operates on both sides of the dispute. It is true that I wish to avoid the idea that Acts 4:12 wants to exclude most of the people who have ever lived on God's earth from eschatological salvation. I admit to finding such a notion utterly repugnant. But I would claim the silence of the text in defense of my interpretation. It does not demand restrictive exclusivism. Perhaps there are other verses in the New Testament that do demand it and for which I am not responsible in this chapter. All I can say is that Acts 4:12 is not one of them.

Put positively, Peter is telling us of the power of God to save, of a divine power at work in limited ways during Old Testament times before Jesus came, and that has now been released into the world with unique eschatological strength. It is not Peter's intention to deny that God has been at work saving people before (that would be an absurd position for a Jew to take), but to affirm that God is now saving people in a unique, new, messianic way through Jesus. Peter is telling us that God's act in Jesus was absolutely decisive; he is not telling us to think of it as something entirely discontinuous with his saving work in the history of Israel, and indeed, I would add, throughout the entire historical process.[14]

According to Acts 4:12, then, Jesus has done a unique work for the human race, the good news of which needs to be preached to the whole world. But this uniqueness does not entail exclusivity. Think of the way John thinks of Jesus as the unique incarnation of the Logos, which nevertheless also enlightens everyone (John 1:9). I believe Peter also may be thinking in this way. God was at work in ancient Israel before Christ came. People like Abraham knew God even though they did not know Jesus. The Son through whom all things were made is

and Free-will Theism," in *The Grace of God, the Will of Man,* ed. Clark H. Pinnock (Grand Rapids: Zondervan, 1989), 121–39.

13. Richard H. Drummond tries to shift theological thinking from the narrow perspective to one that recognizes the universality of God's covenants (*Toward a New Age in Christian Theology* [Maryknoll, N.Y.: Orbis, 1985]).

14. The point is made by Geoffrey W. H. Lampe in his Bampton Lectures, *God as Spirit* (Oxford: Clarendon, 1977), 31.

constantly at work in the world. The Spirit of God broods over the whole creation and over history. We should not think of God as absent from the world except where the name of Jesus of Nazareth is pronounced. Although for many evangelicals the finality of Christ spells exclusivism, I believe that our high Christology can also create space for openness and generosity to the world's peoples. We do not need to think of the church as the ark of salvation, leaving everyone else in hell; we can rather think of it as the chosen witness to the fullness of salvation that has come into the world through Jesus.[15] I do not mean by this a blanket endorsement of all human religion, but rather I affirm that God is not limited to working only through human preachers.

I find encouragement in the way even exclusivists practice leniency occasionally in their own interpretations. For example, I am glad they find it possible to hope for the salvation of children who die in infancy, even though babies cannot call on the name of Jesus and the Bible never actually states such a hope clearly.[16] In a similar way they find it possible to accept the salvation of Old Testament saints who lived before Jesus and therefore could not have called upon his name for salvation. In both cases, exclusivists allow large groups of people to enter into eschatological salvation without naming Jesus in this earthly life. This means that even they do not always interpret Acts 4:12 strictly when it comes to certain extraneous issues. I applaud their qualifications of the application of this text and urge them to extend them more upon further thought.

I realize that exclusivists are reluctant to apply the same line of reasoning to the plight of the unevangelized that they apply to infants and Jews before Christ. But I hope they will think about doing so. Surely God's goodness and justice imply that God will not expect people to invoke Jesus' name who cannot possibly do so, since they are ignorant of it through no fault of their own. Surely we all want to confess that God is the rewarder of those who diligently seek him in the ways they can seek him (Heb. 11:6).[17] I have always been impressed by the view put forward at the Second Vatican Council to the effect that the person who dies having sincerely sought after God, but not having learned about Jesus, will not be automatically condemned in the judg-

15. William J. Abraham provides insight into this in *The Logic of Evangelism* (Grand Rapids: Eerdmans, 1989), 217–23.

16. See, for example, Robert P. Lightner, *Heaven for Those Who Can't Believe* (Schaumberg, Ill.: Regular Baptist, 1977).

17. Evangelicals holding this view include Charles Kraft, *Christianity in Culture* (Maryknoll, N.Y.: Orbis, 1979), 253–57; James N. D. Anderson, *Christianity and World Religions* (Downers Grove, Ill.: Inter-Varsity, 1984), chap. 5; and John E. Sanders, "Is Belief in Christ Necessary for Salvation?" *Evangelical Quarterly* 60 (1988): 241–59.

ment but will be given the opportunity to plead the blood of Christ.[18] My main point is that Acts 4:12 can be intelligibly read in a more lenient framework and says nothing that requires us to adopt an exclusivist stance.

Earlier I claimed that Acts 4:12 did not comment on the status of other religions, before Christ had been preached among them. Adding to that, I do find Luke saying things later in the Book of Acts that might bear lightly upon this matter. For example, in Acts 10 Cornelius enjoys a positive relationship with God before he is saved by Christ and used by God to change Peter's narrowmindedness; in Acts 14, at Lystra, Paul acknowledges divine revelation and providence in the past history of the pagan peoples he was dealing with; and in Acts 17 Paul recognizes the Greeks of Athens to be worshiping the unknown God (notice that Paul speaks of the unknown God, not of a false god or an idol). Certainly the other religions, including Judaism, do not have messianic salvation to offer, but that does not mean God has no dealings at all with non-Christian peoples. On the contrary, God is drawing all nations into his kingdom.

If So, Why Missions?

One reason I think evangelicals reject the lenient tradition of interpretation is their fear that such a view might negate the necessity of world missions. I take such a fear seriously but do not believe it is warranted. Paul taught that Abraham was justified by his faith although he never called on the name of Jesus—but that did not stop Paul from thinking it necessary to preach Christ to Abraham's descendants (Rom. 9:1–3). Obviously, Paul thought it was crucial that they learn of the fullness of salvation in Jesus now that it had become available. He felt he was debtor to Jew and Gentile alike to tell them what God had done. Should any of them have already responded positively to God out of the light they had received in the past, then they would need to know the true source and nature of that light. They would want to have access to the full measure of God's grace and power in Jesus and be initiated into the kingdom of God.[19] On the other hand, in the case

18. *The Church,* par. 18. Further, I recall how some of the church fathers, including Augustine, spoke about a *limbus* in which believers before Christ were placed to await the proclamation of salvation when Christ descended into hell. Since they had no opportunity to confess Christ during their lifetime, the fathers thought they were given the opportunity after death. Such thinking holds promise and we need to extend it further.

19. A corollary to this idea is that a mark of those who truly responded in the past is their readiness to accept the gospel when they hear it. On this, see Abraham, *Logic of Evangelism,* 221–22, and David K. Clark, "Is Special Revelation Necessary for Salvation?" in this volume.

of those who may have rejected God previously, it is only right that they too should be confronted with a fresh opportunity to respond to Jesus. Who knows but that the proclamation of the fullness of messianic salvation in Jesus' name will awaken them from their slumbers and bring them to the knowledge of eternal life? It is easy to see the necessity of world missions in the exclusivist paradigm, and admittedly less easy in the lenient framework. But world missions can be seen to be vitally important once one moves away from the hell-fire insurance concept of salvation to the fuller concept outlined above.

Acts 4:12 makes a strong and definitely exclusive claim about the messianic, holistic salvation Jesus has brought into the world. It is a salvation that is incomparable and without rival. It is available through no other name than Jesus the incarnate Son of God. But the text does not exclude from eternal salvation the vast majority of people who have ever lived on the earth. I myself do not believe they are automatically excluded, although to prove it would require a larger assignment than I have been given.

9

Athenians Who Have Never Heard

Darrell L. Bock

T he declaration of the gospel is a major theme in the New Testament. But because much of the New Testament is written to the church, we have few examples of evangelistic messages. What messages there are appear in Acts; yet even these are mostly to Jewish audiences in the synagogue. One exception is Paul's speech at Athens (Acts 17:16–34), where he offers the message of resurrection to a pagan audience. But this is not any pagan audience; it is a highly cultured and respectable pagan audience, with a rich philosophical and religious heritage. Here is the Bible's equivalent of those who have "never heard." Does Paul's message to a religious people who have never heard of Jesus help us with a similar question today?

An Overview of Acts 17:16–34

Paul's remarks in Acts 17:16–21 place the speech in context. We hear that he is "provoked" by the many idols he saw in the city. The ancient city of Athens had a rich history—it was a world power under Pericles (495–429 B.C.), a place of civilized culture, and a center of reli-

117

gious and philosophical reflection. Her streets were filled with monu-
ments honoring a wide variety of gods, a "veritable forest of idols."[1] To
the Jews idol worship was abominable:

> And so retribution shall fall upon the idols of the heathen, because
> though part of God's creation they have been made into an abomina-
> tion, to make men stumble and to catch the feet of fools. The invention
> of idols is the root of immorality; they are a contrivance which has
> blighted human life. (Wisd. of Sol. 14:11–12 NEB; compare Isa. 44:9–20)

To be sure, the tone of the Wisdom of Solomon differs from Paul's
speech, but it does reveal Jewish attitudes toward idols and suggests
why Paul was disturbed by what he saw.[2] The highest form of religious
paganism still falls short of the knowledge of God (1 Cor. 1:18–25).

Luke describes the audience for Paul's remarks in Acts 17:17–18.
Standing in the crowd are Jews, the devout, Epicureans, and Stoics.
The term *devout* is important because it shows that some are seeking
God. In Acts, Luke applies this term to several groups (13:43, 50;
16:14; 17:4; 18:7, 13; 19:27), recognizing that just because people are
not Christians or Jews does not mean they are uninterested in God.

The Epicureans and Stoics were the two major philosophical schools
in Paul's time. The followers of Epicurus (341–270 B.C.) were indifferent to the gods, regarding them as too removed to worry about. Here
is the ancient equivalent to an agnostic secularist. The Stoics, founded
by Zeno (340–265 B.C.), were pantheists, who argued for the unity of
humankind and kinship with the divine. Reason and the world-state,
the "cosmopolis," were their central themes. Paul's audience, therefore, represented the spectrum of religious opinion.

These people saw Paul as a "babbler," a derisive term that referred to
birds that picked up spare seeds.[3] He was a preacher of "foreign divini-
ties," because he preached Jesus and the resurrection. So they brought
Paul to the Areopagus, also known by its Latin name, Mars' Hill. The
locale was named after the Roman god of war and was noted for its
"market-square" quality, where anything and everything could be discussed (v. 21). Paul did not shy away from discussing Jesus with people
of diverse religious and philosophical points of view.

1. F. F. Bruce, *The Book of Acts,* rev. ed., New International Commentary on the New
Testament (Grand Rapids: Eerdmans, 1988), 330. Livy (59 B.C.–A.D. 17) says, "Athens . . .
has . . . statues of god[s] and men-statues notable for every sort of material and artistry"
(45.27). See R. E. Wycherley, "St. Paul at Athens," *Journal of Theological Studies* 19 (1968):
619–21.

2. For further information on Jewish attitudes toward idolatry, see James G. Sigountos,
"Did Early Christians Believe Pagan Religions Could Save?" 231–33, in this volume.

3. Walter Bauer and Kurt Aland, *Wörterbuch zum Neuen Testament,* 6th ed. (Berlin: de
Gruyter, 1988), 1522.

The speech itself has four parts: introduction (vv. 22b–23), God as Creator (vv. 24–25), God and people (vv. 26–29), and the call to repent (vv. 30–31). The reactions come in verses 32–34.

Paul addresses the crowd as "religious" (*deisidaimonious*), a difficult word to translate. Used positively *deisidaimonious* means "religious," but when used negatively it means "superstitious."[4] Paul plays off both senses here. They have a religion, he says, but it is wrongheaded (vv. 23, 30). The God they worship is unknown to them and the opportunity to plead ignorance has passed. Paul informs them about the God they "feel after" and "seek" but do not know (vv. 24–27). Thus, in the introduction of the speech, he recognizes their altar inscribed "to an unknown god" (v. 23) as an effort to be religious. Nonetheless, the Athenians have not found the true God. So Paul proclaims God to them, by means of common ground.

He starts out with God the Creator who, as Lord of heaven and earth, does not live in shrines nor is served by human hands (vv. 25–26). Here Paul politely but firmly criticizes the pagan cult and worship, emphasizing that God is the Creator and people are the creatures. There is nothing they can do to help God live.

The sovereignty of God is also emphasized in verses 26–29. God has created the nations, the times, and the boundaries of residence. The purpose of the creation of humankind comes in verse 27; they are created to seek God. In fact, he is not far away. Paul then cites two ancient writers, Epimenides (ca. 600 B.C.) and Aratus (ca. 315–240 B.C.), who acknowledge that humanity is God's offspring. Paul uses these authors to show that everyone is created by God. But the relationship of Creator and creature does not imply salvation, as the call to repentance and the threat of judgment clearly demonstrate. God is not found in images of gold, silver, and stone. Idols are useless. They reflect ignorance of the greatness and omnipresence of God.

Thus, while Paul's introduction respectfully treats the Athenian effort to be religious, he concludes that their effort has not found the true God. The difference is important. Paul offers no word of acceptance or comfort to the "highly religious" of Athens. They are sincere, but are headed in the wrong direction and have not found God (vv. 23, 30).

Some argue that Luke's portrait of Paul's respecting pagan religion is historically inaccurate. Paul's speech, they say, could never have come from the man who wrote Romans 1:18–32. It more likely was created

---

4. Bauer and Aland, *Wörterbuch zum Neuen Testament*, 347. Josephus, *Against Apion* 2.130, calls the Athenians "the most pious of the Greeks." See also Bruce, *Book of Acts*, 335 n. 54.

by Luke and reflects his thinking, not Paul's.[5] This view, however, fails to note two realities: (1) Paul often shifts emphases as his audience changes (1 Cor. 9:20–22), and (2) although Paul establishes common ground in his speech through the rhetorical device *captatio benevolentiae* ("currying of favor"), he nevertheless criticizes his audience's approach to the divine. In effect he says, "You Greeks search for the divine, but your idol-worship is wrong, an affront to the great Creator. You attempt to worship someone you do not know." This condemnation of idolatry is indeed similar to Romans 1. To say the opposite is to ignore the comment that Paul was provoked by the idols in Athens (17:16). Moreover, Paul's call to repentance shows that there is no endorsement of sincere religion here. The speech reveals Paul's missionary strategy of "being all things to all people," but still fits well with his theology in Romans 1.

Paul closes his speech with a call to repentance. God's grace allowed a period of ignorance, but this period is now over. All people everywhere are commanded to repent. The universality of the demand is stressed by the use of "all" and "everywhere." Acts 17:31, the key verse, gives the reason why one must repent. God has fixed a day of judgment *and* he has appointed a judge. Everyone is ultimately responsible to God *and* to Jesus. In other words, the sovereign God has a sovereign assistant. All are subject to both this God and the one who will wield the gavel on the final day. Paul's speech does not stress the suffering Savior or forgiveness of sins; rather, it argues a more fundamental relationship between God and humankind. Because Jesus is God's appointed judge, if we are subject to God, then we are also subject to Jesus. "He has given proof of this to all men," Paul says, "by raising him from the dead."

At this point the speech ends. Some mocked Paul; others wanted to hear more; a few believed (vv. 32–34). The closing remark here is significant. Paul did not say everything in this speech—only the fundamental point, that when one approaches God, one also approaches Jesus. Attempts to separate the two are wrongheaded—just as wrongheaded as trying to confine God to a building or portraying him in an idol. To get to God, one must go through Jesus: this is the kingship of Jesus Christ. Paul is not interested in the death of Jesus here. He is interested in the living Christ, the resurrected and exalted Lord who exercises authority at the side of God (Acts 10:42–43).

The inability to separate what God is doing from what Jesus did is the major point of Paul's speech in Acts 17. Resurrection, which inter-

---

5. For example, Hans Conzelmann, *Acts of the Apostles,* trans. James Limberg, A. Thomas Kraabel, and Donald H. Juel; ed. Eldon J. Epp and Christopher R. Matthews; Hermeneia (Philadelphia: Fortress, 1987), 138–49.

ested the crowd, serves only as an indicator of the importance and centrality of Jesus. What God has joined together in his plan, we are not to put asunder. When one looks to God, Paul says, one will find Jesus. When Paul makes known the unknown God, he speaks of God and Jesus in the same breath (1 Cor. 8:5–6).

Thus, Paul's speech establishes a fundamental approach to the "religious" world of those who do not know Jesus, but is this all that can be said of Acts 17? What about the possibility that some might reach God apart from Jesus? Such positions usually rest on two ideas: the claim of ignorance and the appeal to piety. The first idea is that ignorance excuses culpability, and the second, that some are pious enough to be received by God. We must therefore look at these two themes in Luke–Acts, both of which are alluded to in Acts 17. How does Luke view these two areas? Is it possible that, although Jesus judges all, some will get in without knowing him, either because they were ignorant or because they were sufficiently devout? To look at the question from the Lucan angle is important, because many regard Luke as the most sympathetic of the biblical writers on such matters.

Does Ignorance Excuse Those Who Have Never Heard?

The theme of ignorance appears rarely in Luke–Acts. In fact, besides Acts 17:30, the only other occurrence is in Acts 3:17. Nevertheless, the theme is important. In Acts 3, Peter says that Israel acted in ignorance when they executed Jesus. But how can this be when the nation acted willfully in slaying Jesus? Luke 23 documents their conscious choice to slay the innocent Jesus while letting the criminal Barabbas go. "Ignorance" here means that they acted outside the truth. They acted consciously, but they did not really know what they were doing. In Acts 3:19 Peter, calling on the people to repent, speaks of the return in authority of Jesus Christ. These themes match Acts 17:30–31. What Acts 3 shows is that ignorance is not an excuse. One is still culpable before God for actions that are outside the truth. Those in ignorance must repent.

The term *ignorance* in the rest of the New Testament is no different. Particularly instructive are uses in Pauline materials and in Peter's epistles. In 1 Timothy 1:13, Paul speaks of his own actions when he persecuted the church, saying that he acted in ignorance. Yet again, Paul is not absolved of blame or responsibility as a result of his ignorance. Rather, he needed God's grace to save him from his sinful past as the "worst of sinners." Grace means experiencing the forgiveness God offered in Jesus. Ignorance was no excuse. What God graciously offers to the ignorant is knowledge of the truth, not a loophole to avoid judgment. Ignorance means a lack of knowledge about the true God and the need to come to him in truth.

In the Epistles, the term *ignorance* most often describes the lifestyle of the saved before conversion. Christians are exhorted not to live as they once did. Paul calls their former lifestyles (or the current lifestyles of some) lives lived in ignorance (Eph. 4:18; compare 1 Pet. 1:14; 2 Pet. 2:12). Yet, the immoral life, although it reflects ignorance, still remains culpable for its acts before God.

A final interesting use of the term occurs in Romans 10:2–3, where Paul discusses the ignorance of his Jewish kinsmen. He recognizes their zeal in pursuing God, but says their pursuit is not according to knowledge. In fact, they are ignorant of the righteousness that comes from God. So zeal and the pursuit of self-righteousness are not good enough. It involves a wrongheaded approach to God. Again, ignorance is not an excuse. Those who are ignorant are still culpable before God for their actions. As Acts 17:31 says, each will meet the one appointed to judge the world in righteousness. The concept of ignorance gives no comfort or hope of salvation. It is no excuse.

If ignorance is no excuse elsewhere in the New Testament, then it not surprising that ignorance provides no excuse in Acts 17:31, which mentions a past period of ignorance. But now that Jesus has come times have changed; it is time for all people everywhere to repent. When Paul speaks to "those who have never heard," lack of knowledge is no excuse. All must respond to the returning King who will surely sit in judgment on the last day.

Someone could object that those who have never heard are in a different category. They are not responsible because they have had no opportunity to hear the gospel. Only when Jesus is preached is one responsible to believe. But if this is true, then at Mars' Hill Paul puts nonhearers at risk. In their ignorance they had a chance, but now that he has told them about Jesus they must respond or be destroyed. We are driven to the absurd conclusion that Paul should never have mentioned Jesus, because as "nonhearers" they had a chance! But clearly, the apostle believed it was essential to mention Jesus to those who had never heard. The idea that some would enter the kingdom through ignorance is unacceptable to Paul.[6]

Do God-Fearers Have Any Hope?

When one looks at the devout or "God-fearers," an interesting situation develops. There are various ways in which the New Testament

---

6. There is only one Pauline passage that could allow this suggestion—Romans 2:1–16. Douglas Moo, "Romans 2: Saved Apart from the Gospel?" (in this volume) discusses this text and allows two possible interpretations. He prefers to see Romans 2 as a description of hypothetical "sinless Gentiles" who please God (while Rom. 3 states that

expresses this concept of devotion. The noun *eulabēs* ("devout") is uniformly positive (Luke 2:25; Acts 2:5; 8:2; 22:12), as is its synonym *eusebēs* ("godly") (Acts 10:2, 7; 2 Tim. 3:12; Titus 2:12; 2 Pet. 2:9). These terms refer to believers or to those about to become believers. But these positive terms are absent from Acts 17. In Acts 17:17 we find a decidedly mixed term, *sebō* ("worship"). Negatively, Acts 13:43 uses it of the devout converts to Judaism, while 13:50 uses it to describe the devout women who persecute Paul. We even find the term used in Acts 19:27 of those who worship Artemis, so it can be applied to pagan worship. Positively, Lydia is described with this term (Acts 16:14), as is Titius Justis (Acts 18:7). The point is that the term can be used to describe the religiously zealous, whether or not they are accepted by God.[7]

The theme of the God-fearer needs more development, since Acts 17 only raises the issue. The phrase, which in Greek involves the verb *phobeō* with the object *theon,* is rare and does not appear in Acts 17. Yet, the concept is present in Acts 17:17. The phrase is found in Acts 10:2, 22 as a description of Cornelius. The Jewish synagogue audience in Acts 13:16, 26 is addressed with this description. These are the only uses of the phrase.

The use of God-fearers in Acts 13 is crucial. Here Paul addresses the Gentiles in his audience as God-fearers. Does this mean that they are in God's blessing? The answer is, No, at least, not yet. In the speech Paul presents Jesus and warns his God-fearing audience not to reject the message. To scoff at the message is to perish (Acts 13:40–41). The God-fearer for Luke is interested in the divine, but the God-fearer is not in the kingdom until he or she responds to the message. What is said explicitly in Acts 13 applies as well in Acts 17, or else Paul's call to repent makes little sense. God-fearers are treated with respect because they are sympathetic to divine matters; but they are not eternally blessed by God simply because they express an interest in God. Entry requires a specific kind of response. In Luke's terms, it requires turning to God as found in Christ. In Paul's terms, it requires turning "to [the living] God from idols, to serve a living and true God, and to wait for his Son from heaven, whom he raised from the dead, Jesus who delivers us from the wrath to come" (1 Thess. 1:9–10 RSV). Note how well Paul's words fit the conclusion of his speech in Acts 17.

---

no such people exist). I prefer the other option, that Paul foresees Gentile Christians who "do . . . things required by the law" (Rom. 2:14) through the indwelling of the Spirit (Rom. 8:4). Either way, there is no exception for the ignorant.

7. An exceptional use is the charge of the Jews that Paul worshiped God contrary to the law (Acts 18:13). The God-fearer is receptive to divine things, but does not necessarily know God. His acceptance by God depends on factors that go beyond the description of the person as a God-fearer. The sentiment of the term is not unlike Romans 10:2–3.

The Bible records some sincere people who are devoted to God—and even accords them a certain respect. But it is still considered wrong-headed devotion or "worship in ignorance." Neither devotion nor fearing God without fearing Jesus is good enough. Ignorance is no excuse. At Mars' Hill, Paul preaches Jesus to those who have never heard his name, because the ignorant need to hear about the risen King.

Acts 17 shows how Paul approached an audience who had never heard of Jesus. He acknowledged their devotion and attempt to approach God and even offered a critique of their worship, but he did not accept their religion as true. God has appointed Jesus to judge the world, he said, and anyone who approaches God must recognize the sovereign, mediatorial function of his Son Jesus. God and Jesus are inseparably linked in the divine plan.

Ignorance and "God-fearing devotion" in themselves provide no hope that one can enter God's presence outside of Jesus, as the New Testament shows. Devotion to God must be according to knowledge. In other words, one must believe in the righteousness that comes from God through faith in Jesus. Perhaps Acts 17:30–31 (RSV) says it best: "The times of ignorance God overlooked, but now he commands all men everywhere to repent, because he has fixed a day on which he will judge the world in righteousness by a man whom he has appointed, and of this he has given assurance to all men by raising him from the dead." To know God one must know the appointed one. In short, to be a part of the kingdom, one must know the King.[8]

8. Clark Pinnock has contributed an interesting chapter ("Acts 4:12—No Other Name under Heaven") on this same theme in this volume. He is right to argue that Acts 4:12 affirms a "holistic salvation" and, as such, does not *directly* touch this theme. But he is wrong in the implications he draws from the silence of that text. My handling of the themes of ignorance and God-fearer shows that respect for those who seek God is not the same as acceptance of their faith as "true" or "saving." Luke knows the difference. Acts 4:12 is not "unfairly manipulated" by exclusivists; rather it is related properly by them to the assertions and implications of the speeches in Acts 13 and 17. In short, I am more confident than Pinnock that Acts 10:35, 14:17, and 17:23 answer the "salvation-in-Christ" question in an exclusivist direction, and that as a result the implication of Acts 4:12 falls into a similar category.

10

Romans 1: Finding God in Creation

Aída Besançon Spencer

The first wedding I ever performed was in Trenton, New Jersey. The couple had been referred to my husband and me. We had never met them before. When we asked if they believed in God, the man paused and replied: "When I look up to the sky at night and see all the stars, which are so beautiful, I know God must exist." This man always comes to mind when I think of Paul's words to the Roman Christians: "What can be known of God is manifest among humans; for God made it manifest to them. For God's unseen attributes, namely God's everlasting power and deity, are being seen thoroughly since the creation of the world, being perceived by means of the things God has made" (1:19–20).[1] This man perceived God's deity by looking at what God had created.

Finding God in creation is at first thought a delightful and endless topic. Here is a mystery that is reasonable. God who is a Spirit and therefore unseen, invisible, or incomprehensible to the senses of sight,

---

1. Unidentified Scripture translations are mine.

125

touch, taste, smell, and sound nevertheless can be known (or becomes visible) by seeing, touching, tasting, smelling, and hearing all that God has created.[2]

Can Humans Clearly See God in Creation?

God has been revealed in nature to all humans. Theologians call this "general revelation."[3] In Romans 1:19–20 Paul stresses that this general revelation is *visible* because God made it visible to them. God communicates to every person individually ("to them") through what can be seen in the world. Paul suggests a comparison between *to gnōston* ("the known") of verse 19 and *ta aorata* ("the invisible") of verse 20 by beginning both clauses similarly. What can be known of God is God's invisible or unseen nature. The author may be known by the creation.

To gnōston is used elsewhere in the New Testament of personal friends (Luke 2:44; 23:49).[4] More significantly, it also can be used in proclamations: "Let it be known to you" (Acts 2:14; 28:28). "What can be known of God" is, in effect, God's self-proclamation. Furthermore, God's self-proclamation is "clear or manifest."[5] The adjective *phaneros* is from the same word family as the verb *phaneroō*, translated "has shown" (RSV) or "has made it plain" (NIV). *Phaneros* refers to outward or visible things (e.g., circumcision) as opposed to inward or not so self-evident things (e.g., obedience to the law, Rom. 2:28–29). *Phaneros* functions as a synonym of *gnōstos* in Matthew 12:16 and Philippians 1:13. *Phaneros* is what is proclaimed or publicized as opposed to what is secret (Mark 4:22; 1 Cor. 14:25). The verb *phaneroō* can refer to bringing light on an object (Eph. 5:13), a visible proclamation, as part of a parade (2 Cor. 2:14) or as a present body (incarnation, 1 Tim. 3:16), or a verbal proclamation (Titus 1:3). The opposite is a mystery or lack of clarity (Col. 1:26; 4:4). In other words, God's self-proclamation *to* (*gnōston*) is proclaimed clearly (*phaneros*) because God made it clear and self-evident "to them."

---

2. Of course, God can choose in a theophany to be heard (e.g., Samuel, 1 Sam. 3:4) or seen (e.g., Moses, Exod. 3:2–4), and God chose to become incarnate (Phil. 2:6–7). God is Spirit, however, and inherently not limited by the five senses (John 4:24; Deut. 4:15–19). Paul declares that Jesus is the living image of the "invisible" God (Col. 1:15).

3. See further, Millard J. Erickson, *Christian Theology* (Grand Rapids: Baker, 1983), 1:153–54.

4. *To gnōston* is an abstract substantive (a neuter adjective with an article used as a noun). See Archibald T. Robertson, *A Grammar of the Greek New Testament in the Light of Historical Research,* 3d ed. (New York: Hodder & Stoughton, 1919), 763.

5. James Hope Moulton and George Milligan, *The Vocabulary of the Greek Testament* (London: Hodder & Stoughton, 1930), 663.

Both God's *ta aorata* ("invisible qualities," 1:20)[6] and the verb *kathorao* ("has been clearly perceived") are formed from the same root verb, *horao* ("I see"). Paul writes here of what "cannot be seen." Even as the God who cannot be seen became visible in Jesus (Col. 1:15–16), the God who cannot be seen is visibly proclaimed by what God created. Beginning with the time of the creation of the world,[7] God's unseen qualities have been demonstrated "by means of what is created." Paul specifies that God's invisible qualities can be (and are being) perceived clearly. *Kathorao* is a verb in which *horao* ("I see") is intensified by the prefix *kath* (*kata*, "down"). Literally, *kathorao* signifies "look down, see from above, view from on high." Because one "sees from above," one "sees distinctly" and "sees thoroughly."[8] Paul therefore accentuates what he said in Romans 1:19: "The known of God is *clear*." He uses the present passive, "is being perceived clearly," to communicate that God's invisible nature continues to be seen.

Paul therefore considers that God's invisible qualities not only can be seen, but seen *clearly*. They are seen clearly "being perceived by means of things God has made." Paul uses *noeo*, a synonym of *kathorao*, which, according to Bauer's *Lexicon*, is "of rational reflection or inner contemplation."[9] In the Gospels, Ephesians 3:4, and Hebrews 11:3, *noeo* refers to more than knowing a fact; it refers to perceiving the *significance* of the fact, as in: "Why do you discuss among yourselves the fact that you have no bread? Do you not yet *perceive?*" (Matt. 16:8–9 RSV). In such cases of complete understanding, the will is involved (John 12:40). In other words, when creation is contemplated with a receptive will, which looks to discern the significance of creation, then God's unseen nature can be seen distinctly.[10]

6. *Ho aoratos* is also an abstract substantive like *to gnōston*.

7. The preposition *apo* ("from") usually suggests a general starting point (Robertson, *Grammar of the Greek New Testament*, 577).

8. Henry George Liddell and Robert Scott, *A Greek-English Lexicon*, 9th ed. (Oxford: Clarendon, 1968), 856; Joseph Henry Thayer, *A Greek-English Lexicon of the New Testament* (repr., Grand Rapids: Zondervan, 1962), 314.

9. Walter Bauer, *A Greek-English Lexicon of the New Testament,* trans. William F. Arndt and F. Wilbur Gingrich, 2d rev. ed. by F. Wilbur Gingrich and Frederick W. Danker (Chicago: University of Chicago Press, 1979), 540.

10. The Jewish philosopher Philo develops a similar thought. Superior classes of people envisage the world as a "well-ordered city":

They have beheld the earth standing fast, highland and lowland full of sown crops and trees and fruits and all kinds of living creatures to boot; also spread over its surface, seas and lakes and rivers both spring fed and winter torrents. They have seen too the air and breezes so happily tempered, the yearly seasons changing in harmonious order, and over all the sun and moon, planets and fixed stars, the whole heaven and heaven's host, line upon line, a true universe in itself revolving within the universe. Struck with admiration and astonishment they arrived at a conception

What are those unseen or invisible qualities? They are God's everlasting or eternal power and deity. "Power and deity" is a pleonasm, two synonyms joined by "and" to heighten one thought.[11] What is God's "everlasting" power? *Aidios* is formed from the root *aei* ("ever, always"). It refers to "without beginning" or "without end." It contrasts with *aiōnios* ("the immeasurableness of eternity . . . especially adapted to supersensuous things") or with *aeizōos* ("everliving").[12] God's unseen attributes have been perceived since the creation of the world because God's power had no beginning and it has no end. The world may have a beginning and an end but God has no beginning or end. Peter explains that the divine power results in life and godliness (2 Pet. 1:3–4). Only God has a truly "everlasting" deity (*theiotēs*), unlike the deity assigned to Roman emperors.[13] Therefore, Paul can conclude in verse 21 that humans "have known" (*ginōskō*) God, the same word used for the intimacy of knowledge in marriage (e.g., Gen. 4:1 LXX).

Ginōskō is similar to *noeō* in that both types of knowledge generally have more involved than mere facts. *Ginōskō* is a broad word. According to Thayer *ginōskō* is "a discriminating apprehension of external impressions, a knowledge grounded in personal experience."[14] It is opposed to *eidenai* ("mental perception") in 1 Corinthians 14:7, 9, where understanding comes as a result of hearing clear and audible words. *Ginōskō* can refer to personal experiential knowledge of theolog-

---

according with what they beheld, that surely all these beauties and this transcendent order has not come into being automatically but by the handiwork of an architect and world maker; also that there must be a provider, for it is a law of nature that a maker should take care of what has been made.

Another early Jewish writer also said: "For the greatness and beauty of created things give us a corresponding idea of their Creator" (Wisd. of Sol. 13:5 NEB). These ideas all have an Old Testament basis, as we shall see later in this chapter. In secular Greek thought, see also Pseudo-Aristotle, *De Mundo* 6: "The invisible God is made visible by his works themselves," cited by William Sanday and Arthur C. Headlam, *A Critical and Exegetical Commentary on the Epistle to the Romans*, 5th ed., International Critical Commentary (Edinburgh: T. & T. Clark, 1902), 43. The Stoics also used the "argument from design," as in Cicero, *De Natura Deorum* 2.95.

11. Robertson adds that when one article is used for two distinct groups they are treated as one for the purpose in hand. *Te* and *kai* also have a closer unity than *kai* . . . *kai* (Robertson, *Grammar of the Greek New Testament*, 787, 1178–79). Contrast Richard C. H. Lenski: "The use of *te* helps to show that 'everlasting' modifies only 'power' and not also 'divinity'" (*The Interpretation of St. Paul's Epistle to the Romans* [Minneapolis: Augsburg, 1936], 98).

12. Thayer, *Lexicon of the New Testament*, 14, 21; Liddell and Scott, *Greek-English Lexicon*, 26, 36.

13. For example, a certain Abinnaeus, wanting to be appointed as tax collector, addressed the Emperor Augustus as "our Divine [*theiotēs*] eternal [*aiōnios*] master" (Moulton and Milligan, *Vocabulary of the Greek Testament*, 286).

14. Thayer, *Lexicon of the New Testament*, 118.

ical truths as in knowledge of peace (Rom. 3:17), sin (Rom. 7:7; 2 Cor. 5:21), grace (2 Cor. 8:9), God's will (Rom. 2:18), or God's wisdom (1 Cor. 2:8), or it can refer to experiential knowledge of a person.[15] Paul is saying that humans can have an experiential knowledge of God by contemplating God's creation.

Examples of God's Power and Deity

In Romans, Paul cites no clear example of how God's everlasting power and deity may be perceived clearly in the created world. The created world probably would include the humans,[16] birds, four-footed animals, and reptiles of 1:23 because these created beings were believed by some to be gods, rather than to reflect God. Jesus said that the person who gave food and drink, welcomed a stranger, clothed the naked, visited the sick or the inmate "did it to me," therefore showing that Christ is present in the person in need (Matt. 25:34–40). Similarly, since humans have been created in God's image, God's power and deity may be "perceived clearly" in them. Humans need, desire, and have the ability to interrelate with each other, reflecting the one God who is in three persons (Gen. 1:26). The ability of humans to think, speak, procreate, and be moral would reflect God's own power.[17]

How do birds, four-footed animals, and reptiles illustrate God's power and deity? Jesus uses ravens to illustrate an apparently self-sufficient being (Luke 12:24). God tells Job about animals that reflect God's power and deity: the wild ox whose strength is great and who will not serve humans; the ostrich who knows no fear; the war horse who leaps like the locust and cannot stand still at the sound of the trumpet; the hawk who soars and spreads its wings toward the south; the eagle who mounts up and makes its nest on a high rocky crag, where it spies out the prey from afar; the hippopotamus (Behemoth) whose strength is in its loins and power in the muscles of its belly, who is not afraid of a turbulent river and cannot be taken with a snare; and Leviathan, who sneezes forth fire and smoke, whose back is made of rows of shields ("he counts iron as straw, and bronze as rotten wood" [Job 39:5–41:34 RSV; Heb. 39:5–41:26]).

In several of Paul's sermons, especially when speaking to Gentiles, he uses illustrations testifying of God's power and deity. For instance, at Lystra, Paul speaks of "rains and fruitful seasons" as proof of God's good-

15. God: 1 Cor. 1:21; Gal. 4:9; God's mind: Rom. 11:34; Christ: 2 Cor. 5:16; a person: 1 Cor. 8:3; a person's thoughts: 1 Cor. 2:11; a person's power: 1 Cor. 4:19.

16. In Col. 1:23 and Mark 10:6 *ktisis* ("creation") refers to humans.

17. See, for example, the humans' adaptation of God's revelation in the writing of mystery novels in William David Spencer's *Mysterium and Mystery: The Clerical Crime Novel* (Ann Arbor: University Microfilms International Research Press, 1989).

ness (Acts 14:17). At Athens, Paul highlights the nascent (and custom-ary) belief in an unknown god in order to introduce the Athenians to the God who gives "to all life and breath and all things" (Acts 17:25).

Certain psalms develop the theme to which Paul alludes, such as Psalms 19, 104, and 148.[18] David personifies creation as a human with a powerful voice or with the shofar, the ritual horn, proclaiming a wedding:

> The heavens are telling the glory of God;
>   and the firmament proclaims his handiwork.
> Day to day pours forth speech,
>   and night to night declares knowledge.
> There is no speech, nor are there words;
>   their voice is not heard;
> yet their voice goes out through all the earth,
>   and their words to the end of the world.
> In them he has set a tent for the sun,
> which comes forth like a bridegroom leaving his chamber,
>   and like a strong man runs its course with joy.
> Its rising is from the end of the heavens,
>   and its circuit to the end of them;
>   and there is nothing hid from its heat. (Ps. 19:1–6 RSV)

God's greatness, honor, and majesty in Psalm 104 are illustrated by the immenseness of light and sea and by personifying the winds as messengers. Psalm 148 pictures the sun, moon, shining stars, and waters above the heavens as all praising the Lord; the sea monsters, fire and hail, snow and frost, and stormy wind as all obeying the Lord. Even

> Mountains and all hills,
>   fruit trees and all cedars!
> Beasts and all cattle,
>   creeping things and flying birds

all praise the Lord together with the rulers of the earth (Ps. 148:9–11 RSV)! "Everything that breathes" praises the Lord (Ps. 150:6a).

Is General Revelation Sufficient?

The reader may raise two questions about general revelation. First, since creation does illustrate the presence of God, is any additional type of communication necessary? Why have special revelation such as the Bible? Before Paul ever introduces the topic of creation, he men-

18. See also Ps. 97.

tions the necessity of the prophets and of personal, individualized communication. The good news, he says, was promised beforehand by prophets (Rom. 1:2; 3:21–22; 16:26). Paul desires to visit the Romans personally for their mutual benefit (Rom. 1:11–13). Moreover, even though the creation presents an image of the Creator, the image is insufficient. The structure of Paul's argument shows that by itself the creation condemns; it does not affirm.

Paul's main purpose in writing this letter is to appeal to Jewish and Gentile believers to live in harmony with one another because the good news "is the power of God for salvation to everyone who believes, to the Jew first and also to the Greek."[19] Paul explains the principle of righteousness through faith in chapters 1–4. Since Paul's goal is to bring harmony to the warring Jews and Gentiles, he begins by explaining that everyone, Gentile and Jew, needs salvation. The Gentiles need the good news that righteousness can come through faith because although they can "perceive clearly" God in the created order, they did not glorify or thank God. They are "without excuse."

In the Greek text Romans 1:18–19 is one sentence and 1:20–21 is another. Thus the positive statement of nature reflecting God's power and deity (1:19–20) is embedded in a negative introduction and conclusion:

> For the anger of God is revealed from heaven against all godlessness and injustice of humans, the ones suppressing the truth with injustice . . . in order that they may be without excuse; because having known God not as God they glorified or thanked, but they were given to worthless speculation in their thoughts and their dull hearts became darkened. (1:18, 20–21)

Paul wants to explain that the Gentiles are without excuse for their godlessness because they can perceive God clearly in the created order (1:18–32). But, as well, Jews are also without excuse for their (hypocritical) godlessness because of the law (2:1–24).[20] The Gentiles who are irreverent and unjust are not so out of ignorance, according to Paul (1:18).

Asebeia and *adikia* are a pleonasm, two synonyms highlighting one thought (human sin). *Asebeia* means "impiety" or "want of reverence towards God."[21] It is related to the verb *sebomai* ("worship"). In other

---

19. See my arguments in *Paul's Literary Style: A Stylistic and Historical Comparison of II Corinthians 11:16–12:13, Romans 8:9–39, and Philippians 3:2–4:13,* Evangelical Theological Society Monograph 1 (Winona Lake, Ind.: Eisenbrauns, 1984), 108–11.

20. Paul uses *asebēs* and *asebeia* to refer not only to Gentiles but also to all people (Rom. 4:5; 5:6).

21. Liddell and Scott, *Greek-English Lexicon,* 255; Thayer, *Lexicon of the New Testament,* 79.

words, *asebeia* means, literally, not to worship. *Adikia* is, literally, "not just," or the violation of justice. The root *dikē* can include both injustice (as a judge, Rom. 9:14) and evil or sin.

Human injustice or sin suppresses ("cripples") the truth that God can be known by what is created. *Katechō* means possess,[22] and technically refers to legal ownership of lands possessed. It can also mean "arrest," "put in irons," "lay hands on," "impress for a public duty," and "hold back," "detain," "restrain," as to detain in town.[23] In other words, these humans are the ones restraining or taking possession of the truth, and they do so by means of their own injustice or sin.[24] Therefore, they are "without excuse" or defense (1:20; 2:1).[25] Paul returns to this theme in Romans 3: "Jew and also Gentile are all under sin" (v. 9), and "all the world has become answerable to God's judgment" (v. 19).

Although Paul could say that humans "knew God" from what God created, they did not respond in praise or thanksgiving (1:21). Instead they began "worthless or futile speculation," which led to the darkening and dulling of their wills. The verb *mataioō* occurs only here in the New Testament. The related *mataios* is used by Paul in 1 Corinthians, however, to speak of "worthless" things: If Christ is not raised, faith is worthless and the thoughts of the wise are worthless (15:17; 3:20). A *mataios* expense is a "useless" expense. A worthless speculation would be one that has no reality to it. It leads to no realistic goal. Idols are worthless, in contrast to the living God who made heaven and earth and sea (Acts 14:15; 1 Pet. 1:18). Dwelling upon substitutes for the living God would certainly be an example of what Paul has in mind. These futile speculations occur in their "thoughts" (*dialogismos*) or "arguments." *Dialogismos* always carries negative connotations in the New Testament. Literally it refers to a judicial argument in court.[26] By not confessing God through praise people became less like God. Their thoughts and wills were incapacitated. Unlike the God who brings

---

22. *Echō* ("have") perfected by *kata* ("down").

23. Robertson, *Grammar of the Greek New Testament,* 606; Moulton and Milligan, *Vocabulary of the Greek Testament,* 336–37.

24. *En* basically has the idea of rest or motion "within." In 1:18 *en* can be locative, in the sphere of (humans suppress the truth "in the sphere of injustice") or instrumental, by means of (humans suppress the truth "with injustice," i.e., suppression is located in injustice). See Robertson, *Grammar of the Greek New Testament,* 585–90. Although the instrumental use is less common than the purely locative use in the New Testament, I think it corresponds well with the active verb *katechō*; see Lenski, *Romans,* 93–94.

25. *Eis to* plus the infinitive (1:20) is a result or purpose clause. God's unseen qualities being perceived clearly *results* in humans not having any excuse for not acknowledging God as God.

26. Moulton and Milligan, *Vocabulary of the Greek Testament,* 391, 151. For example, Luke 5:21–22; 6:8; James 2:4.

light and clarity, their wills became darkened. Unlike the "only wise God" who can "put things together," who "has insight and comprehension" (Rom. 16:27), their hearts or wills became stupid. Why? Because they chose to worship the creation rather than the Creator.[27]

Since Paul had been writing from Achaia or Macedonia,[28] he might well be thinking of the many statues to gods in the cities of these lands: the temple to the sun god Apollo at Corinth, the imposing temples to Athena and Artemis at Philippi, or the smaller temples of Hermes, Aphrodite, and Tyche at Corinth. Or, he could have been thinking about the many portrayals of Pan, the half-goat, or of Cheiron, the half-horse. A dining-room floor would often picture Dionysus, the god of nature. The charlatan prophet Alexander took advantage of a snake cult at Abonuteichos to claim that his snake, Glycon, was an incarnation of Asclepius. Fish and doves were held sacred to Atargatis, the fish-goddess, at Hierapolis and Aphrodisias.[29] The gods could become incarnate in any form. These people have neglected the maxim that Charles Williams phrases so well: "This also is Thou; neither is this Thou."[30] Even today, whenever people get carried away serving someone or something of their own creation, they have in effect worshiped "idols."[31]

Why then is general revelation insufficient? The created order is insufficient because it ends up as bad news.[32] The good news that the

27. To think that God is known by learning about the different gods of other religions would be to think that God is known by learning about idols or "false gods." Idols or false gods tell us about God's creation, which indirectly teaches us about God's attributes. However, to confuse the means (creation) with the end (Creator) is to commit blasphemy.

28. Romans may have been written anywhere from the provinces of Achaia through Macedonia. For my arguments see *Paul's Literary Style,* 93–97.

29. Ramsay MacMullen, *Paganism in the Roman Empire* (New Haven: Yale University Press, 1981), 35, 121; John Ferguson, *The Religions of the Roman Empire,* Aspects of Greek and Roman Life (Ithaca: Cornell University Press, 1970), 19–20; 187–89 (Chap. 4, "The Divine Functionaries," discusses how, for the ancient, "all nature was life, spirit, divinity").

30. Mary McDermott Shideler, *The Theology of Romantic Love: A Study in the Writings of Charles Williams* (Grand Rapids: Eerdmans, 1962), 21.

31. Paul J. Achtemeier has a fine discussion on contemporary idolatry. He adds that people become like the lord they serve. Like the ancients who worshiped statues of animals, our society today "shows signs of bestiality": "If in our desire to overcome a competitor in whatever area, whether as student or professional, whether as husband or wife, whether as business man or woman, we take as our model the rapacious drive of the beast of prey, sweeping all aside in our desire to overcome, is it any wonder that our society becomes bestial?" (*Romans,* Interpretation [Atlanta: John Knox, 1985], 38).

32. Having perceived God's nature from creation, can any human being respond in thanks rather than in worthless speculation? Paul clearly says in Romans 1–2 that Gentile, as well as Jew, can perceive some aspect of God's nature and that faith is needed

Old Testament prophets and Paul want to declare is that now all who believe can have God's righteousness through faith in Jesus Christ (Rom. 3:21–22). The Gentiles' godlessness provides no excuse because godliness is attainable through faith in Christ, for both Jew and Greek.

Is General Revelation Clear?

The second question that can be raised about creation is whether it succeeds in making visible God's power and deity. What about natural disasters such as earthquakes and floods? What about great examples of inhumanity of humans against one another? What about animals killing weaker animals? What does Paul have to say about the evil and injustice in the created order?

Paul writes about this aspect of nature in 8:19–22: "The creation was subjected to futility" (8:20 RSV). It is in "bondage to decay" (8:21 RSV). What was created by God is now part of a fallen world. When Adam sinned he affected the innocent bystander, the earth. The ground did not sin, but because of Adam's sin, it became "cursed," "bringing forth thorns and thistles" (Gen. 3:17–18). Eve and Adam, created in God's image, now had antagonism in their marriage (Gen. 3:16).[33] The serpent would eat "dust" all the days of its life (Gen. 3:14). What God created has become enslaved to sin. Paul is aware of the way human sin has affected nature. Nevertheless, he still can write that even such an "enslaved creation" yet speaks clearly about its Creator.

The hymnist Maltbie D. Babcock writes:

> This is my Father's world,
> And to my listening ears
> All nature sings, and round me rings
> The music of the spheres.
>
> This is my Father's world:
> I rest me in the thought
> Of rocks and trees, of skies and seas;
> His hand the wonders wrought.[34]

---

in righteousness. In Romans 3:9–12 Paul adds that neither Jew nor Greek seeks God (quoting Ps. 14:3). I do not think that Paul clearly addresses the situation of the eternal state of the *devout* human who has not been told by another human that Jesus is Lord and that God raised him from the dead (Rom. 10:9) because Paul is, after all, writing to the *churches* in Rome. My personal response is to rely on God's loving and just character to judge such people and to preach all the more the good news.

33. For more information, see chap. 1 in my book *Beyond the Curse: Women Called to Ministry* (Peabody, Mass.: Hendrickson, 1985).

34. *The Worshipbook: Services and Hymns* (Philadelphia: Westminster, 1972).

Babcock can find scriptural support for his psalm in Romans 1:18–21. God may be experientially known from creation, not only from inanimate nature, but also animate nature, humans, birds, four-footed animals, and reptiles. Although creation is fallen, Paul still has stressed the clarity of God's self-revelation by word order (*phaneros* precedes its verb) and by the use of many synonyms for clarity (*phaneros*, "manifest"; *phaneroō*, "make clear"; *gnōstos*, "known"; *kathoraō*, "see thoroughly"). God who "cannot be seen" (*aoratos*) is proclaimed by means of what God created. Therefore, God's "everlasting" (not temporary) power and deity can be seen thoroughly when contemplated by receptive wills (*noeō*). Nevertheless, special revelation is still indispensable. Because of the testimony of creation, humans are left with the bad news that they are accountable for their impiety to God. They have no defense. Therefore, Gentiles (and Jews alike) need to hear the good news that they may become righteous through faith in Jesus the messiah, proclaimed by the prophets of old, and by believers in face-to-face proclamations.

11

Romans 2: Saved Apart from the Gospel?

Douglas Moo

To those who by persistence in doing good seek glory, honor and immortality, he will give eternal life. (Rom. 2:7)

For it is not those who hear the law who are righteous in God's sight, but it is those who obey the law who will be declared righteous. Indeed, when Gentiles, who do not have the law, do by nature things required by the law, they are a law for themselves, even though they do not have the law, since they show that the requirements of the law are written on their hearts, their consciences also bearing witness, and their thoughts now accusing, now even defending them. (Rom. 2:13–15)

If those who are not circumcised keep the law's requirements, will they not be regarded as though they were circumcised? The one who is not circumcised physically and yet obeys the law will condemn you who, even though you have the written code and circumcision, are a lawbreaker. (Rom. 2:26–27)

These passages from Romans 2 appear to teach that people can be saved by doing good things. "Persistence in doing good" can bring eternal life, "obeying the law" can lead to being declared righteous before God, "doing by nature the things required by the law" can result in thoughts that "defend" a person on the day of judgment (see v. 16), and "keeping the law's requirement" can mark a person as belonging to God's people (i.e., be considered as circumcised). Nothing is said in either these texts or the larger context about responding to the gospel or about faith in Christ. Romans 2, in other words, seems to furnish considerable exegetical ammunition to those who think that people can be saved without responding in faith to the gospel of Jesus Christ.

Many have drawn just this conclusion from Romans 2. Several church fathers and the reformer Zwingli thought these passages referred to "enlightened" pagans who lived before the time of Christ. Others go further, saying Paul opens the door here to the possibility that people after Christ's coming, who have never heard the gospel in any form, can be saved by a sincere and obedient response to the "light" they have received.

I will show in this chapter that this interpretation of Romans 2 is incorrect. First, I will give my reasons for rejecting the conclusion that Paul is teaching salvation apart from the gospel and faith. I will then present two more satisfying interpretations of the relevant texts and indicate my own preference between them.

Does Paul Teach Salvation by Works?

The biggest problem for anyone arguing that Romans 2 allows for salvation by works is that such a reading conflicts with other texts in this same letter. "No one will be declared righteous in his sight by observing the law" (3:20a). "For we maintain that a man is justified by faith apart from observing the law" (3:28). "However, to the man who does not work but trusts God who justifies the wicked, his faith is credited as righteousness" (4:5). In these texts Paul seems to say that a right relationship with God comes only through faith, and that nothing a person does can contribute in any way to establishing this relationship.

Some boldly cut the knot of paradox and state that Paul simply contradicts himself. He usually teaches salvation by faith alone, but for some reason, teaches salvation by works in Romans 2.[1] These interpreters can claim Paul's authority for "salvation apart from the gospel," but in so doing they destroy the value of appealing to the apostle as an authority. What kind of authority should Paul have for

---

1. See, e.g., Heikki Räisänen, *Paul and the Law* (Tübingen: Mohr, 1983), 99–108; and E. P. Sanders, *Paul, the Law and the Jewish People* (Philadelphia: Fortress, 1983), 123–32.

us if he so blatantly contradicts himself at so fundamental a point for his theology and preaching? We may, then, dismiss this view from consideration because it leads to no certain conclusions about how a person is to be saved.

Those who think that Romans 2 teaches salvation by doing, and that such a teaching does not contradict Paul's teaching elsewhere, argue in different ways, and I do not intend here to rehearse all the possibilities. Rather, I will take one recent and well-argued article as an example. Klyne Snodgrass insists that Paul is teaching "salvation to the doers" in Romans 2 and that nothing in Paul's letters contradicts this conclusion. First, suggests Snodgrass, the "doing" that God rewards with salvation in Romans 2 is a doing that springs from the work of God's grace in the life of a person. Paul's "by grace alone" is, then, preserved. Second, in texts like Romans 3:20 and 3:28, Paul is not denying that works or doing can justify—only that certain *kinds* of works do not justify. Specifically, Snodgrass argues that the phrase used in both these verses, *erga nomou* ("works of the law"), refers to works done in a legalistic spirit, "works done in the flesh." Paul resolutely denies that such works, done apart from God's grace in a desire to gain favor with God, can save. But there is nothing in Paul against the idea that the "right" kind of doing can bring a person into relationship with God. God, Romans 2 teaches, is impartial and will reward every person according to what that person has done; and the one who responds sincerely and obediently to that "light" will be saved.[2]

Quite apart from questions about whether this interpretation gets at what Paul is doing in Romans 2, I am not convinced that it escapes the charge of Pauline inconsistency. For Snodgrass's view to work, *erga nomou* must have a restricted meaning and Paul must not elsewhere teach that justification is by faith alone. Both are questionable. Despite recent claims to the contrary, there is no good reason to confine Paul's "works of the law" to a certain kind of works, such as "works done in a 'legalistic spirit,'" or "works done to claim covenant status."[3] *Erga nomou*, which Paul uses eight times (also in Gal. 2:16 [three times]; 3:2, 5, 10), is clearly equivalent to the simple *erga* ("works") of Romans 4:2 and 4:6. The addition of the phrase *of the law (nomou)* simply denotes the source that demands the works; it does not change the meaning of the word *works* from the way Paul uses it elsewhere—of

2. Indeed, Snodgrass suggests that some passages such as Rom. 3:31; 8:4; 13:8, 10; Gal. 5:14; 6:2 support this idea. See Klyne R. Snodgrass, "Justification by Grace—to the Doers: An Analysis of the Place of Romans 2 in the Theology of Paul," *New Testament Studies* 32 (1986): 72–93, esp. 85.

3. The latter is the way that James D. G. Dunn interprets the phrase; see *Romans 1–8*, Word Biblical Commentary 38a (Waco, Tex.: Word, 1988), 158–60.

anything a person does (see Rom. 9:11–12). This is confirmed by the equivalent Jewish phrase, which also denotes anything done in obedience to the law.[4] In Romans 3:20 and 3:28, then, Paul rejects any place for human "doing," however motivated or directed, in the justification of sinful human beings, as the majority of Protestant interpreters have correctly seen. Nothing we can do, not even the works of Abraham (Rom. 4), can bring us to God.

Moreover, justification by faith is, for Paul, the necessary corollary to "by grace alone." Any work that a human does, however it is motivated (and Abraham's were surely rightly motivated!), creates an "obligation" on God's part. Therefore, since God gives his salvation in an act of pure grace, there can be no place for works in the process. (This is the logic of Rom. 4:4–5.)

If this is so, then any interpretation of Romans 2 that allows for people to be saved apart from faith runs head-on into the bedrock of Paul's theology: justification by faith alone, as the necessary corollary to salvation by grace alone. We have put the matter negatively: salvation apart from faith contradicts salvation by faith alone. But it can also be defended positively when we recognize the place of chapter 2 in the argument of Romans. Romans 1:18–3:20 is a long, but necessary "interruption" in the basic train of Paul's thought. In 1:16–17, Paul affirms that the gospel mediates saving power to everyone who believes, both Jew and Gentile. Romans 3:21 resumes and develops this theme. The intervening argument (1:18–3:20) is intended to show why human beings need this "revelation of the righteousness of God" and why it can be experienced only through faith. What is the reason? Sin. It holds every person, Jew or Gentile, under its power (3:9). And because of sin, no person can be justified before God by obeying the law or by doing any other good work (3:20). Boiled down to its essentials, then, Paul is claiming that people must respond in faith to the revelation of God's righteousness because it, and it alone, breaks the stranglehold of sin. And the revelation of God's righteousness occurs, he says, in the gospel.

Romans 2 cannot mean that people are saved apart from faith or apart from the gospel. But my case will not be convincing unless I can demonstrate a plausible alternative interpretation. In fact, two such interpretations exist.

The Gentile Christian Interpretation

The first holds that Paul is speaking, in each of the verses quoted at the head of this chapter, of Gentile *Christians*. It is they, and they only,

4. For more detailed argument, see my article "'Law,' 'Works of the Law,' and Legalism in Paul," *Westminster Theological Journal* 45 (1983): 73–100.

who persist "in doing good" (2:7), who are justified by observing the law (2:13), who "do by nature things required by the law" (2:14), and who are accounted as God's people by keeping the requirements of the law (2:26). They do not have the law "by nature," that is, by being born as Jews under the Mosaic law. Yet, their faith incorporates them into Christ, gives them the indwelling Spirit (see 2:28–29), and makes them able to "fulfill" the demands of the law. Thus is brought to pass the circumstances predicted by the prophet Jeremiah for the "new covenant," when God's law is written on the hearts of his people (Jer. 31:31–34; compare Rom. 2:15). On this view, of course, Romans 2 says nothing about the possibility of salvation apart from the gospel, for all of Paul's statements about those who are saved by doing refer to people who have already responded to the gospel.

This view, which has a long and distinguished history,[5] succeeds in harmonizing Romans 2 with 3:20 and 3:28. Paul would be saying that faith alone justifies and is the necessary presupposition of the works that count before God in the final judgment. Still, while this interpretation may be theologically sound, it has problems satisfying the data in Romans 2. First, the introduction of Gentile Christians at this point in Paul's discussion would interfere with his purpose. Romans 2 is part of Paul's indictment of humankind, an indictment that reaches its climax in 3:9: "Jews and Gentiles alike are all under sin." Throughout 1:18–3:8, Paul shows that Jews and Gentiles are on the same footing before God, because they have been exposed to the revelation of God, but have turned from that revelation. To compare Jews and Gentile Christians at this point in his indictment would disrupt this carefully argued equation between the two.

The second problem with the Gentile Christian view is the description of the "Gentiles" (*ethnē*) in verse 14 as those who "do by nature things required by the law." Gentile Christians certainly fulfill the law (see Rom. 8:4), but they do it through the Spirit, not "by nature" (*physei*), a word that alludes to natural, inborn capacities.

Third, we are required on this view to assume that when Paul says people will be saved by doing good or by their obedience to the law, he really means "by their faith which is manifested in their doing good." This is a big assumption to make, for Paul appears to be saying that it is the doing itself which is the criterion for the judgment of God.

While the Gentile Christian view should be taken seriously, I do not think it is the best interpretation of Romans 2. The context and thrust

---

5. Held by Augustine, revived by Karl Barth and argued recently by, among others, C. E. B. Cranfield, *A Critical and Exegetical Commentary on the Epistle to the Romans*, International Critical Commentary (Edinburgh: T. & T. Clark, 1975), 1:151–58, 172–74.

of Paul's argument are better explained if these people are identified as Gentiles apart from Christ. Does this mean, then, that Paul opens the door to the salvation of Gentiles apart from the gospel? In a sense, yes, he does—but only to slam it decisively in the next chapter. Let me explain by examining Romans 2, paragraph by paragraph, in light of the hypothetical interpretation.

The Hypothetical Interpretation

The paragraph in verses 6–11 begins and ends with statements that God will impartially render to each person "according to his works." Paul breaks down this general statement into two possibilities: punishment for doing wrong (vv. 8–9) and eternal life for doing good (vv. 7 and 10). Paul's purpose in this paragraph is to set forth the standard by which God judges each person, whether Jew or Gentile. He is not teaching how a person can be saved, but why God's judgment is truly a "righteous judgment" (v. 5). Here, apart from Christ, is the standard of judgment: works. Doing evil will be punished, but doing good, *if persisted in sufficiently* (v. 7) will be rewarded with eternal life. But Paul does not say that anyone outside of Christ meets this standard. In 3:9 ("all are under sin") and 3:20 ("no one can be justified by 'works of the law'") he plainly denies that it is possible. The standard is set forth, and it embodies a genuine promise—but it is a promise that the power of sin, unleashed in the world through Adam (Rom. 5:12–21), prevents any person from attaining.[6]

The paragraph that follows takes the matter a step further. One might well respond at this point: Paul, you have said that God will judge each person, impartially, according to that person's works. But do not the Jews have a decisive advantage at this point? Has not God given them in the Mosaic law a clear description of the works he expects, while the Gentiles have been left without such guidance? In the face of this potential objection, Paul makes two main points in verses 12–16: (1) having the Mosaic law does not help the Jews, and (2) the Gentiles have not been left without guidance from God. The former point emerges clearly in verses 12b–13. Jews ("those under the law," i.e., under its authority) will be judged according to the Mosaic law that has been given them (v. 12b), and it is not possessing, learning, or teaching that law which will clear them at the judgment, but *doing* it (v. 13). Here again, Paul is setting forth the standard by which Jews will be judged—he is not showing the Jews how

6. This line of interpretation is taken by, among others, Charles Hodge, *Commentary on the Epistle to the Romans* (repr., Grand Rapids: Eerdmans, 1950), 49–50, 54–55, 64–65; and Richard N. Longenecker, *Paul, Apostle of Liberty* (repr., Grand Rapids: Baker, 1976), 116–22.

they may be saved. Romans 3:20 makes it clear that no person will be justified (*dikaioō*, the same verb as is used in 2:13) by doing the law. The logic of Paul in chapters 2–3 may be summarized in three key statements:

1. Doing the law can bring justification (2:13).
2. All are under the power of sin (3:9).
3. No one can be justified by doing the law (3:20).

The second of these assertions explains why the promise embodied in the first never becomes a reality and why the third, therefore, states the situation as it really is.

The description in verse 14 does not fit Gentile Christians. Paul is referring to non-Christian Gentiles who, though they do not "have the [Mosaic] law," show, by their "natural" conformity to many of the law's demands, that God has put within them a knowledge of "right and wrong." Verses 14–15, then, do not explain verse 13b—as if Paul were describing those who are justified by obeying the law—but they qualify verse 12a. Those Gentiles who perish "apart from the [Mosaic] law" are not without access to God's law in a more general sense: they have the basic moral law of God written on their hearts (note the reference to the conscience in v. 15).

Thus, Paul hints again at what he has taught in Romans 1:19–22: that in some way God confronts every person and, when judgment falls, each is "without excuse"—whether that person be a Jew who has the law of Moses or a Gentile who has the law of the heart. But does Paul in verse 15 allow that such Gentiles may follow the law of the heart so well that they are "excused" in the judgment? The verse could be read this way, but makes no sense in the context, since verses 14–15 explain why the Gentiles are condemned in verse 12a. Rather than reading verse 15b as if Paul were saying that some Gentiles may have thoughts that "accuse" them, while others have thoughts that "excuse" them, we should understand the point to be that all Gentiles have some thoughts that "accuse" and some that "excuse" (the NIV translation implies this). Every Gentile who stands before God in the judgment will be able to plead that he or she has occasionally, and maybe even often, done what "the law on the heart" demanded: honored parents, refrained from stealing, murder, adultery, and so on. But no Gentile will be able to stand before God without many "thoughts" that reveal a frequent lack of conformity to God's demand. Such lack of conformity is sufficient basis for the wrath of God.

The last paragraph of Romans 2 is parallel to verses 12–16. Both show that the covenant privileges of the Jews do not shield them from the judgment of God and that they are in the same situation as the

Gentiles. While verses 12–16 make this point in light of the Jews' possession of the Mosaic law, verses 25–29 make it with reference to circumcision, the "sign of the covenant." Paul argues that mere possession of
this blessing has no "value," unless it is accompanied by obedience to
the law (v. 25). Again, we find Paul making what is actually *done* the
decisive criterion in God's verdict. And assessment by this criterion can
have positive as well as negative results, for even uncircumcised
Gentiles, if they obey the law, will be considered as belonging to the
people of God (v. 26). The case for identifying these Gentiles as Gentile
Christians is stronger here than in any of the other debated texts in
Romans 2.[7] Two reasons support this position. First, verse 27, which
continues the thought of verse 26, appears to predict an actual situation
in which the Gentiles who follow the law judge the Jews who do not.
Second, the latter part of the paragraph identifies the Holy Spirit, the
agent of new covenant regeneration, as the one who accomplishes the
circumcision that stamps people as God's own (see vv. 28–29).

Yet the argument is not conclusive. The realism of verse 27 may
simply reflect the hypothetical circumstance of verse 26. If uncircumcised Gentiles were to meet the law's demand, at the judgment they
would be able to condemn the Jews who had the law, but did not do
it. It is true that Christian experience is "foreshadowed" in verses
28–29, for Paul always uses "Spirit," when contrasted with "letter"
(*gramma*), to refer to a specifically Christian situation (see also Rom.
7:6 and 2 Cor. 3:5–6). But it is not clear that verse 29 describes the
same individual as verse 26. Paul's description of the "true Jew" in
verses 28–29 contrasts with the law-breaking Jew of verses 25 and 27
and does not further describe the uncircumcised Gentile of verse 26.
Paul's main point in verses 25–27 is that Jews cannot rely on their circumcision to shield them from the judgment of God. In verses 28–29,
he contrasts this "ineffective" circumcision with the only circumcision
that counts before God: the circumcision of the heart, accomplished
by God's Spirit. Here Paul anticipates his teaching later in Romans that
Christians who fulfill the law through the Spirit are the true people of
God (see 8:2–4).[8]

---

7. For instance, John Murray adopts the interpretation of vv. 7, 10, 13, and 14–15
argued above, but still thinks that here Paul is referring to Gentile Christians; see *The
Epistle to the Romans*, New International Commentary on the New Testament (Grand
Rapids: Eerdmans, 1959), 1:86–87.

8. Another factor makes it unlikely that Paul is referring to Gentile Christians in v.
26. As in the earlier texts, it is conformity to the law that here qualifies one to be a
member of God's people. But Paul makes clear that it is faith, not conformity to the law,
that turns a Gentile into a Gentile Christian. Paul insists that any form of doing or obedience to the law is distinct from faith (e.g., Rom. 4:4–5, 13–14; Gal. 3:12). He would
never describe faith under the rubric of "keeping the requirements of the law."

Paul never says that Gentiles apart from the gospel can be saved by meeting the demands of the law, or by doing good works. The texts could mean this only if they are ripped out of context. Once the context is recognized, Paul's purposes understood, and his theology of justification taken into account, we quickly see that Gentiles cannot be saved apart from the gospel.

12

Eternal Consequences or Eternal Consciousness?

Scot McKnight

I grew up in the sort of Christianity that did not shy away from poking fun at unbelievers and, when the preacher led them to it, the congregation on occasion cackled at those who wanted to "burn in hell forever and ever." In the process of becoming socialized into that fundamentalist movement with its unabashedly strong self-consciousness, I confess I rarely reflected on the ghastly nature of hell or on the haughty, insensitive, and repulsive way we spoke of fellow humans (see James 3:10). Universalism was not even a tolerable thought; but the bold vision of hell was. That condescending, jovial attitude we had toward unbelievers changed significantly during two crucial summers.

In my college days, I spent two summers as part of an evangelistic team in Austria, going door to door, passing out tracts, holding tent meetings, seeking to convert as many Austrians as possible. We were noticeably unsuccessful—so unsuccessful that my faith was challenged, if not shaken. The hardest part for me to handle was the massive unbelief and widespread apathy. Rarely did we meet fellow Christians, even more rare was the opportunity to see someone surrender his or her life to Jesus Christ. More frequently we were harassed, ridiculed, and asked to leave; often the response was a sad stolidity. The consequences of rejecting Christ did not phase them at all. For me hell was real; for them it was a myth. Convinced that they were sadly wrong and yet compassionate enough to hope for something good, I groped for answers. I confess that one cognitive model that sustained me in all my encounters with unbelief was the hope that hell would not be eternal for these people. I say "hope" because it was my hope that these people would not "burn in hell" forever. To me it seemed grossly unfair for a finite human being to suffer infinite consequences for a finite act: unbelief. I had to find a solution because hell for the masses was intolerable for me. I concluded that God could not be the "Eternal Torturer" and, after visiting the Mauthausen concentration camp, hell as an "eternal torture chamber" was too repulsive even to imagine.

Since then I have arrived at a slightly different position, a position that believes in final (conscious) exclusion from God's presence but that cringes at the thought of fellow human beings—people I talk to, girls my daughter walks home with, boys my son plays ball with, friends in the here and now—remaining eternally conscious of their separation from God, their Creator and Father, from his Son, the Savior of the world and the wisest teacher of mankind, and from his Holy Spirit, who makes love, peace, and joy possible for each of us. I believe, in other words, in endless conscious pain caused by the absence of everything good, but this thought is so unbearable that I can only take consolation in God's goodness and in the hope of conversion. To poke fun at recalcitrant unbelievers is disgusting and, I believe, never to be a part of a Christian's conversation.

In short, I believe in final judgment, that Jesus Christ shall come "to judge the living and the dead." Further, I believe that this judgment has eternal consequences and that those who are damned are eternally conscious of their separation. And this confession is not said gleefully; I believe it because I am convinced that Jesus taught it. Yet some respected biblical scholars differ with me and so, before I look at what Jesus teaches, I shall briefly sketch their views.

Conditional Immortality and Annihilationism

What is the sensitive evangelical soul to do? Universalism is clearly ruled out by Scripture![1] An attractive alternative to eternal, conscious

---

1. See the essays in this volume: Aída Besançon Spencer, "Romans 1: Finding God in Creation"; Douglas Moo, "Romans 2: Saved Apart from the Gospel?"; William V. Crockett, "Will God Save Everyone in the End?"; and Carl F. H. Henry, "Is It Fair?"

separation from God is conditional immortality, sometimes called annihilationism.[2] It is true that these two terms are fraught with difficulties of definition and so some brief comments are in order. Conditional immortality has at least two forms: (1) all human beings will live endlessly but only Christians become "immortal" and receive "eternal life," a view argued for on the basis of how the New Testament uses the term *immortal*,[3] and (2) some form of annihilationism. Annihilationism, likewise, has at least two forms: (1) all humans are (or begin to be) annihilated at death and (2) all human beings are raised to experience God's judgment, some of whom inherit eternal life and others of whom experience God's destruction that eventuates in endless extinction and nonexistence.

Annihilationism, in its "Christian" form,[4] argues that "man . . . fulfills his destiny in salvation, while the reprobates fall into nonexistence either through a direct act of God or through the corrosive effect of evil (annihilationism proper)."[5] Or, as Alan Johnson defines it, "all men were created immortal but . . . those who do not repent and believe in Christ will by a positive act of God be deprived of immortality and reduced to nonexistence at death."[6] Put differently, this kind of annihilationism believes that all humans will be called to account finally before God, that those who are believers will be granted (or will

2. My colleague Murray J. Harris rightly contends that immortality is a final condition only of believers in the sense that it is "a divine gift that will be acquired only by the righteous and only through a future resurrection or resurrection transformation." He distinguishes his view clearly from annihilationism and shows that traditional theological explanations of the notion of immortality (=natural immortality) are indebted more to Plato and Aristotle, for whom immortality was the inevitable result of having within the soul an immortal subsistence, than to the biblical evidence. Hence, Harris's several publications are studies in the biblical usage of this and other terms; see Harris, "Immortality," in *New Dictionary of Theology*, ed. Sinclair B. Ferguson, David F. Wright, and James I. Packer (Downers Grove, Ill.: Inter-Varsity, 1988), 333; for a complete defense, see Harris, *Raised Immortal: Resurrection and Immortality in the New Testament* (Grand Rapids: Eerdmans, 1983), 237–40; Harris, *From Grave to Glory: Resurrection in the New Testament, Including a Response to Dr. Norman L. Geisler* (Grand Rapids: Zondervan, 1990).

3. For a recent proponent, see Harris, *Raised Immortal*, 180–85, 197–99. This kind of conditional immortality is the positive sharing in God's immortality and one shares this through faith in Jesus Christ.

4. In contrast to the view that all human beings pass eternally from existence at death. This view cannot claim any Christian heritage while "conditionalism" of some sort has been argued by some Christian theologians.

5. As defined by Roger Nicole, "Annihilationism," in *Evangelical Dictionary of Theology*, ed. Walter A. Elwell (Grand Rapids: Baker, 1984), 50.

6. Alan F. Johnson, "Conditional Immortality," in *Evangelical Dictionary of Theology*, ed. Walter A. Elwell (Grand Rapids: Baker, 1984), 261. Johnson here expresses a slight variation: (1) natural immortality is assumed, (2) at death or judgment unbelievers are stripped of immortality and consequently annihilated, and (3) believers continue in their immortality.

retain their) immortality (eternal life with God) and those who are unbelievers will be judged and then ultimately annihilated.[7]

There is nothing necessarily unworthy of Christian reflection in the annihilationist's construction of the final state of unbelievers; Scripture does not give us that much revelation on the final state. But a lack of information about something ought not to keep us from thinking about it. Nor do I necessarily question the motivation of those who come to this conclusion.

In fact, I admire the candor of John R. W. Stott:

> Emotionally, I find the concept ("eternal conscious torment") intolerable and do not understand how people can live with it without either cauterizing their feelings or cracking under the strain. But our emotions are a fluctuating, unreliable guide to truth and must not be exalted to the place of supreme authority in determining it. As a committed Evangelical, my question must be—and is—not what does my heart tell me, but what does God's word say?[8]

Now this way of discussing the matter is what I believe, too. And for that very reason Dr. Stott and I can enter into dialogue. If I could be persuaded that the Bible does not teach eternal consciousness in torment, I would gladly embrace annihilationism—if only for the emotional strain it would release. And, in turn, if I could persuade Dr. Stott that the Bible teaches eternal, conscious torment then I am convinced he would not believe in annihilationism. And so it is appropriate that we turn to one passage in the Bible, a verse that has convinced me that Jesus taught conscious, eternal torment.[9]

---

7. Proponents of this view include John R. W. Stott. In an engaging book, David L. Edwards and John R. W. Stott, *Evangelical Essentials: A Liberal-Evangelical Dialogue* (Downers Grove, Ill.: Inter-Varsity, 1988), 312–29, Stott sets forth his case in a balanced and reasoned manner. Evangelicals need to discuss this matter openly, but are rightly squeamish and modest about "consultations on hell!" Stott's view may well owe some of its inspiration to Basil F. C. Atkinson, *Life and Immortality: An Examination of the Nature and Meaning of Life and Death as They Are Revealed in the Scriptures* (Taunton: Goodman, 1962), esp. 82–112. Another recent statement of this view can be found in Stephen H. Travis, *Christ and the Judgement of God: Divine Retribution in the New Testament* (Basingstoke: Marshall Pickering, 1986), 65–77 (who is quite cautious).

8. In Edwards and Stott, *Evangelical Essentials,* 314–15. See M. J. Harris, *Raised Immortal,* 184–85.

9. Stott discusses Matt. 25:46 (*Evangelical Essentials,* 317) in the context of "imagery" where he argues that "eternal" does not necessarily mean eternal consciousness. He writes, "On the contrary, although declaring both [punishment and life] to be eternal, Jesus is *contrasting* the two destinies: the more unlike they are, the better." The problem here is that what is in contrast is not the time factor (eternal) but the nature of the eternality (punishment versus life); this contrast could hardly be more unlike. His view, and the many who agree with him here, requires equivocation on the meaning of "eternal."

Exegesis of Matthew 25:46

The interpretation of the parable of the sheep and the goats (Matt. 25:31–46) has a long and debated history.[10] Here a climactic and tragic scene is sketched before the reader's eyes: a scene of summoning before God all humankind (25:32: "all the nations") for final judgment. As the shepherd separates the sheep from the goats, so God will separate the righteous (those who have lived in Christ and God's will) from the unrighteous (those who have lived apart from Christ and God's will). And, just as the righteous are given place in God's kingdom (25:34–40) so also the unrighteous, or "the cursed" (25:41), will be assigned to "eternal fire prepared for the devil and his angels" (25:41). Here there are expressions of both deprivation and retribution.[11] The final criterion for judgment is a life that reflects a relationship to Jesus Christ, exhibited in deeds of mercy to "the least of these brothers of mine" (25:40, 45; see also Rom. 2:7; Gal. 6:8; 1 Tim. 6:12).[12]

But the crucial expressions for our discussion about annihilationism are found in Matthew 25:46, which reads, "And they [the wicked] will go away to eternal punishment [eis kolasin aiōnion], but the righteous to eternal life [eis zōēn aiōnion]." The issue here can be resolved to one simple, though crucial, question: Does "eternal" refer to "temporally unlimited consciousness and consequences" or is there evidence that "eternal" refers to "temporally unlimited consequences but temporally limited consciousness"?[13]

To answer this question, two further questions must be asked: (1) What does eternal refer to, especially in the context of Jesus' (and

---

10. For this section, see the commentaries of D. A. Carson, *Matthew*, Expositor's Bible Commentary 8, ed. Frank E. Gaebelein (Grand Rapids: Zondervan, 1984); Robert H. Gundry, *Matthew: A Commentary on His Literary and Theological Art* (Grand Rapids: Zondervan, 1982); Robert H. Mounce, *Matthew* (San Francisco: Harper & Row, 1985). More technical studies are referred to in the notes of these commentaries and in the volume by Friedrich listed in n. 12.

11. Harris, *Raised Immortal*, 181.

12. A heated debate continues to rage regarding the identity of the "least of these brothers of mine"; on this see especially Carson, *Matthew*, 518–21. More complete discussion may be seen in James Friedrich, *Gott im Bruder* (Stuttgart: Calwer, 1977), 1:220–57, esp. the useful table of interpretation at 2:186–89. On the issue of Matthew and the final judgment, see Roger Mohrlang, *Matthew and Paul* (Cambridge: Cambridge University Press, 1984), 48–71 with notes.

13. The term *kolasin* is a graphic metaphor for "punishment," in spite of Atkinson's attempt to see an image of separation (*Life and Immortality*, 101–2). For support of the meaning "punishment," see Walter Bauer, *A Greek-English Lexicon of the New Testament and Other Early Christian Literature*, trans. William F. Arndt and F. Wilbur Gingrich, 2d ed. rev. F. Wilbur Gingrich and Frederick W. Danker (Chicago: University of Chicago Press, 1979), 440–41. It is foolhardy, however, to speculate on the nature of this punishment.

Matthew's)[14] teachings? and (2) what does eternal refer to in the context of final-judgment scenes?[15]

I begin with the meaning of eternal in Jesus' (and Matthew's) teachings.[16] The standard Greek lexicons divide the meaning of *aiōnios* into two major categories: (1) lasting for a long but definite period (aeonial), an age or lifetime, and (2) perpetual, immeasurable time (eternal), forever, or a temporally unlimited period.[17] Context must decide whether a given word should be interpreted according to the first (aeonial) or second (eternal) definition. But the matter is largely resolved when one recognizes that this present age is temporally limited (because it is not the perfected age) and the future age is temporally unlimited (because it shares in God's immortality). The distinction between "this age" (limited time) and "the age to come" (unlimited time) is central to New Testament eschatology: in Jesus Christ God has broken into time, separating the old from the new, inaugurating the kingdom of God that will be consummated in an endless glorious reign of God. God's time is essentially endless and eternal, and it follows that the final age is an eternal (endless) age. In the exegesis of New Testament texts, this distinction must be observed.

14. This methodological point is crucial; since those who are concerned to establish their views on the basis of the Bible are willing to take the text as it stands, we must understand the author of this text (Matthew). To go to Jesus' original words, in the original Aramaic, is not without importance but will not supplant the words of Matthew for those who hold to their authority. Finally, to go to John's usage of eternal is to explain one author by another author, when the two authors use different categories and meanings. John's idea of "qualitative new life" ought not to be used to define eternal in Matthew unless Matthew's text suggests the same. I suspect this methodological failure is at the root of Colin Brown's suggestion that eternal in Matt. 25:46 need not mean endlessness; rather, he says, it can have qualitative and quantitative senses; see Brown, "Punishment," in *The New International Dictionary of New Testament Theology,* ed. Colin Brown, 3 vols. (Grand Rapids: Zondervan, 1975–78), 3:99.

15. For the meaning of eternal, see esp. William G. T. Shedd, *The Doctrine of Endless Punishment* (New York: Scribner, 1886; repr., Minneapolis: Klock & Klock, 1980), 75–90.

16. For the broader discussion of condemnation in the teachings of Jesus, see Travis, *Christ and the Judgement of God,* 135–41.

17. See Henry G. Liddell and Robert Scott, *A Greek-English Lexicon,* 9th ed. (Oxford: Clarendon, 1968), 45; James H. Moulton and George Milligan, *The Vocabulary of the Greek Testament* (Grand Rapids: Eerdmans, 1930), 16 (who conclude that the term(s) is used for something for which the horizon is not in view); Bauer, *Greek-English Lexicon of the New Testament,* 28 (who agrees with definition 2 above); Geoffrey W. H. Lampe, *A Patristic Greek Lexicon* (Oxford: Clarendon, 1961), 56–57; see also the important discussion of Nigel Turner, *Christian Words* (Edinburgh: T. & T. Clark, 1980), 449–57. More detailed analyses can be found in Joachim Guhrt, "Time," in *The New International Dictionary of New Testament Theology,* ed. Colin Brown, 3 vols. (Grand Rapids: Zondervan, 1975–78), 3:826–33; Hermann Sasse, "αἰών, αἰωνιοζ," in *Theological Dictionary of the New Testament,* ed. Gerhard Kittel and Gerhard Friedrich, trans. Geoffrey W. Bromiley, 10 vols. (Grand Rapids: Eerdmans, 1964–76), 1:197–209.

Matthew respects this distinction in his use of the term *aiōn*. Both temporal and eternal senses of *aiōn* are present in 12:32 when he says that sin against the Holy Spirit "will not be forgiven, either in this age [*aiōn*] or in the age [*aiōn*] to come" (compare Eph. 1:21). Here there are two ages, the word *aiōn* being used for a definite period of time, clearly limited; the duration of the second age is unspecified. Since the second instance describes life with God, and since God is eternal (see e.g., 1 Tim. 1:17), this second age is endless. Matthew uses the term age (*aiōn*) for a limited duration in 13:22, 39, 40, 49; 24:3; 28:20. In each of these something tips off the reader to an ending of some kind, whether it be "the worries of this life" (13:22), the "end of this age" (13:39, 40, 49; 24:3), or the spread of the gospel until the return of Christ (28:20). But in the absence of such limiting indicators the exegete should take the term *eternal* to mean endless.

Matthew also uses the term *aiōn* and its related adjective *aiōnios* ("eternal") to indicate endlessness. When Matthew reports the rich young ruler's request, "Teacher, what good thing must I do to get eternal life?," he has in mind a life of *endless acceptance* with God (19:16). The same connotation undoubtedly arises in Matthew 19:29: those who follow Jesus receive blessings now and inherit a life that is *permanent, endless, and eternal (zōēn aiōnion)*. Against this, one might argue that these passages refer to "life that pertains to the final age" and thus aeonial, or limited. But since the final age is inextricably bound up with God's immortality, it is endless. So then, there is nothing in these texts to suggest that the final age has an end in view, or that there is some limitation to the time involved (see Rev. 11:15).[18]

Further, Matthew never uses the adjective *aiōnios* ("eternal") in the sense of "belonging to this temporally limited age." Such a sense, for Matthew, is reserved for the noun *aiōn,* as the evidence discussed above shows. This suggests, then, that in Matthew the adjective *aiōnios* refers to something eternal and temporally unlimited. So when Matthew says that someone will acquire eternal life or suffer eternal punishment, it follows that he has in mind endlessness. The burden of proof is upon the one who argues that *aiōnios* does not mean endlessness. Since Matthew uses the term characteristically as endlessness, evidence must be offered to argue that he means temporal limitedness.

---

18. This is the view of Turner, *Christian Words,* 449–57. Further support may be found in other passages. This meaning is found plausibly at 21:19, though here the notion present may simply be a "permanent or irreversible curse." Endlessness is not so much in view as is "permanence" or "perpetuity" for as long as the thing lasts. I would argue that there is nothing that suggests an end to the eternal fire of 18:8 and 25:41, though it might be plausibly argued that "fire pertaining to the final age" (aeonial) in is view.

Thus, to say someone will acquire eternal life or suffer eternal punishment, if that time period is the final state (and here there is no doubt), it follows that Matthew has in mind endlessness.[19]

Because *aiōnios* ("eternal") modifies both punishment and life in Matthew 25:46, it stands to reason that the same quality and temporal connotations are in view. That is to say, however long the life extends is how long the punishment lasts; the durations are identical. It is grammatically unsuitable to drive a wedge between the two uses of the term *eternal* in Matthew 25:46, suggesting that one refers to endlessness (eternal) and the other to temporal limitation (aeonial).[20] So far as I know, no one has ever suggested that there is some temporal limitation to the life that the righteous enjoy with God after God's final judgment. Since it is clear to say that the eternal life is temporally unlimited it follows that eternal punishment is also temporally unlimited.[21] In addition, if the expression *weeping and gnashing of teeth* in Matthew refers to the final state, then eternal consciousness again is implied (Matt. 8:12; 22:13; 24:51; 25:30). Weeping and gnashing of teeth, then, conforms neatly with eternal (not aeonial) punishment in Matthew 25:46. But it must also be said (in our desire to say what Scripture states and no more) that it is possible for this weeping and gnashing of teeth to be a temporary experience of punishment after the verdict of God is revealed.

To summarize thus far: Though *aiōnios* at Matthew 25:46 could refer to a period of limited time (aeonial; and thus support annihilationism), it is more likely that the adjective refers to endless, or more plausibly pertaining to the final age, an age that partakes in God's eternality. But before we can draw this conclusion with certainty, we must look at the terms *age* and *eternal* through a different lens.

We turn now to the meaning of eternal (and age) in the context of

---

19. Shedd writes: "If anything belongs solely to the present age, or aeon, it is aeonian in the limited signification; if it belongs to the future age, or aeon, it is aeonian in the unlimited signification. If, therefore, the punishment of the wicked occurs in the present aeon, it is aeonian in the sense of temporal; but if it occurs in the future aeon, it is aeonian in the sense of endless. The adjective takes its meaning from the noun" (*Doctrine of Endless Punishment,* 84–85).

20. So Stott in Edwards and Stott, *Evangelical Essentials,* 317; the comments of Richard T. France, *The Gospel According to Matthew* (Grand Rapids: Eerdmans, 1985), 358, are ambiguous but seem to support Stott.

21. So Harris, *Raised Immortal,* 183; Carson, *Matthew,* 522–23; Mounce, *Matthew,* 244; Floyd V. Filson, *The Gospel According to St. Matthew* (San Francisco: Harper & Row, 1960), 268; Heinrich A. W. Meyer, *Critical and Exegetical Hand-Book to the Gospel of Matthew* (1883; repr., Winona Lake, Ind.: Alpha, 1980), 477. See also the extended note of John A. Broadus, *Commentary on the Gospel of Matthew* (Philadelphia: American Baptist Publication Society, 1886), 512–15. The classic defense of the traditional viewpoint remains Shedd, *Doctrine of Endless Punishment.*

judgment scenes in the New Testament.[22] It goes without saying that the final age is endless because God is endless; the final age is the age toward which God has directed history and the age during which Jesus Christ is forever praised (1 Tim. 1:17; 1 Pet. 4:11; 2 Pet. 1:11; Rev. 1:18; 4:9–10; 5:13; 7:12; 10:6; 11:15). Also, it is clear that the final state of believers, those who live by virtue of the sacrifice of the Lamb of God, is an endless state (Rev. 22:5). God is eternal and his life is endless; the final state of his people is eternal and endless as they share in his immortality.[23] It remains to ask if the final state of the wicked is also of the same nature. And it can be said that the evidence of the New Testament, when temporal factors are involved, never suggests anything but endlessness for the final state of the unbeliever.[24]

Paul, in 2 Thessalonians 1:9, states that "they [the persecutors of Christians] will be punished with everlasting destruction and shut out from the presence of the Lord." The emphasis here is on the nature of that final judgment: it is eternal, it is destructive, and it excludes one from the presence of God. Eternal separation from God is the essence of God's punishment on the wicked, as eternal fellowship with God is the essence of God's final deliverance of the faithful. But separation from God's presence must be defined as nonfellowship, not annihilation. In other words, it could be argued that since God is omnipresent, then banishment from his presence means extinction. It is more likely, however, that Paul has in mind an irreversible ver-

22. The notion of eternal torture is seen also in numerous noncanonical texts (Judith 16:17; 1 Enoch 27:1–5; 48:9; 53:2; 91:9; 2 Enoch 40:12–13; 4 Maccabees 12:12; Dead Sea Scroll 1QM 15:1). On the other hand, there are also texts from the same body of literature that suggest annihilation (4 Ezra 7:35 [61]; perhaps Dead Sea Scroll 4Q171 2:6 [on Ps. 37:10]). Clearly, the choice between annihilation and eternal torment was a first-century one. I cannot agree with Atkinson (*Life and Immortality*, 99–100) that several Old Testament passages speak of extinction in the sense of annihilation (Ps. 37:20; Prov. 10:25; Isa. 41:11–12; Ezek. 28:19; Obad. 15–16). In each of these the inference he draws is possible; in each, however, it must be said that the metaphor used may have other implications.

23. So also Shedd, *Doctrine of Endless Punishment*, 79–80.

24. Although it goes beyond the scope of this chapter to examine the connotations of various other metaphors for the final state of the wicked (e.g., fire, destruction, decay), it can be said that the analogies often break down at the point where the inferences are drawn. For instance, it is argued that since fire eventually consumes (or destroys) what it burns, then it follows that annihilation is the inference to be drawn from the metaphor. Less weight, however, should be placed on the metaphors themselves (since in many cases they are mutually exclusive—how can the final place be described with both "fire" and "utter darkness"?), and more on the temporal terms used. Some of the evidence used from Judaism to support annihilationism assumes this kind of inference (e.g., 1 Enoch 48:9; 53:2; 91:9). On the use of metaphors in this regard, see Shedd, *Doctrine of Endless Punishment*, 77–79.

dict of eternal nonfellowship with God. A person exists but remains excluded from God's good presence.

The same conclusion ought to be drawn from Jude 7: the cities (i.e., the people) of Sodom and Gomorrah "serve as an example of those who suffer the punishment of eternal fire." That judgment was final and permanent; those cities are an example of permanent judgment by God. Again, the point pertains to irreversibility, permanence, and finality.

Going even further, in a judgment text, the seer of Revelation states the "the smoke of their torment rises for ever and ever [*eis aiōnas aiōnōn*]." And, to clarify the meaning of for ever and ever, he adds, "there is no rest day or night for those who worship the beast and his image" (Rev. 14:11). Temporal indicators are present here. They point to unlimited duration, without end, and ceaselessness. Further, there is the notion of consciousness here in the words *there is no rest*. It is not a pretty picture; sin leaves behind harsh, unforgiving consequences and tragic consciousness. That the judgment of God on sinful humankind has eternal consequences is further supported by the eternal smoke of Revelation 19:3. Obviously, this means that fire is eternal and that the consequences are irreversible (compare Isa. 34:10), not necessarily that there is eternal consciousness. But the connection of torment, eternal fire, and eternal smoke is found elsewhere (4 Ezra 7:36; 2 Enoch 40:13; Dead Sea Scroll 1QS 2:7–8; Matt. 8:11–12; 13:42, 50; 22:13; 24:51; 25:30; Mark 9:42–48) and does not suggest temporality.

The judgment of the devil, the beast, and the false prophet are described with similar language: "And the devil, who deceived them, was thrown into the lake of burning sulfur, where the beast and the false prophet had been thrown. They will be tormented day and night for ever and ever" (Rev. 20:10). Here we have the term *basanizō* ("torment") associated with endlessness. Endless torment requires endless consciousness, otherwise God is reduced to pouring out his judgment on lifeless objects. It follows that for ever and ever, though undoubtedly referring to consequences, also refers to endlessness and to eternal consciousness when agents (such as Satan and unbelievers) are in view.[25]

So when the writers of the New Testament use the concept of eternal in the context of a judgment scene, they refer to the final state of affairs and to its finality. This naturally involves an endless state of existence, whether it be eternal life with God or eternal punishment away from God. Those who refuse to submit to God suffer endless torment.

25. Against the argument that eternal punishment for temporal sin is unjust, it could be argued that those who deserve eternal punishment might be sealed in their sin from which they never repent. Consequently, they never turn to God in true repentance but persist in their pride and rebellion. But this is not taught in Scripture and is speculative; see Shedd, *Doctrine of Endless Punishment*, 145–52.

We are driven to one conclusion. The terms for eternal in Matthew 25:46 pertain to the final age, and a distinguishing feature of the final age, in contrast to this age, is that it is eternal, endless, and temporally unlimited. It follows then that the most probable meaning of Matthew 25:46 is that just as life with God is temporally unlimited for the righteous, so punishment for sin and rejection of Christ is also temporally unlimited. Since it is unthinkable that God would punish an unconscious being, the final state of the wicked is conscious, eternal torment. I believe that Jesus teaches this truth, and therefore I am obligated to affirm it. It is painful to me, yet in the words of John Stott, "our emotions are a fluctuating, unreliable guide to truth." We can be thankful to God that his Word transcends our fluctuations.

The doctrine of eternal punishment has a long history in the church. Its rhetorical significance cannot be wiped away, either from the memory of many Christians who turned to Christ under the gravity of a threatening punishment or from the pages and pages of those whose works have stimulated the church to faithfulness. In the words of William G. T. Shedd:

> Take the doctrine of eternal perdition, and the antithetic doctrine of eternal salvation, out of the Confessions of Augustine; out of the Sermons of Chrysostom; out of the Imitation of à Kempis; out of Bunyan's Pilgrim's Progress; out of Jeremy Taylor's Holy Living and Dying; out of Baxter's Saints' Everlasting Rest; and what is left?[26]

May our prayer be that of a former edition of the Book of Common Prayer:

> Keep in our minds a lively remembrance of that great day in which we must give a strict account of our thoughts, words, and actions, and according to the works done in the body be eternally rewarded or punished by him thou hast appointed the Judge of quick and dead, the Son, Jesus Christ our Lord.[27]

---

26. Shedd, *Doctrine of Endless Punishment*, vii.

27. From *The Book of Common Prayer,* section: Forms of Prayer to be used in Families (Shedd refers to this prayer). I am grateful to my colleagues, Drs. Walter C. Kaiser, Jr., Murray J. Harris, and K. J. Vanhoozer, for commenting on an earlier draft of this chapter.

13

Will God Save Everyone in the End?

William V. Crockett

Many Christians wonder about people who have never heard the gospel. They are bothered by the thought that a loving God might dispatch large numbers of humanity—who seemingly never had a chance—to hell. They are bothered by the inherent unfairness of it all and wonder whether there might not be other doors to salvation. These are reasonable concerns and throughout this book the question of the "heathen" has been addressed from many perspectives.

But there is another possibility. Perhaps God will save not only the "heathen," but everyone. If this were the case, then it would be of little concern whether or not someone heard the name of Christ. God in his infinite mercy would gather all creation into one huge, harmonious family. It might not happen immediately upon death, but ultimately the irresistible love of God would draw all creatures to himself. Those who hold this hope (universalists) typically appeal to the apostle Paul for support because the Gospels paint a negative picture for the wicked and because Paul seems to hint that eventually God will reconcile everyone to himself.[1]

Usually, when the question of universalism surfaces, people on both sides cite texts to support their positions.[2] This is, of course, as it should be. Sometimes, however, over-zealous people misuse verses and unwittingly distort the truth. They become "prooftexters" and create what Frederic W. Farrar calls an "ignorant tyranny of isolated texts."[3]

Here I try to avoid some of these problems by approaching universalism from the perspective of what modern sociologists would call group boundaries.[4] Every group, whether religious or not, has boundaries. They use these boundaries to distinguish themselves from other groups. In fact, without clear boundaries a group cannot exist because it will eventually merge with other groups. An understanding of boundaries reveals how difficult it would have been for Paul and his readers to have been universalists.

The Meaning of Boundaries

Groups or sects use boundary lines to distinguish themselves from other groups with competing lines. At the same time, groups strive to preserve themselves, and an important aspect of survival is the maintenance of clear boundaries. Boundaries are essential if distinct communities are to continue.

Sociologist Peter Berger has shown that all human societies, including religious ones, are enterprises of world-building. They build their own worlds complete with boundaries. Societies may differ but each has its "official" interpretation of reality, and this interpretation passes for "knowledge" in the community. "To participate in the society," says Berger, "is to share its 'knowledge.'"[5] Sharing knowledge involves a socialization process and members of a group, whether they know it or not, are participants. They continually build and reinforce their understanding of reality.

1. For example, at first glance Rom. 8:19, 21; 11:32; 1 Cor. 15:22; Eph. 1:10; and Col. 1:20 do sound universalist, but in light of their contexts and background settings, they are consonant with Paul's harsh judgment terminology. I have discussed these issues fully in *Universalism and the Theology of Paul* (Ph.D. diss., University of Glasgow, 1986).

2. Arguments often range beyond the circle of the Bible. For example, would a loving God destroy his children? And what must a just God do in face of rebellion? These are worthy questions, but cannot be considered in this chapter.

3. Frederic W. Farrar, *Eternal Hope: Five Sermons* (New York: Dutton, 1885), 75.

4. Peter L. Berger and Thomas Luckmann, *The Social Construction of Reality: A Treatise in the Sociology of Knowledge* (Garden City, N.Y.: Doubleday, 1966); Peter L. Berger, *The Sacred Canopy: Elements of a Sociological Theory of Religion* (Garden City, N.Y.: Doubleday, 1967); James M. Gustafson, *Treasure in Earthen Vessels: The Church as a Human Community* (Chicago: University of Chicago Press, 1961), 26–29.

5. Berger, *Sacred Canopy,* 21.

But every community is in constant danger of collapse. It is an island in the center of chaos, a ship battered by angry waves. Alien forces—potent and destructive—are everywhere. They surround the community like a hostile army constantly probing the boundaries for weakness. For a society to survive, say sociologists, it must provide its members with a "plausibility structure"—a system of beliefs that helps an adherent to understand and make sense of the world. The most desirable structure is one that is taken for granted. It must seem obvious. "Only a lunatic would deny the universal truth of my religion," a model adherent might say. The adherent must think that truth—his or her truth—is clearly written in the fabric of the universe for all to see. The more obvious a belief system looks to the insider, the more clearly defined will be its boundaries. "It is not enough that the individual looks upon the key meanings of the social order as useful, desirable, or right," says Berger. "It is much better . . . if he looks upon them as inevitable, as part and parcel of the universal 'nature of things.'"[6]

The Apostle Paul and Boundaries

Christianity began as a tiny branch of Judaism. During the first fifteen to twenty years, outside groups such as the Romans made little distinction between Jews who believed in Jesus the Messiah (Nazarenes; Acts 24:5) and Jews who thought he was a fraud. From the Roman perspective, Jews were Jews; they all believed in the same God whether they called themselves Nazarenes, Pharisees, Sadducees, or Essenes.

Within the Jewish faith itself, however, there were distinct boundaries between these groups. Each group saw itself as unique and the sole arbitrator of truth. As time passed, the gulf widened between Jews and Christians, especially during the time of Paul (A.D. 50s and 60s) when Gentile converts flooded the church.

As far as Christians were concerned, there was a gulf not only between them and Jews, but between them and anyone who had not embraced the gospel of Jesus Christ. Sociologists, as we have seen, call this kind of gulf a "boundary." In the early Christian community boundaries were clear and fixed. Christians enthusiastically proclaimed the gospel because their belief system seemed obvious to them. The rich and famous might laugh at their message, but no matter. "The message of the cross is foolishness to those who are perishing," said Paul, "but to us who are being saved it is the power of God" (1 Cor. 1:18).

Because Christians believed they were the only group that possessed the full truth of God, they experienced an intense sense of belonging.

6. Ibid., 24, 37–39.

At the same time their plausibility structure created borders against the intrusions of outside ideas. In Paul's letters there were a number of ways he set up boundaries between members of the sect and the outside world. Wayne Meeks observes how the Pauline community maintained its boundaries.[7] One of the ways Paul was able to keep sect members within acceptable bounds was his use of belonging-separation language, that is, the language the community used to include or exclude. Note how such language sharply distinguished insiders from outsiders. *Insiders* were "saints" (Rom. 1:7; 1 Cor. 1:2), "loved by God" (1 Thess. 1:4), "known" by God (1 Cor. 8:3), "brothers and sisters" (Rom. 16:1, 17), "children of light" (Eph. 5:8; 1 Thess. 5:4–11), "believers" (Rom. 4:11; 1 Cor. 1:21; Gal. 3:22). *Outsiders* were "outsiders" (1 Cor. 5:12–13; 1 Thess. 4:12), "unrighteous" (1 Cor. 6:1, 9), those who "did not know God" (Gal. 4:8; 1 Thess. 4:5), the "world" (1 Cor. 1:20–28; Gal. 1:4; 4:3), "children of darkness" (Eph. 5:8; 1 Thess. 5:4–11), "unbelievers" (1 Cor. 6:6; 7:12).

"By this kind of talk," says Meeks, "members are taught to conceive of only two classes of humanity: the sect and the outsiders."[8] As far as Paul and the Pauline community were concerned, insiders and outsiders were complete opposites. Like the two solidarities pictured in 1 Corinthians 15:22, those in Christ received life, those in Adam found only death.

Meeks finds the language of family "especially striking."[9] Members of the Pauline community saw themselves as a family: children of God, brothers and sisters. Those outside were not part of the family but "enemies," "idol-worshipers." Yet the boundaries between the two groups were permeable; these former "enemies" (Rom. 5:10) and "idol-worshipers" could penetrate the barrier and join the family (1 Thess. 1:9). This last point is important and I will return to it shortly.

Those who became part of the Pauline community began a new life and adopted a new family. They had to break with the past. "Whatever else is involved," says Meeks, "the image of the initiate being adopted as God's child and thus receiving a new family of human brothers and sisters is a vivid way of portraying what a modern sociologist might call the resocialization of conversion."[10] (An evangelist might call it being "born again into the family of God.") No longer did converts define their place in society in terms of their natural fam-

7. Wayne A. Meeks, *The First Urban Christians: The Social World of the Apostle Paul* (New Haven: Yale University Press, 1983), 84–107; and Meeks, "Toward a Social Description of Pauline Christianity," in *Approaches to Ancient Judaism*, ed. William Scott Green, Brown Judaic Studies 9 (Chico, Calif.: Scholars Press, 1980), 2:27–37, esp. 32–41.
8. Meeks, *First Urban Christians*, 86.
9. Ibid.
10. Ibid., 88.

ilies or former relationships. They had a new family. This new set of relationships created a new solidarity. Believers were now "in Christ." "If anyone is in Christ, he is a new creation; the old has passed away, the new has come" (2 Cor. 5:17).

There were other means of integrating new believers into the community. Baptism and the Eucharist were powerful symbols of the new life. As with any group ritual, baptism and eucharistic rituals established boundaries and promoted group solidarity.[11] Believers were "one in Christ" (Gal. 3:28) because they had been "baptized into Christ" (3:27) and because they had "put on Christ" (3:27). Believers continually rehearsed the Eucharist (1 Cor. 11:23–26). By means of this ritual they reminded themselves of Christ's sacrifice for them and his promise to return to gather them to himself. This "common memory," as James Gustafson calls it, fostered solidarity. Under such circumstances, the sense of common purpose and life would grow, he says, and the historical community would deepen.[12]

In Paul's churches, then, there was a sharp distinction between the insider and outsider. Paul continually contrasted the family of God with the "world." Boundaries were clear. Everything was used to promote group solidarity. When believers sinned they were reminded that they were no longer part of the world (Rom. 6:1–11; Gal. 4:8–10; Col. 2:20). If they sinned egregiously, they were banished from the community—into the realm of Satan (1 Cor. 5:1–5). When believers died, their relatives were reminded that their grief was not like the hopeless grief of the world (1 Thess. 4:13). When believers suffered for their newly found faith (Rom. 8:17–18; 2 Cor. 1:5; 1 Thess. 1:4–6; 3:3–4), the suffering further united them with the community. Suffering was just another indication of the dangers outside the camp. New converts were taught to expect suffering (1 Thess. 3:3–4). Powerful models of endurance in the face of suffering—such as Paul, fellow workers, and Christ himself—were given to assure converts that suffering was part and parcel of the faith.[13]

The result was a sharp distinction between God's chosen disciples and those outside the faith. In the case of suffering, outsiders were ever bent on tormenting the righteous. Paul's allusions to opposition and suffering, says Meeks, were "a compelling picture of a world hostile to

---

11. Gustafson, *Treasure in Earthen Vessels*, 11, 72–73; Meredith B. McGuire, *Religion: The Social Context* (Belmont, Calif.: Wadsworth, 1981), 12–13, 150–51; Anthony Thiselton, "Knowledge, Myth and Corporate Memory," in *Believing in the Church: The Corporate Nature of Faith* (London: SPCK, 1981), 45–78, esp. 52–67. See also Meeks, *First Urban Christians*, 88–89, 102–3.

12. Gustafson, *Treasure in Earthen Vessels*, 73–74.

13. Meeks, *First Urban Christians*, 96.

God's intentions and to his chosen agents."[14] The apostle maintained clear lines of demarcation between the righteous and the wicked. Indeed, these boundaries are significant even in the end (the eschaton). Suffering for Christ would bring "glory" (Rom. 8:18; 2 Cor. 4:17), but those who afflicted the faithful would be destroyed (1 Thess. 5:3).

Universalism and Boundaries

One wonders, therefore, how reasonable it is to claim that Paul was a universalist. Or, harder still, that his readers understood him to mean that one day even outsiders would join the insiders in a harmonious union. Obscure hints of a final, universal homecoming would hardly be picked up by a community steeped in separation language. Boundaries were designed to include and exclude. They intensified belief in the community, hardened distinctions between true believers and the outside world, and, in general, made particularism (the belief that only some will be saved) easier to believe than universalism. A sect member would have found it natural to exclude outsiders. After all, truth resided only in the community; salvation therefore must have been the exclusive possession of those in the sect.

What did these boundaries mean to Paul? His language depicts two classes of people, with demarcation lines fixed even into the eschaton. Paul, we must conclude, believed in a *permanent* separation of insiders from outsiders. If he were a universalist, it would be difficult to account for his sharp insider-outsider language. Someone might suggest that he had practical reasons for fixing clear borders—perhaps he wanted to maintain discipline in the community or preserve group identity in the center of an alien world. But why, if he wanted to teach universalism, would he use such misleading, exclusivist language? Would he not have avoided the harsh warnings of judgment, and toned down the "two-classes-of-people" language?[15]

The universalist might respond that Paul used harsh warnings and exclusive language because the apostle believed there would be a temporal separation of the wicked from the just. He might have thought

14. Ibid.
15. One possibility, though unlikely, has classic antecedents. Origen and Gregory of Nyssa argued that Paul, though a universalist, avoided saying flatly that all would be saved. But this was good. The fear of eternal punishment, they reasoned, restrained the multitude from plunging further into wickedness. It would be unwise—even dangerous—to teach the many anything other than the traditional view of everlasting punishment (Origen, *Against Celsus* 3.79; 4.10; 6.26; Gregory of Nyssa, *Catechetical Oration* 8). But we have no reason to think that Paul held views similar to Origen and Gregory of Nyssa. Even if Paul were a universalist, there is no evidence he used judgment terminology simply to prod the wicked to do good.

that the wicked would be removed to a place of severe (though not endless) punishment, in short, a purgative hell. This view has the advantage of keeping universalism intact, while at the same time preserving the integrity of Pauline judgment language.

But the solution seems out of place. It does not match the grave nature of Paul's judgment terminology. When Paul warned that the wicked were doomed to wrath, destruction, and death, or when he used the language of belonging and separation to create solidarities (1 Cor. 15:22), there is good reason to think that he had a permanent condition in mind. He never suggested that eschatological wrath (*orgē*), for example, reformed the wicked. Wrath never prodded or encouraged the wicked to do good; it was reserved by Paul to stress the utter hopelessness of the wicked. The same is true with destruction and death. They allowed for no hope beyond the grave.[16]

But more than this, group boundaries have, as Meeks calls it, a "soteriological contrast pattern."[17] They reminded believers that in the past their eschatological future was bleak, but now in Christ they had eternal hope. Their future was secure. The point is that Paul distinguished sharply between those who perished and those who obtained salvation (1 Cor. 1:18; 2 Cor. 2:15; 4:3; Phil. 1:28; 2 Thess. 2:10). If we ask what happens when the wicked are destroyed, part of the answer must surely be that they lose all that salvation and eternal life implies. The stark contrast between the two groups removes the possibility that Paul thought the wicked would be destroyed and then rise again. In other words, we should not think that Paul's destruction terminology implied hope; it was the opposite. When contrasted with salvation and life, it implied eschatological death. And this appears to be a final, hopeless condition.

Still, we must not forget the goal of Paul's missionary enterprise: to bring others to faith in Christ (Rom. 9:10–19; 11:14; 1 Cor. 9:19–23). Outsiders could be converted to insiders. The boundaries were not so hardened that outsiders were unable to cross over into the community of believers. But in so doing outsiders had to accept the truth of the Messiah and the strictures of their new family.

So Paul's division of humanity into insiders and outsiders did not necessarily exclude the wicked. They were excluded only as long as they remained wicked. If they repented and believed, they would then be insiders.

But what does this mean? Certainly it means that outsiders (as Paul

---

16. A fuller treatment of Paul's judgment language may be found in William V. Crockett, "Wrath That Endures Forever," *Journal of the Evangelical Theological Society* 34 (1991):195–202.

17. Meeks, *First Urban Christians*, 95.

himself once was) had opportunity to be justified by faith in Christ. The gospel he preached was "the power of God for the salvation of everyone who believes" (Rom. 1:16). But was salvation available for those under eschatological wrath? Here we must say that in Paul's mind the wicked in the eschaton were forever doomed.

In Paul's letters members of the community were taught an exclusive view of the world. There were only two classes of people: those who believed in Christ (insiders) and those who did not (outsiders). Insiders looked forward to a glorious future with Christ; outsiders would be destroyed in the eschaton. This is the way the Pauline community viewed the world—through its tinted glasses of group solidarity. The groups never merged, even in the afterlife.

Today, some might see the "heathen" as victims who never had the opportunity to hear the gospel. Paul, however, argues that they did hear God's voice—in nature (Rom. 1:18–20) and in their hearts (Rom. 2:15–16). But they, like all people (Rom. 3:23),, turned their backs on the eternal One, preferring the things of this age to the things of God. Paul describes them as "wicked" and under the "wrath of God" because they willingly "suppressed the truth" (Rom. 1:18–32).[18] From Paul's vantage, they were not part of the Christ solidarity, nor would they be in the eschaton. They were outsiders who actively resisted the will of God and the efforts of his church.

With such a rigid view of the world, it is difficult to imagine that the apostle Paul expected outsiders ever to unite with insiders in glory. He and his fellow believers would be more inclined to think that in the end the righteous would go the way of life; the wicked the way of death.

18. See Aída Besançon Spencer, "Romans 1: Finding God in Creation"; and Douglas Moo, "Romans 2: Saved Apart from the Gospel?" both in this volume, for a more complete discussion of these ideas.

Part

3

Missiological Issues

14

Do All Roads Lead to Heaven? An Examination of Unitive Pluralism

Timothy D. Westergren

The question "Do all roads lead to heaven?" seems at first glance to enjoin a simple and emphatic no. For most of Christian history this reaction has been reflexive, but within the modern era a good number of Christians have responded with a strong yes. Indeed, outside conservative Christian circles, popular sentiment feels that all religions are basically the same or, at least, equally valuable. A scholar might put such religious relativism this way: all religions are equally valid paths to one divine reality.[1]

---

1. To quote one such scholar exactly: "Each of the great world faiths constitutes a perception of and a response to the ultimate divine reality which they all in their different ways affirm" (John Hick, "Pluralism and the Reality of the Transcendent," *Christian Century* 98 [21 Jan. 1981]: 46). Indeed, what scholars propose first in theory often takes time to become popular sentiment. In this regard, John Hick can be justifiably called the major "prophet" of unitive pluralism. He first confessed back in 1973 to his growing discomfort with the exclusion of most of humanity from Christian salvation. He published the

Unitive pluralism[2] is a sophisticated form of religious relativism. It does not simply assert the validity of any religious experience[3] or of each major world religion. Instead, its goal is a relationship among religions that allows for differences, yet fosters a "unity of vision"[4] through interreligious dialogue. This means then that "what is true will reveal itself mainly by its ability to *relate* to other expressions of truth and to *grow* through these relationships."[5]

For an evangelical to speak kindly of other religions is a dangerous practice; to consider truth in places other than the Bible is risky business. Thus I struggle even to keep the attention of "my own kind" long enough to make a point. But I must try, for the diversity of human experience will not lessen as we head toward the third millennium, but multiply. This pluralism will call for true disciples of Jesus Christ to deal squarely with those who now call for a relativist perspective on other religions.

Paul Knitter is currently the major popular proponent of unitive-pluralist thinking. He reasons with explicitly Christian concepts toward a "theocentric model" which allows "many ways to the center."[6] Though this chapter serves only as an introduction to Knitter's arguments, it is possible, I think, to explain accurately and to critique fairly the lines of his model.

---

first systematic treatment of "those left outside" in *God and the Universe of Faiths*. In this landmark treatise, he draws on an analogy from the history of science, arguing for a "Copernican revolution" in a Christian understanding of other religions. He characterizes as "Ptolemaic" the traditional doctrine—both Roman Catholic and Protestant—which proclaims, in his words, that "all men, of whatever race or culture, must become Christians if they are to be saved" (*God and the Universe of Faiths* [New York: St. Martin's, 1973], 121).

2. This term was coined by John A. T. Robinson in *Truth Is Two-Eyed* (Philadelphia: Westminster, 1979), 39.

3. Unitive pluralists clearly want to distance themselves from an unbridled relativism which accepts any personal claim for divine encounter—cults and religious quacks do not count. On the contrary, all religious experience that has a claim to a true conception of the Real can be evaluated by a positive criterion of truth: "That which has come out of a great revelatory religious experience and has been tested through a long tradition of worship and has sustained human faith over centuries of time and in millions of lives, is likely to represent a genuine encounter with divine reality" (Hick, *God and the Universe of Faiths*, 141).

4. Ibid.

5. Paul F. Knitter, *No Other Name? A Critical Survey of Christian Attitudes toward the World Religions* (Maryknoll, N.Y.: Orbis, 1985), 219.

6. Ibid.,145. By "theocentric" Knitter means that God's ultimate nature is not revealed conclusively in Christ; God has spoken for himself in other historical revelations. John Hick would put it like this: "We shift from the dogma that Christianity is at the center to the realization that it is God who is at the center, and that all religions, including our own, serve and revolve around him" (*God and the Universe of Faiths*, 131).

What Unitive Pluralists Are Saying

Knitter, a Roman Catholic professor at Xavier University in Cincinnati, Ohio, joined the pluralist chorus with *No Other Name? A Critical Survey of Christian Attitudes toward the World Religions*. His lucid overview presents a spectrum of Christian responses, including the "conservative evangelical model" which holds to "one true religion."[7]

Evangelical concerns are explained fairly by Knitter, even congenially so. Rather than nose-punching and running to safety, Knitter wants to engage and persuade positively. While he obviously disagrees that Christ is the absolute way to God, he concedes that evangelicals may be right: "Both critical Christians and skeptical humanists must be open to the *possibility* that *what* they are saying may be true."[8] And he truly does understand the claim of God incarnate as the scandal of particularity: "In one particular person and event, God has overcome the relativizing conditions of history; in one event God has offered a truth and a grace found nowhere else, on which the salvation of the world hinges. If God be God, this is possible."[9] Nevertheless, he remains unconvinced. On what basis can he reject Christ's uniqueness and normativity? He answers by attempting to show that we misunderstand the Bible and its limits.

Many conservatives would brand Knitter a "flaming liberal" and shut the door. Though he may be, tagging him negatively does not bring us closer to understanding him. I can, however, unmaliciously describe his treatment of the Scriptures as liberal, because he overtly wants to "free" us from Scripture as absolute authority. According to Knitter, while we may start with what the Bible has to say about other religions, no final conclusions about their ultimate truth or value should be reached without an equal dependence on shared human experience.[10] He makes this move openly, calling to his defense our century's "profound experience of historical relativity" and consequent "contemporary New Testament scholarship"—scholarship that demythologizes and "descandalizes" a divine Christ.

Knitter wants so badly for us to realize that the books of the New Testament are primarily human books written by persons who experienced God in the man Jesus of Nazareth and that the authors were naturally inspired to communicate this excitement to others. Knitter espouses the myth-of-God-incarnate theology where "God *is* truly encountered in Jesus, but not only in Jesus."[11] In the twentieth cen-

---

7. Knitter, *No Other Name?* 75.
8. Ibid., 89.
9. Ibid.
10. Ibid., 92.
11. Ibid., 152.

tury, perhaps no better statement of this thinking can be found than that by the New Testament scholar Wilhelm Bousset in his magisterial work, *Kyrios Christos*. Bousset taught that "the view of Jesus found in the New Testament was not historically true of Jesus himself."[12]

Since this is offensive to us, Knitter takes a more positive, persuasive approach. He prefers to call the New Testament euphemistically a "transformation" of Jesus' religion.[13] This shift is easy to trace and even a necessity in Knitter's mind. Moreover, he claims that because of this shift, "a nonnormative, theocentric Christology does not contradict the New Testament proclamation of Jesus and is therefore a valid interpretation of that proclamation."[14]

He defends this with two substantial statements that deserve scrutiny. First, borrowing from Stanley Samartha, he asserts that "although the witness of the New Testament writers is Christocentric, Jesus Christ himself is theocentric."[15] Undisputedly, the core of Jesus' original message was the kingdom of God. Jesus was consumed with announcing that God's reign and rule had broken into human existence. But after the death and resurrection of Jesus, Knitter thinks the focus shifted. Jesus' disciples made the proclaimer the proclaimed. Knitter implies that Christ's claims about himself cannot be taken at face value but need to be tempered by contemporary biblical research that casts doubt on Jesus' own self-awareness. Jesus was not conscious of his own divinity or preexistence because he was not divine. In fact, we cannot even reconstruct a psychological profile of his actual self-consciousness.

What value, then, do New Testament statements about Jesus have? This is our question. Knitter asks a similar but presumptive one: "How did Jesus' original message about the kingdom of God come to be translated into the early communities' proclamation of Jesus as Messiah, Lord, Word, Savior, Son of God?"[16]

He answers with his second basic statement: New Testament statements about Christ are "mythic-symbolic."[17] This technical term from New Testament studies could be translated roughly as "meaning-giving fiction." It certainly implies that titles given Jesus are not revelatory denotations of his identity; rather they are symbolic and interpre-

---

12. Wilhelm Bousset, *Kyrios Christos: A History of the Belief in Christ from the Beginnings of Christianity to Irenaeus*, trans. John E. Steely (Nashville: Abingdon, 1970). The quotation is from Hendrikus Boers, "Jesus and the Christian Faith: New Testament Christology since Bousset's *Kyrios Christos*," *Journal of Biblical Literature* 89 (1970): 452.

13. Knitter, *No Other Name?* 174.

14. Ibid., 172.

15. Ibid., 158.

16. Ibid., 175.

17. Ibid., 180.

tive names that find "their origin in the *saving experience* of Jesus by individuals and the community."[18] In communicating that experience, the earliest Christians were confessing radical, personal commitment, not defining their creed with analytic, scientific language. Moreover, the seemingly exclusive claims about Christ have been accidentally interpreted by traditional Christianity[19] in that way because of the kind of love language used. Knitter explains:

> Exclusivist christological language is much like the language a husband would use of his wife (or vice versa): "You are the most beautiful woman in the world . . . you are the only woman for me." Such statements, in the context of a marital relationship . . . are certainly true. But the husband would balk if asked to take an oath that there is absolutely no other woman in the world as beautiful as his wife. . . . That would be using a different kind of language, in a very different context.[20]

In a similar way, Christians have accepted this religious love language and, based on it, have erroneously taken "an oath that there is absolutely no other" way to salvation.

From Knitter's perspective, Christ as the "one and only" could mean "I am fully committed to you" rather than "no one else is worthy of commitment." The apostle's cry in Acts 4:12, "there is no other name . . . by which we must be saved," could then be an enthusiastic description of Christ's reliability as God's instrument rather than an exclusive declaration of Christ as God's only instrument.

An Evaluation of Unitive Pluralism

We must criticize Knitter on the boundaries of biblical truth-claims. Unfortunately, the scope of this exercise excludes a debate over scriptural exegesis of specific passages. Certainly we could marshal plenty of New Testament scholarship to challenge Knitter's claims.[21] We choose to believe—and have increasingly positive scholarship to

18. Ibid. New Testament scholars speak of these different but simultaneously developing interpretations of Jesus' significance to early believers as "trajectories."

19. As early as 1977 the current unitive-pluralist movement challenged the centrality and universality of Christ through the well-known book, *The Myth of God Incarnate*, ed. John Hick (London: SCM, 1977). John Hick and other contributors believe that the Chalcedonian Creed, which confesses Christ as having both divine and human natures, makes an unwarranted deification of an otherwise human Jesus. This is the source of Christianity's intolerable exclusivism.

20. Knitter, *No Other Name?* 185.

21. One argument of note bears directly on our topic: Christopher J. H. Wright, "The Christian and Other Religions: The Biblical Evidence," *Themelios* 9 (Jan. 1984): 4–15. See also the remarks of Frederick W. Schmidt, "Jesus and the Salvation of the Gentiles," 99–102 in this volume.

ground our belief—that the apostles wrote accurately and authoritatively about Jesus. We grant the humanness of the authors and their
cultures, but claim divine inspiration of the message and divine super-
intendence over their works. Knitter has made his choice about
Scripture; we must make ours.

We do not solely depend on the New Testament either. Surely the
older testament reveals to us the God who has become Immanuel
(God present with us) in Jesus Christ. And we have recorded what
Jesus himself claimed about his relationship with Yahweh: "No one
comes to the Father except through me. If you really knew me, you
would know my Father as well. From now on, you do know him and
have seen him" (John 14:6–7). The apostles' witness goes beyond
Peter's assertion of "no other name . . . by which we must be saved"
(Acts 4:12) to Paul's declaration that Jesus' name is "above every
name" and will be recognized eventually as such by all people of all
times (Phil. 2:9–10).

Truly it is difficult to believe what Knitter asks of us: That some little sect of Judaism, beleaguered by fellow Jews and Gentile Greeks and
Romans, made the bold claim that "Jesus is Lord" because they were
"in love" and not because they were ruling out the possibility of other
saviors. It would help convince us if the early Christians had proclaimed that the one transcendent divine reality was revealed relatively through Jesus and the law, or Jesus and the gods. Or perhaps
that Jesus was an authoritative rabbi, an outstanding Jewish mystic, or
a new god in the pantheon.

But no, the apostles denied these relations and were attacked precisely because of their intransigence. Christ's own claim to sonship of
the one true God, Yahweh, and his resurrection did not permit such
compromise. As one Lutheran scholar summarizes, "He is the one and
only Christ, or he is not God's Son at all. He is the one and only
Savior, or he is no Savior at all. The exclusive claim is not a footnote to
the gospel; it is the gospel itself."[22]

Therefore, whenever a Buddhist or Muslim or fellow Christian disagrees with us, we can and must be true to what we have received.
Indeed, how can we honestly dialogue with a Buddhist about our

---

22. Ted Peters, "Confessional Universalism and Inter-Religious Dialogue," *Dialog* 25
(1984): 147. Steven Neill also has a well-said comment on Christian claims:

[The] Christian faith claims for itself that it is the only form of faith for men. By its
own claim to truth it casts the shadow of imperfect truth on every other system. This
Christian claim is naturally offensive to modern man, brought up in the atmosphere
of relativism, in which tolerance is regarded almost as the highest of the virtues. But
we must not suppose that this claim to universal validity is something that can be
quietly removed from the Gospel without changing it into something entirely different from what it is. (*Crisis of Belief* [London: Hodder & Stoughton, 1984], 30)

faith, if—as Knitter wants—we first surrender the very heartbeat of our experience and tradition? After all, the reason we are Christians is because we feel that no one else is worthy of our commitment!

Moreover, by diluting Jesus' universality and normativity, we actually destroy true interreligious dialogue. A genuine dialogue involves two persons with two fundamentally different claims to truth. Though different religions all encourage openness to some higher reality, the conceptions and descriptions of the divine that they promote are mutually exclusive and contradictory. What kind of God is God if he is conceived both theistically and nontheistically, both personally and nonpersonally? If the Christian gives away his or her convictions about ultimate reality, the non-Christian is left to a monologue. If the non-Christian also dilutes his or her claims, the result is what Ted Peters calls "two empty chairs." He continues,

> What actually happens in practice is that we end up with two history-of-religions scholars filling the chairs . . . reenforcing one another's prejudices about how narrow-minded and exclusivist are all those people who are still committed to the symbols that they . . . have risen above. . . . This is just what happens frequently at so-called dialogue meetings.[23]

Unitive pluralists would deny this characterization, even as they deflate the importance of creed and doctrine in religion. Statements about God's nature and activity from various traditions are mythic, but they are powerful in that they spawn genuine religious experience. The central affirmations of world religions are cultural products, and as such they can be discussed. They precede divine encounters, not follow them. Sacred texts have systematized the experiences for others' vicarious assimilation.[24]

Ironically, propositional truth—the very stuff pluralist arguments are made of—is somehow stabbed in the back. If we take seriously the concepts and beliefs of various religions and portray them accurately, and if we adhere to the law of noncontradiction (that is, two conflicting truth claims cannot both be true), it is hard not to view one's own religion as ultimately true to reality. Our claim to exclusivity is really not so odd. Since the world religions are radically different, each has an appeal or makes more sense to different people. True, no one has exhaustive knowledge of God or conclusive evidence to destroy another's faith; yet, that is the nature of faith: to commit oneself wholeheartedly to a distinct, coherent understanding of God. Those who have no interest in faith, those who have grown indifferent

---

23. Peters, "Confessional Universalism," 147.
24. These ideas are developed in John Hick, *God Has Many Names* (New York: Macmillan, 1980), 11, 53, 83.

should be the only ones naive enough to say, "Oh, I think that all religions are the same."

Let us return to the unitive pluralists' treatment of the Scriptures and then posit another response. Gavin D'Costa, an Indian theologian, objects to Hick's and Knitter's selective use of the Bible. D'Costa observes that the driving theological axiom behind their inclusiveness is the universal salvific will of the God who desires that no one should perish (2 Pet. 3:9).[25] He wonders how they can use this Christian teaching without another one which grounds it: that "salvation and grace come from God alone in Christ."[26] How can pluralists assume the concept of God's love for humanity and rip it from the fabric of Christian truth?[27] God desires for all people to be saved, but the revealed nature of his holiness and justice necessarily limits the valid response, and consequently the numbers saved. We cannot espouse the universal salvific will of God without allowing that the events on which this belief is grounded —namely God in Christ—are real, historical and normative. Unitive pluralists make revelation about Christ relative while claiming that their belief, derived from the same revelation, is absolute.[28] Haddon Wilson

25. Knitter wants to give this venerable Christian teaching a quantitative meaning by extending God's actual scope of salvation to millions of people of other religious convictions. He reaches this conclusion, however, not by evidence from scriptural revelation, not by a Rahnerian scheme of "anonymous Christians," not by an empirical investigation of the various religious traditions, but by a simple and magnanimous proclamation that each religion can save equally. Knitter does not know irrefutably that every religion saves, but he must grant this across the board in order to establish mutual respect and equality. See Peters, "Confessional Universalism," 146.

26. Gavin D'Costa, "The Pluralist Paradigm in Christian Theology of Religions," *Scottish Journal of Theology* 39 (1986): 214.

27. Pluralists have a bias toward a certain kind of God. Above all, God is good and loving. Hick argues that if we accept a perfectly good God, it follows that he always acts justly and without partiality. Accordingly, no perfect, just God would set certain standards for salvation and then give only some the opportunity to even know of them. Christianity, therefore, cannot claim to be the sole possessor of truth. This would consign the majority of humankind to hell, which certainly seems neither fair, impartial nor just. (This analysis is adapted from Peter Byrne, "John Hick's Philosophy of Religion," *Scottish Journal of Theology* 35 [1982]: 289. Byrne, a British critic, contends that Hick's argument was the kind used by eighteenth-century deistic writers to show the superiority of natural religion over revealed. Whether or not the parallel holds, surely Hick does lean heavily on his own reasoned perception of God and less on Christian revelation.)

28. Knitter and Hick find themselves on the horns of the dilemma of modern New Testament Christology. If the Christology of the New Testament is not the expression of *some* truth about the historical Jesus, then, "to recognize that christology is a composite product of the early Christian communities and not the truth about the historical Jesus is a dissolution of christology itself; yet, to justify a christology by attempting to confirm that its claims about Jesus are somehow valid is possible only at the expense of not recognizing the early Christian communities as their true authors" (Boers, "Jesus and the Christian Faith," 452).

notes that pluralists want "to put the emphasis on the God that is revealed in Christ as though we can know him apart from Jesus Christ. Then we can make statements like 'God is love' and use them apart from and even against much of the history of Jesus and the history from Jesus."[29]

And that is what Knitter does. The intense religious diversity overwhelms him so that no longer does the scriptural testimony of God revealed in Christ judge human experience, but the reverse. He asks, "Can such a claim be made on the authority of tradition when tradition seems to contradict our present experience?"—which is for him "the relativity of all revelations . . . the truth and goodness of other religions, the encounter with other believers who also state that their experience and revelation is a message for all times and all peoples."[30] So we see that Knitter's all-important criterion is religious experience, that is, interaction with a sacred text, worship and ritual, and personal encounter.[31] We are left as the judges of truth on the stage of human religious activity; yet no one can possibly declare a clear winner here.

If Jesus Christ and the testimony about him are not the criteria, further, if no divine revelation from any religion should be the sole criterion for anyone, all that is left are pragmatic measures: effects on human behavior, satisfaction of human need, and promotion of psychological health. But are these measures any more compelling than that of a Creator God revealed to humankind in Christ? They are if God, in all his pluralistic revelations, is simply a good concept for promoting human peace and happiness. Knitter devalues the crucial quest: What is the truth?

Must Exclusivists Be Bigots?

The unitive pluralism of Paul Knitter asserts that exclusivism is unnecessary and unwarranted in today's world. I have defended the necessity of commitment from the nature of faith and the warrant for absolute truth-claims from the nature of truth.[32] I cannot leave this

---

29. In C. F. D. Moule, *Origins of Christology* (Cambridge: Cambridge University Press, 1977), 166.

30. Knitter, *No Other Name?* 143.

31. With experience as his principal guide, Hick limits truth and falseness to talk about mere appearances—the similarity of activity. If no one religion can "capture" God or even claim the correct angle from which to view him, it follows that any judgments are not conclusive on how the Real is but only on how the Real appears. And it appears to Hick that all world religions provide adequate means of salvation and revelation to their respective adherents.

32. The nature of truth presents two challenges to unitive pluralists. First, truth relativized can empty the very term *truth* of any real shared meaning. Second, the challenge of truth to unitive pluralism is the contradictory truth-claims of different religious traditions.

discussion, however, without examining the accusation that Christian exclusivists are narrow-minded and intolerant and without exhorting ourselves to appropriate change.

When unitive pluralists castigate conservative Christians for their exclusive stand, they do so from the history of church mission—the record of conscious Christian interaction with other cultures and religions. And they are horrified by what they read and see. In their mind's eye, they see the passionate appeals to Christians, especially in North America, to engage in a concerted evangelistic effort on a global scale as a continuation of imperialistic attitudes toward other faiths. These active proselytizers are Hick's "immoral Christians,"[33] who condemn the majority of humanity to hell. Knitter, though less harsh, believes exclusive Christians, in an age of relative truth-claims, have lost all moral and intellectual credibility through their insistence that Christ is the one fixed and eternal point.

These accusations are not empty. They sting. If Christians believe in a compassionate and merciful God, if we bear the good news of Christ, why does our history convict us of insensitivity, intolerance, and ethnocentrism toward nonbelievers? We have condemned ourselves by relational arrogance.

Unfortunately, the unitive pluralists want to cure Christian arrogance with theological compromise. Diluting the urgency of Christian truth will surely lessen the excessive zeal, they believe. But they have made a fundamental mistake. It is wrong to assume that tolerance is an issue of truth when, in fact, it is an issue of character and cultural awareness in a culturally and religiously diverse world.[34]

First, we must concede our guilt. Hans Küng accurately states that "blind zeal for truth in all periods and in all churches and religions has ruthlessly injured, burned, destroyed and murdered."[35] I admit with a fellow Christian that

> though I stand in the long train of Christians who have taken the message of Christ to places where it has not previously been heard, I know the history of the missionary movement too well not to recognize its blemishes—its caricatures of the gospel, its outright denials of the faith of Christ *crucified*. A crucified Lord can—in the hands of dominant elites—become an imperious idol of culture. I am aware of the prob-

---

33. Hick declares "that it is not a morally or religiously acceptable view that salvation depends upon being a member of the Christian minority of the human race" ("The Philosophy of World Religions," *Scottish Journal of Theology* 37 [1984]: 229).

34. I am indebted to Mark Horst's investigation of tolerance; see "The Problem with Theological Pluralism," *Christian Century* 103 (1986): 971–74.

35. Hans Küng, "What Is the True Religion?" *Journal of Theology for Southern Africa* 56 (Sept. 1986): 4.

lems "younger Christians" worldwide have in achieving, as Christians, a sense of cultural authenticity and their liberation from western superiority.[36]

Truly, we as evangelicals should regret the marriage of Christian mission and Western ethnocentricity.

I venture to say that much of unitive pluralism's emotive force stems from a deep-seated guilt for corporate Christianity's cultural "imperialism." Liberal churches admitted much earlier than we that Western Christianity was not the only enculturated biblical response to biblical claims. But in their quest to avoid blind zeal, they exhibited a "weary forgetfulness of truth that has had as a consequence a loss of orientation and norms so that many no longer believed in anything."[37]

Unitive pluralists believe, nevertheless, that they are seeking truth, but not at the expense of sensitivity. And this is commendable. Much of the interreligious dialogue abhorred by evangelicals is actually an honest attempt to respect others by listening to *them* say what *they* believe. Peter Berger calls this the "anti-defamation" approach.[38] For example, a Buddhist might say, "You think we believe so-and-so but you're mistaken. We believe thus-and-such." This kind of dialogue attempts to avoid misunderstandings that often lead, in our own evangelistic zeal, to condescension and rejection. We should personally engage in this kind of conversation with nonbelievers. It allows an opportunity to hear the perspective of another accurately, and to share the gospel more relevantly.

But unitive pluralists ask for a far more radical change from Christians and missionaries than just becoming culturally sensitive. They want us to revise our normative declaration—"Jesus Christ is Lord of all"—for the sake of "Christian tolerance." Missiologists who write from a unitive-pluralist perspective strongly echo Knitter's call to accept as a human fact the relativity of all religious truth.

But again we say that this confuses character with truth. Tolerance has been redefined by pluralists to mean "an open-minded acceptance of all religious truth."[39] This is suspect. Tolerance actually involves real

36. Alfred Krass, "Accounting for the Hope That Is in Me," in *Christian Faith in a Religiously Plural World,* ed. Donald G. Dawe and John B. Carman (Maryknoll, N.Y.: Orbis, 1978), 157.

37. Küng, "What Is the True Religion?" 4.

38. Peter Berger, "The Pluralistic Situation and the Coming Dialogue Between the World Religions," *Buddhist Christian Studies* 1 (1981): 39.

39. See Harold A. Netland, "Exclusivism, Tolerance and Truth," *Missiology* 15 (1987): 77–95; and Keith Yandell, "Some Varieties of Relativism," *International Journal of Philosophy* 19 (1986): 61–85.

disagreement. It means that despite real commitment to conflicting truth-claims, the oppositions can treat one another with dignity. As Christians who are judged by the Word of God, we bear the burden of proof to show that we can commit ourselves to the exclusive truth of salvation through Christ alone *and* also be genuinely loving, respectful, and humble before those of other faiths.

A Methodist minister recently brought to light John Wesley's example in this regard.[40] Wesley encouraged believers to develop a "catholic spirit"—a way of describing Christian humility and compassion. In his mind, the truths of Christian faith should develop this catholic character in the believer. They are part of the "process by which a person becomes loving and appropriately tolerant." The person of a truly catholic spirit is not double-minded about the truth. "It is the believer who is tolerant, not the believer's opinions. Wesley judges catholic spirit not by what the believer says about accepting others, but by the gifts of tolerance and love exhibited in the believer's life."[41]

In our evangelism, therefore, this means our claim to truth about God in Christ should be neither defensive nor offensive, but positively candid. Since we have the Spirit that leads into all truth, we can communicate what we believe simply and sincerely. This is what Paul commends in 2 Corinthians 4:2: "We have renounced secret and shameful ways; we do not use deception; nor do we distort the word of God. On the contrary, by setting forth the truth plainly we commend ourselves to every man's conscience in the sight of God. We are exhorted, then, not to use manipulative persuasion techniques such as unfair comparing, belittling, cajoling, a condescending tone, and generalizing. These deny the integrity of persons who are, like us, created in God's image and loved by him. "In the long run, truth for both ourselves and for our friends in other religious traditions must be a matter of the heart, and a conviction of the heart cannot be won by force or trickery."[42]

Moreover, we are plainly told by our Lord Jesus how others will recognize us for who we are: "By this all men will know that you are my disciples, if you love one another" (John 13:35). Nonbelievers should recognize us first as charitable people. We could cite other Scriptures that remind us of the intense value our Lord placed on the practice of truth.

So while the most significant question about any religion remains that of truth (e.g., Are Buddhist claims about God true?), this question is moot if we who ask it act differently than the truth of God's love in Christ demands. We cannot possibly make a valid testimony for truth until "we can show that we have learned our lesson: that we under-

40. Horst, "Problem with Theological Pluralism," 972.
41. Ibid.
42. Peters, "Confessional Universalism," 148.

stand the difference between bearing witness to the truth and pretending to possess the truth; that we understand the witness (*marturia*) means not dominance and control but suffering."[43] Precisely this contrast between bearing witness and possessing that truth is where we need to be self-critical. Once Christians of any time and culture fall under the illusion that they "possess" the truth of God incarnate as a commodity, the distinctions between faith and culture begin to blur. Our American mode of worship becomes the only way of Christian worship; our view of successful Christian living becomes the ultimate; our Western missionary efforts become a special "manifest destiny" in God's economy that are irreplaceable. But God is not an American. And most of God's people do not speak English! Our announcement of forgiveness and a call to repentance is a call to new life, yes, but a new life that can—indeed must—take many cultural forms.

Furthermore, this bearing witness to the truth is not only a proclamation to others but a self-convicting message: Western Christians must be continually "converted."[44] Repentance is a hallmark of Christian life. Our American Christian culture must come under the scrutiny of God's Word, communicated to us by Christians and non-Christians of other cultures. This is the point of personally engaging with those of other cultures and religion: they force us from cultural blindness; they test the actual resonance of our Christian love and tolerance.

M. M. Thomas, an Indian missiologist, presents two commitments that Christian exclusivists need to make in the face of unitive pluralism.[45] First, we must admit the legitimacy of different cultural incarnations of our one faith. In this we are not abandoning universal truth for an unlimited pluralism, but accepting positive cultural expressions of the universal Christ.[46]

The first commitment leads to the second: we must allow Christianity to be truly incarnated in other cultures by the believers of that culture. How can they know if they have not heard, and how can they hear if there is no culturally authentic and relevant proclamation—not just an "American" witness in disguise?[47] A foreign mission-

43. Lesslie Newbigin, "Can the West Be Converted?" *International Bulletin of Missionary Research* 11 (Jan. 1987): 7 (for many years, Newbigin was an Anglican bishop in South India).

44. Ibid.

45. Madathilparampil M. Thomas, "The Absoluteness of Jesus Christ and Christ-Centered Syncretism," *Ecumenical Review* 37 (1985): 387–97.

46. The risk of syncretism is obvious, but relevant communication is always risky. Truly biblical Christians are open-minded culturally but allow no deviation from their ultimate allegiance.

47. Emilio Castro, "Mission in a Pluralistic Age," *International Review of Mission* 75 (July 1986): 209.

ary must become a Jew to the Jews, a Czech to the Czechs, and a Chinese to the Chinese—and then allow Christians to live out their faith as Jews, Czechs, or Chinese. If Christ was truth incarnate and was a Jew who revealed God's salvation in Jewish terms, then we can do no less as culture-bound witnesses than to incarnate the truth authentically in each people-group. Our fear of syncretism too often prevents us from taking real cultural risks for the sake of the gospel. But if we bear witness to the truth, we cannot afford not to take risks.

Paul Knitter and others present a sophisticated system of religious relativism that moves inevitably toward universalism. Constrained by this age, they have traded in Christianity's unique claims about God for some visionary gain. But the vision distorts the basic human understanding of truth. If religious truth is relative, indifference often replaces commitment, chronic uncertainty replaces stability.

Knitter asks us to reconceive our commitment to Christ in terms of human love language; yet this very change deflates the awesome and divine love of a God whom we believe has revealed himself uniquely in Christ. The nature of truth about God for us is primarily revelatory and not natural. Therefore, the One in Three and Three in One who has revealed himself excludes the natural (and plausible!) human reasoning of unitive pluralism. We do not know God exhaustively, but what we do know, and how it was communicated, forbids us from compromise.

We admit, nevertheless, that we cannot simply shout our claims all the louder. This inhibits sensitive listening to others, no matter how antagonistic their claims might be. Shouting is abrasive, rude, and intimidating; unitive pluralists say that exclusivists cannot help but shout.

On the contrary, the kind of truth we are committed to demands excellent character. Tolerance has more to do with behavior than beliefs, more with open-handedness than open-mindedness. In short, we tolerate those who believe differently, even unitive pluralists.

Finally, causes of past arrogance and ignorance may be traced to a close identification of Western Christian practice with universal Christian belief. We mistakenly place our cultural expression of Christian faith above all others. In turn, our dominance over poorer, less-educated Christians around the world decreases our willingness to listen to those committed to other religions founded in foreign places. We are ignorant of how their faith works for them and dismiss learning about it because it is mistaken.

But God's standard of love demands learning about it. And unless we, on a personal level, listen attentively to another's faith, we have few valid points of contact in communicating the gospel of Jesus Christ.

15

The Effect of Universalism on Mission Effort

Charles Van Engen

U niversalism and mission would seem to be mutually exclusive terms—or are they? Certainly the ideas represented by the two camps have not been seen as compatible with each other. Universalists often hold negative opinions of traditional missionary practice. For example, when John Hick called for a "Copernican revolution in theology," he began by degrading the idea of *extra ecclesia nulla salus* (outside the church there is no salvation). He referred to it with terms like "arrogant," "cruel," "entirely negative attitude," "ignorant," "blinded by dark dogmatic spectacles," and an "attitude of rejection" which comes from a "radically questionable" concept of God. As Hick sees it:

> The first phase—the phase of total rejection—was expressed in the dogma that non-Christians, as such, are consigned to hell. As the expression of an attitude to other human beings the dogma is as arrogant as it is cruel; and it is a sobering thought that such a dogma was at one time almost universally accepted among Christians. . . . The Roman Catholic Church today has passed decisively beyond this phase, but the

183

earlier dogma still persists within evangelical-fundamentalist Protestantism. For example, one of the messages of the Congress on World Mission at Chicago in 1960 declared: "In the years since the war, more than one billion souls have passed into eternity and more than half of these went to the torment of hell fire without even hearing of Jesus Christ, who He was, and why He died on the cross at Calvary. . . ."

This entirely negative attitude to other faiths is strongly correlated with ignorance of them. . . . Today, however, the extreme evangelical Protestant who believes that all Muslims go to hell is probably not so much ignorant . . . as blinded by dark dogmatic spectacles through which he can see no good in religious devotion outside his own group.

But the basic weakness in this attitude of rejection lies in the doctrine of God which it presupposes. If all human beings must, in order to attain the eternal happiness for which they have been created, accept Jesus Christ as their Lord and Savior before they die, then the great majority of humanity is doomed to eternal frustration and misery. . . . To say that such an appalling situation is divinely ordained is to deny the Christian understanding of God as gracious and holy love.[1]

Missionary spokespersons, on the other hand, have reacted against the undermining of missionary motivation represented by such universalist perspectives. Already in the 1930s Hendrik Kraemer responded to William E. Hocking and the "Laymen's Foreign Mission Inquiry" by strongly affirming a deeply biblical missionary motivation. Opposing the religiously pluralistic position advocated by Hocking and Protestant liberalism of the day, Kraemer stated:

The only valid motive and purpose of missions is, and alone can be, to call men and peoples to confront themselves with God's acts of revelation and salvation for man and the world as presented in Biblical realism, and to build up a community of those who have surrendered themselves to faith in and loving service of Jesus Christ.[2]

1. John Hick, *God Has Many Names* (Philadelphia: Westminster, 1980), 29–31, quoting from John O. Percy, ed., *Facing the Unfinished Task: Messages Delivered at the Congress on World Mission* (Grand Rapids: Zondervan, 1961), 9. See also Eugene Hillman, *The Wider Ecumenism: Anonymous Christianity and the Church* (London: Compass, 1968), 25–27. Hick's antimissionary assessment echoes Ernst Troeltsch's negative perspective, articulated in a lecture at the University of Oxford in 1923; see "The Place of Christianity among the World Religions," in *Christianity and Other Religions,* ed. John Hick and Brian Hebblethwaite (Glasgow: Fount, 1980), 26–28.

2. Hendrik Kraemer, *The Christian Message in a Non-Christian World* (New York: Harper, 1938; repr., Grand Rapids: Kregel, 1969), 292; quoted by Edmond J. Dunn, *Missionary Theology: Foundation in Development* (Lanham, Md.: University Press of America, 1980), 52. Kraemer wrote against Hocking's *Rethinking Missions: A Layman's Inquiry after One Hundred Years* (New York: Harper, 1932). A good place to enter this conversation is the July 1988 issue of *International Review of Mission* commemorating the fiftieth anniversary of the International Missionary Council conference at Tambaram,

During the past several decades mission theorists and practitioners have emphasized the dangers of universalism in the way it undermines the motive and urgency for mission. Michael Griffiths even called it a "Trojan Horse" that

> gained entrance into Christendom and threatens to destroy missionary motives and hinder the effectiveness of Christ's soldiers and their readiness to continue the battle . . . perhaps there is no battle! . . . If all men are to be saved in the end why bother to urge men to repent now? They will later in any case. Why bother to be converted oneself for that matter? But the urgency which has characterized missionary endeavor derives not merely from the fear of hell, but from the consciousness that to live even this life without Christ is to be condemned to an alienated, meaningless existence estranged from God.[3]

After citing Daniel T. Niles and Douglas Webster to support his contention that the universalist position destroys missionary urgency, Griffiths states:

> It is this viewpoint which appears to underlie the present swing away from soteriological concern to social concern. Indeed, it is precisely because many leaders in the World Council of Churches believe that God will save all men anyway that "salvation has been given such a firm this-worldly orientation and evangelism often becomes simply irrelevant.[4]

Significantly, as recently as 1989, both Lesslie Newbigin and Johannes Verkuyl expressed concern that if the present universalist/pluralist current in the World Council of Churches continues, the council may become irrelevant to the missiological issues that face us in the future.[5] Clearly the effect of universalism on missionary

---

India. Lesslie Newbigin responds to the *International Review of Mission* in "Religious Pluralism and the Uniqueness of Jesus Christ," *International Bulletin of Missionary Research* 13 (Apr. 1989): 50–54. See also David Bosch, *Witness to the World* (London: Marshall, Morgan & Scott, 1980), 159–75; and Stanley Samartha, "The Lordship of Jesus Christ and Religious Pluralism," in *Christ's Lordship and Religious Pluralism*, ed. Gerald H. Anderson and Thomas Stransky (Maryknoll, N.Y.: Orbis, 1981), 19.

3. Michael Griffiths, *The Confusion of the Church and the World* (Downers Grove, Ill.: Inter-Varsity, 1980), 116, 129.

4. Ibid., 119; quoting N. T. Wright, "Universalism and the World-Wide Community," *Churchman* 89 (July–Sept. 1975): 204; see also Daniel T. Niles, *The Preacher's Calling to Be Servant* (London: Lutterworth, 1959), 32–33; and Douglas Webster, "The Missionary Appeal To-day," *International Review of Mission* 47 (1958): 279–88.

5. Lesslie Newbigin, "Religious Pluralism and the Uniqueness of Jesus Christ," 54; Johannes Verkuyl, "Mission in the 1990s," *International Bulletin of Missionary Research* 13 (Apr. 1989): 55.

motivation and urgency is important.[6] The universalist perspective threatens missionary motivation, reduces missional urgency, and emasculates the biblical message. This matter is especially urgent today when Christians on every continent are rubbing shoulders with neighbors representing a whole range of different religious allegiances.

And yet, we must be cautious in assessing the polemics between the two camps from a missiological point of view. A historical case can be made that the introduction of pluralistic viewpoints into the International Missionary Council from 1938 on (along with the subsequent impact of the "Comparative Religions" movement in North American mainline Protestantism) reduced missionary sending in some churches. A theological argument can also be offered that religious pluralism reduces a Christian sense of missionary urgency.[7] However, neither of these arguments alone may be valid reasons for disavowing the universalist perspective.

In the first place, other religious movements (even relatively pluralistic ones) have been evangelistic in their own right. The Crusades and the Spanish conquest of the Americas could be added to a list that would include Marxism in the 1950s, Transcendental Meditation in the 1960s, militant Islam in the 1970s, the New Age movement in the 1980s, and even Unitarian/Universalism during the last fifty years as perspectives that have been committed to furthering their viewpoints even though they did not represent a biblical understanding of either the gospel or God's mission. To adopt a universalist perspective may not of itself mean the loss of evangelistic energy. The historical argument also ignores numerous other theological and nontheological factors that have contributed to encourage or discourage North American mission-sending (the two world wars, and the Vietnam War, for example).

Second, the presence of strong missionary motivation does not itself guarantee the truth of the message being advocated. The examples above demonstrate that movements we might consider unbiblical may themselves be strongly proselytizing. Militancy often goes hand-in-hand with belief in one's unique (triumphalistic?) perspective, but

6. See Harold Lindsell, "Faith Missions since 1938," in *Frontiers of the Christian World Mission since 1938: Essays in Honor of Kenneth Scott Latourette,* ed. Wilber C. Harr (New York: Harper, 1962), 189–230; John R. W. Stott, *Christian Mission in the Modern World* (Downers Grove, Ill.: Inter-Varsity, 1975), 64–69; Neal Punt, "All Are Saved Except," *Christianity Today* 31/5 (20 Mar. 1987): 43–44; Harold Brown, "Will Everyone Be Saved?" *Pastoral Renewal* 11 (June 1987): 11–16; Carl Braaten, "The Meaning of Evangelism in the Context of God's Universal Grace," *Journal of the Academy for Evangelism in Theological Education* 3 (1987–88): 9–19; William Brownson, "Hope for All," *Perspectives* 3/8 (Oct. 1988): 13–15; and Colin Chapman, "The Riddle of Religions," *Christianity Today* 34/8 (14 May 1990): 16–22.

7. Paul follows a similar line of argument when referring to the resurrection in 1 Cor. 15.

militancy itself does not support the truth of the beliefs that form the foundation of such activism. The truth or falsehood of the universalist perspective must be established by Scripture—not by Christian activism. As Lesslie Newbigin has said, "The Christian goes to meet his neighbor of another religion on the basis of his commitment to Jesus Christ. There is no dichotomy between 'confession' and 'truth-seeking'. His confession is the starting point of his truth-seeking."[8] If we are dealing with a *Christian* approach to other religions, it must begin and end with Scripture. We cannot afford to follow the lead of some of the universalist literature that moves away from its scriptural foundation simply because persons of other faiths do not recognize our Scriptures. This is precisely the point. Our affirmation of Christian truth is based on our experience of Jesus Christ and grounded on the revelation of God as found in Scripture. We need a broader arena of discussion. A study of the relation of universalism and mission should include, among other things, a recognition of the wide variety of topics falling under the concept of universalism, a careful distinction between faith and culture, and an analysis of the apostle Paul's twin concepts of cultural-universalism and faith-particularism. I have space here only to present these issues in a summary, outline form.

A Variety of Topics within Universalism

The term *universalism* indicates an entire constellation of topics that have been discussed for centuries. No one topic by itself covers the range of issues involved in universalism.[9] And each topic in fact relates to a different group of scriptural verses and ideas. The following list represents a sampling of topics and is not intended to be exhaustive.[10]

1. Christianity's view of other religions—past and present
2. Ultimately will all be saved? Is there a second chance?
3. The uniqueness of Christ—exclusive? inclusive? pluralist?
4. Eternal punishment, hell, torment, annihilation

8. Lesslie Newbigin, "The Gospel among the Religions," in *Mission Trends No. 5: Faith Meets Faith,* ed. Gerald H. Anderson and Thomas Stransky (Grand Rapids: Eerdmans, 1981), 4.

9. *The Oxford Dictionary of the Christian Church* defines universalism this way: "The Greek name . . . for the doctrine that ultimately all free moral creatures—angels, men, and devils—will share in the grace of salvation. It is to be found in Clement of Alexandria, in Origen and in St. Gregory of Nyssa. It was strongly attacked by St. Augustine of Hippo and formally condemned in the first anathema against Origenism, probably put out by the Council of Constantinople in A.D. 543" (pp. 69–70).

10. Excellent review essays covering the more recent works on the subject may be found in the July 1989 issue of *Religious Studies Review* 15 (1989): 197–209.

5. Universal/local, objective/subjective views of truth
6. Restoration of all things in Christ
7. Everyone is already an anonymous Christian
8. The necessity of God's love to save all human beings
9. Confusion of the doctrines of creation and redemption
10. Urgency of evangelism and missionary motivation
11. Sociological usefulness of other religions
12. Theocentric world religion—"Copernican Revolution"
13. Theocentric Christology—reductionist local christologies
14. Panentheistic perspectives on the Holy Spirit
15. Soteriological approaches to other faiths
16. Cultural pluralism equated with religious pluralism[11]

Clearly I do not have space here to develop the topics listed above. Merely enumerating them, however, demonstrates how complex the subject is and helps us to see the numerous ways it may be approached, particularly as it relates to the mission of the church. Moreover, the list warns us to be careful and critical in our reading. Because someone brings new questions to bear upon one of the above topics does not necessarily mean that such a person is "universalist" in relation to all the other topics. In the evangelical world, and especially in mission, we have too quickly categorized someone as "universalist" who may be asking questions of only one topic—and may be biblically particularist about the others. So, for example, when Karl Barth offered the hope that one day all humanity would be gathered to God, he never meant to question the uniqueness of Jesus Christ on which his whole dogmatic theology stands or falls.[12] So also when John R. W. Stott suggested that annihilationism might fit the biblical portrait of hell, he was not necessarily advocating more than one salvific path to God.[13] In other words, we evangelical Christians need to understand precisely what a given scholar is asking before we hastily accuse that person of being universalist.

11. An excellent survey of Christian attitudes to other religions over the last century is given by David Bosch, "The Church in Dialogue: From Self-Delusion to Vulnerability," *Missiology* 16 (1988): 131–47. See also David Hesselgrave, "Christian Communication and Religious Pluralism: Capitalizing on Differences," *Missiology* 18 (1990): 131–38; and Carl E. Braaten, "The Uniqueness and Universality of Jesus Christ," in *Mission Trends No. 5: Faith Meets Faith*, ed. Gerald H. Anderson and Thomas Stransky (Grand Rapids: Eerdmans, 1981), 69–89.

12. A synopsis of this matter can be found in Richard Bauckham, "Universalism—A Historical Survey," *Themelios* 4 (Jan. 1979): 48–53.

13. John R. W. Stott, "Taking a Closer Look at Eternal Torture," *World Christian* 8/5 (May 1989): 31–37.

A Distinction Between Faith and Culture

As the church becomes more and more a global community, it is increasingly clear that faith and culture cannot be entirely separated from each other. The gospel does not take place in a cultural vacuum, but is always incarnated in a specific cultural context. And yet we must also affirm that culture and faith are not identical. As Charles Kraft says:

> We deduce, then, that the relationship between God and culture is the same as that of one who uses a vehicle to the vehicle that he uses. But this relationship between God and culture is not a required relationship in the sense that God is bound by culture. On the contrary, God is absolute and infinite. Yet he has freely chosen to employ human culture and at major points to limit himself to the capacities of his interaction with people. . . . Any limitation of God is only that which he imposes upon himself—he chooses to use culture, he is not bound by it in the same way human beings are.[14]

Not only must we distinguish God from culture, but we must also separate the faith of the individual from his or her culture. We need to affirm approaches to contextualization that take seriously the culturally appropriate shape given the gospel in each time and place. But that is a far cry from equating culture and faith. We all know that various persons within the same culture may espouse radically different faiths. And persons of many cultures may share the same faith. At the outset this would seem to be a truism, but it is not always so obvious.

One of the most disturbing aspects of the literature on universalism is the close, nearly synonymous, relationship between faith and culture. This can be seen clearly in Ernst Troeltsch's statement: "But in relation to the great world religions we need to recognize that they are expressions of the religious consciousness corresponding to certain definite types of culture."[15] Whether we are speaking of Wilfred Cantwell Smith, Karl Rahner, Paul Knitter, John Hick, John Cobb, or Wesley Ariarajah, there is a disturbingly close relationship between faith and culture in their writings.[16] Is it not interesting that the strongest proponents of religious pluralism also seem to represent the strands of "Christendom" that tend to be the most culture-affirming, where faith and culture are most closely intertwined?

14. Charles Kraft, *Christianity in Culture* (Maryknoll, N.Y.: Orbis, 1979), 115.

15. Troeltsch, "Place of Christianity among the World Religions," 27.

16. Although I do not have space here to illustrate this, examples abound. See S. Wesley Ariarajah, "Religious Plurality and Its Challenge to Christian Theology," *Perspectives* 5/2 (Feb. 1990): 6–9. Also, see the articles in the reader compiled by Hick and Hebblethwaite, *Christianity and Other Religions*.

Yet the difference between faith and culture is *precisely* part of the question—not something to be unquestioningly assumed. Karl Barth wanted to demonstrate this when he drew a radical distinction between religion and faith.[17] The distinction between faith and culture affirms that creation and redemption, as understood in Scripture, are not the same thing for the Christian. God is the Creator of all human beings, but it is only in Jesus Christ, by the power of the Holy Spirit, through faith, that people are given "the right to become children of God" (John 1:12). It is only through God's grace that we are "predestined . . . to be adopted as his sons through Jesus Christ, in accordance with his pleasure and will—to the praise of his glorious grace" (Eph. 1:5–6). More recently, Lesslie Newbigin in *Foolishness to the Greeks* and *The Gospel in a Pluralist Society* has shown that faith and Western culture cannot and must not be equated.[18] We must carefully and incisively distinguish between faith and culture, no matter if that culture is Jewish, Greek, Roman, European, North American, Asian, African, or Latin American. Unless we draw a radical distinction between faith and culture, we cannot get past the accusation of cultural imperialism in Christian mission. But when we do come to recognize a difference (though close interrelationship) between our faith and our culture, we will be prepared to deal more creatively with the impact of universalism upon mission effort.

I believe this distinction of faith and culture was at the heart of Paul's concept of a universal yet particular gospel, expressed most clearly in Romans. In fact, maintaining a radical distance between faith and culture may be the key to a missiological reading of the "all" passages in Romans, so often cited by universalist writers. So we turn our attention to a brief survey of Romans, seen from a missiological perspective.

Cultural Universality and Faith Particularism in Paul

I do not have the space here to carry out an exhaustive exegetical study of Romans.[19] However, the relationship of universalism to mis-

17. See, e.g., Karl Barth, "The Revelation of God as the Abolition of Religion," in *Christianity and Other Religions,* ed. John Hick and Brian Hebblethwaite (Glasgow: Fount, 1980), 32–51. See also J. Robert Nelson, "Christian Theology and the Living Faiths of Men," in *Christian Mission in Theological Perspective,* ed. Gerald H. Anderson (Nashville: Abingdon, 1967), 109–24.

18. Lesslie Newbigin, *Foolishness to the Greeks* (Grand Rapids: Eerdmans, 1986); Newbigin, *The Gospel in a Pluralist Society* (Geneva: WCC, 1989). See also John R. W. Stott and Robert Coote, eds., *Down to Earth: Studies in Christianity and Culture* (Grand Rapids: Eerdmans, 1980).

19. For an examination of Romans 1–2, see Aída Besançon Spencer, "Romans 1: Finding God in Creation"; and Douglas Moo, "Romans 2: Saved Apart from the Gospel?"—both in this volume.

sion effort cannot ignore the fact that many universalist authors cite the universalist passages in Paul as the scriptural basis for their position.[20] What follows is a cursory outline of Romans that illustrates Paul's unique perspective in the light of universalism and mission. Paul certainly has a universal perspective. But confusion surfaces in the overlapping of faith and culture. Paul demonstrates in Romans that he wants to advocate a *cultural universality,* together with a *faith particularity.*

Romans: A Missionary Team-Leader Writes to a Mission Church

Theme of the letter: The gospel of faith in Jesus Christ is for Jews and Gentiles, Greeks and non-Greeks, wise and foolish, for *everyone who believes* (Rom. 1:14–17; compare 15:8–9, 15–16; 16:26)
The underlying agenda of Romans: A proposed missionary journey to Spain

  I. General revelation demonstrates the unrighteousness of *all* (1:18–32; Paul begins with the worldview of his readers, a viewpoint that designates two kinds of people in the world: Jews and Gentiles; using what Paul Hiebert has called "bounded sets," fig. 1 illustrates this viewpoint).

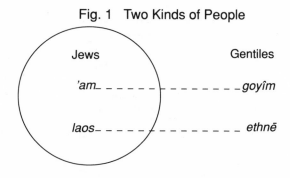

Fig. 1 Two Kinds of People

 II. Special revelation demonstrates the sinfulness of *all* (see fig. 2)
   A. Generally of all humans (2:1–16)
   B. Specifically of Jews also (2:17–3:8)
   C. *All* have sinned, all face judgment (3:9–20)

20. N. T. Wright, "Towards a Biblical View of Universalism," *Themelios* 4 (1979): 54–58.

Fig. 2   The Sinfulness of All

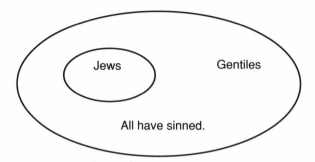

III. Special grace in Jesus Christ is for *all who believe* (Paul's new
    universality, with its new "centered set," is illustrated in fig. 3)
    A. Universality of grace offered to *all who believe* (3:21–31)
    B. Particularity of the response through faith, applicable to
       all (4:1–5:21)
    C. The completeness of the transformation (6:1–23)
       1. The divine-human tension in such transformation—
          faith and culture are, after all, not the same (7:1–25)
       2. The Holy Spirit's role in such transformation (8:1–27)
       3. The universal scope of such transformation (8:28–39)

Fig. 3   Paul's New Universality

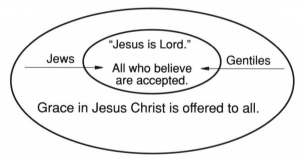

    D. The matter of Israel after the flesh—a question occasioned
       by Paul's redefinition of universality and particularity
       (9:1–11:36)
       1. Against a new exclusivity
       2. God who acts in history is a God of compassion
       3. The instrumentality of the new people of God for the
          nations—and for Israel's salvation as well

Fig. 4   Mission Nature of God's People

IV. The special life of the unique people of God in the world
    (renewing of the mind deals with the difference between
    faith and culture; fig. 4 demonstrates the missional nature of
    the new universal people of God)
    A. The life of the community of faith in the world
       (12:1–15:13)
    B. Paul, a minister of Christ Jesus to the Gentiles; the cre-
       tion of the new universal/particularity (15:14–22)
    C. Paul's long-range plans for Spain (15:23–33)
    D. Paul's concept of teamwork-in-mission illustrated
       (16:1–24).

Concluding doxology (16:25–27):

Now to him who is able to establish you by my gospel and the proclamation of Jesus Christ, according to the revelation of the mystery hidden for long ages past, but now revealed and made known through the
prophetic writings by the command of the eternal God, so that *all
nations* might believe and obey him—to the only wise God be glory
forever through Jesus Christ! Amen. (italics added)

There are two final observations I need to make. First, the reader
should notice that in the final analysis the center around which the
new universal particularity is constructed is the confession, "Jesus is
Lord" (Rom. 10:9). This calls into question all the layers of the onion
of cultural accretions that have been added to that confession through
the centuries by the Christian church. For the gospel to be culturally
universal, all Christians must be willing to divest themselves of everything except that confession. At no time in history has the church's
cultural universality been more evident than in this new day of the
world church. Surrounding the globe in a multitude of cultures, the
church demonstrates its "translatability" in myriads of new and unex-

pected ways.[21] Knitter's thesis, then, is untenable. The *fact* of numerous religious traditions does not make their existence normative —unless the argument is supported by an intimate link with cultural relativity. Instead, the apostle Paul offers God's love and grace to all human beings, representing any and all religious backgrounds. By faith in Jesus Christ, God's love gathers *all people* at the foot of the cross and calls all to experience new life in the Spirit.

Second, this cultural universality develops within a faith particularity that creates a new "Israel" by faith. Not only does this represent a continuity with Abraham (by faith), it also represents a new *missional instrumentality* by the church for the sake of *all* people. These new people of God are now called "ambassadors" (2 Cor. 5:11–21) in the midst of the nations, for the sake of the nations. This instrumentality stresses the faith relationship which transcends all cultural barriers, breaks down the middle wall of partition (Eph. 2), and challenges every form of cultural particularism (even Gentile particularism against the Jews, Rom. 11). This "biblical universality" disavows all other forms of exclusivity: ethnic, sexual, social, education, economic, political. "Jesus is Lord" is for *all persons*. This type of biblical universality represents a common perspective evident in various missions documents, representing a variety of Christian traditions.[22] Such a culturally universal faith calls for "the whole church to take the whole gospel to the whole world."[23]

Are universalism and mission mutually exclusive? If by universalism we mean the range of topics mentioned above used to defend religious relativity and pluralism, the answer is yes. But if by universalism we mean *universality,* that is, Paul's idea of a gospel *available* to all cultures, the answer is no. Rather, the twin ideas of cultural universality and faith particularity support and encourage each other. The invitation that Jesus Christ extends for salvation in him is extended to *all people.* If we take Pauline universality seriously in all its human, cultural, and relational dimensions, our mission effort will be truly revolutionary. Then we will be truly universal, seeking to bring together all peoples, all tribes, all nations in one common faith, confessing together that "Jesus is Lord."

21. Lamin Sanneh has shown this element of the church's missionary nature in *Translating the Message: The Missionary Impact on Culture* (Maryknoll, N.Y.: Orbis, 1989).

22. See Willem A. Visser 't Hooft, *No Other Name* (London: SCM, 1963); "Ad Gentes" and "Lumen Gentium," in *Documents of Vatican II,* ed. Austin P. Flannery (Grand Rapids: Eerdmans, 1975); "The Lausanne Covenant" (1974); "Evangelii Nuntiandi" (Rome, 1974); "Mission and Evangelism: An Ecumenical Affirmation" (Geneva: WCC, 1982); "The Manila Manifesto" (Lausanne Committee for World Evangelism, 1989); "Section I: Turning to the Living God" (Committee on World Mission and Evangelism, San Antonio, 1989). See also *The San Antonio Report* (Geneva: WCC, 1990).

23. This was the theme of the recent Lausanne II meeting in Manila, the largest missionary gathering in history.

16

Do Other Religions Save?

Harvie M. Conn

One of the most serious challenges to the Christian church is expressed in the title of this chapter. If other religions can provide a path to salvation, why bother with evangelism? Where is the distinctiveness of a Christian faith without uniqueness? In this chapter I explore the background for the current discussions outside of evangelicalism. Then, I will examine several theological answers to the question asked in the title of this chapter.

Christian Self-Doubts and the Enlightenment

This is not the first time in recent history that the church has faced an avalanche of information—or questions—about world religions. The first serious encounter of the West with such data can be traced back to the seventeenth and eighteenth centuries, when the church found itself inundated with information on the world's religions and mythical folklore. Travel books fed popular interest and the discovery and translation of sacred texts from the East, especially China, nourished scholarly curiosities.

With this information came a hermeneutical movement, the Enlightenment, whose effects we still feel today. It raised skeptical questions not only about religions in China or India but about Christianity itself. Reasonableness, not revelation, ascended the throne as the criterion of truth.

Gottfried W. Leibniz (1646–1716), for example, was so enamored of things Chinese that he suggested, "In view of the inordinate lengths to which the corruption of morals had advanced I almost think it necessary that Chinese missionaries should be sent to us to teach us the aim and practice of natural theology, as we send missionaries to them to instruct them in revealed theology." Voltaire (1694–1778), charmed by the tolerant humanism of Confucius, saw the period during which his laws were followed as "the happiest and most honorable this earth has ever known."[1]

How were these increasingly acknowledged similarities of "pagan religions" and Christian revelations to be explained? Scholarship turned to the question of the origins of religion. And British Deism heralded the commonalities of "natural religion," not the uniqueness of Christianity, as the answer.

By the middle of the eighteenth century, Deism had lost its argument, but the damage was done.[2] Deism's serious doubts about the uniqueness of the Bible and its willingness to examine all religions before the bar of reason became part of the modern world.[3] An emerging principle of "neutrality" and noncommitment to Christianity was growing.

A new nineteenth-century science, "history of religions" (German, *Religionswissenschaft*), flows out of this skepticism. The Enlightenment mentality had called for the abandonment of any a priori attitude of Christian absolutism over non-Christian religions. *Religionswissenschaft* built on this concept.

E. E. Evans-Pritchard has observed that, with rare exceptions, the most influential formulators of the *Religionswissenschaft* approach were either agnostics or atheists. These "history of religions" scholars concluded that what was then called primitive religion "was with regard to its validity no different from any other religious faith, an illusion."[4] The naturalistic interpretations they offered for the origins of religions undermined any supernatural element.

Max Müller (1823–1900), often called the father of comparative religion, "like the Enlightenment thinkers . . . was concerned with religio

---

1. Quoted in Edgar L. Allen, *Christianity among the Religions* (Boston: Beacon, 1960), 44, 46.

2. Harvie M. Conn, *Eternal Word and Changing Worlds* (Grand Rapids: Zondervan, 1984), 31–33.

3. Henning Graf Reventlow, *The Authority of the Bible and the Rise of the Modern World* (Philadelphia: Fortress, 1985), 411–14.

4. Edward E. Evans-Pritchard, *Theories of Primitive Religion* (London: Oxford University Press, 1965), 14–15.

naturalis, or the original natural religion of reason and assumed that 'truth' was to be found in the most universal essence of religion and not in its particular manifestation."[5] From this higher and more abstract essence, he argued, the first religious conceptions developed out of a corrupted linguistic personification of natural phenomena.

Müller's colleague at Oxford, E. B. Tylor (1832–1917), fathered the science of cultural anthropology with much the same commitments. His 1871 title, *Primitive Culture*, defined religion as "belief in spiritual beings," a belief he called animism. It evolved, he contended, as "primitive man," reflecting on such human experiences as sleep, dreams, and death, made rational inferences about himself or the world.[6]

Cultural anthropology and its studies of religion have moved a long way from these early days, and an even longer way from the earlier questions of Christendom that spawned them. Research methods have been refined and faulty conclusions continue to be corrected. But, as Claude Stipe argues, structural methodologies, however purified, continue to minimize religion.[7] Do other religions save? "An irrelevant question!" cry the strict children of the Enlightenment heritage.

Christian Sincerity and Historicism

This kind of optimism in human reason is not new to the West and to the church. Apologists of the second and third centuries like Justin Martyr and Origen found in the seeds of the rational *Logos* enough light to classify Socrates and Heraclitus as Christians.[8] Their Christian sincerity expected no less.

The Enlightenment, however, expanded Christian sincerity into a rational humanism that transformed Christ's uniqueness into universalism. Reinforcing this movement toward relativism was another issue important for the people of the late nineteenth century (and for us), the problem of "historical consciousness."

Scholars came to recognize that human beings were not just social or rational creatures. We are also historical beings. And since history is limited and always changing, so everything in it is also limited and

5. Joseph Kitagawa, "The History of Religions in America," in *The History of Religions: Essays in Methodology,* ed. Mircea Eliade and Joseph Kitagawa (Chicago: University of Chicago Press, 1959), 17.

6. Fuller expositions of the views of these early scholars and reactions to them will be found in Eric J. Sharpe, *Comparative Religion: A History* (London: Duckworth, 1975), 27–96; Hoffman R. Hays, *From Ape to Angel: An Informal History of Social Anthropology* (New York: Knopf, 1958), 56–83.

7. Claude Stipe, "Anthropologists Versus Missionaries: The Influence of Presuppositions," *Current Anthropology* 21 (1980): 168.

8. For further details, see the later chapter in this volume by James G. Sigountos, "Did Early Christians Believe Pagan Religions Could Save?"

always changing. What is true in one historical situation may not be true in another. The historical quality of life and knowledge, therefore, excludes all claims of unchangeable truth.

This posed serious problems for our understanding of Christianity. How could any historical religion, subject to the relativity and changes of history, claim absoluteness for itself? Gotthold E. Lessing (1729–81) posed the question acutely. The probabilities of history, he argued, cannot yield the certainty required by religious faith. There was, he contended, an "ugly ditch" between universal truths of reason and accidental truths of history.

Ernst Troeltsch (1865–1923) struggled with that issue in his 1901 book, *The Absoluteness of Christianity and the History of Religions.* In so doing he marked a shift in Christian perspective from empathy to what Arnulf Camps calls cultural relativism.[9]

Motivated by German idealism, Troeltsch was unhappy with what he saw as the traditional concept of revelation: a too-transcendent God sweeping down from heaven and intervening as an arbitrary parent in history at significant points. Instead, he claimed, each religion must be seen as a manifestation of the Absolute. Christianity possessed a "qualified superiority" because of the universal appeal of its ethics and its success in holding human hearts amid the buffeting of history.

His own formulations underwent transition before his death. But his significance lies not in his solutions but in the questions he left. If all historical religious forms are relative and limited, what of Christianity? How can we affirm historical relativism and confidence in a unique faith born in history? If salvation is salvation in history, how can any faith, including Christianity, escape the limitations of time and space?

Looking at Some Answers

Modifying the influential categories of Richard Niebuhr's *Christ and Culture* (1951) may help in looking at contemporary nonevangelical responses. But, unlike Niebuhr, we see these views spread out on a spectrum, not a continuum. Niebuhr sees the models as complementing one another, a continuity of solutions. We see the continuity in the problem common to all the models, not necessarily the solutions. Scattered along the spectrum are at least four solutions.[10]

The two polar ends of the spectrum we may call exclusivism and

9. Arnulf Camps, *Partners in Dialogue: Christianity and Other World Religions* (Maryknoll, N.Y.: Orbis, 1983), 27–28.

10. H. Richard Niebuhr, *Christ and Culture* (New York: Harper, 1956), 234–41. Remember that Niebuhr himself ended his creative typology by falling into Lessing's "ugly ditch," acknowledging all solutions as relative in several senses. He also assumed the Bible itself offered no integrated response.

inclusivism. Because of the limitations of this assignment, I must pass quickly over exclusivism, the Christ-against-religions approach of such scholars as Karl Barth (1886–1968) and Hendrik Kraemer (1888–1965). Exclusivists affirm that Christianity draws its origins directly and uniquely from the revelation of God in Christ. But, unlike the evangelical view often mistakenly tied to this terminology, this model also brings a freedom to question the reliability of Christianity as a response to God's revelation in Christ. Even the message of the Bible is said to have been flawed by our human response to the revelation of God.

Inclusivism

At the opposite end of the spectrum is inclusivism, the Christ-of-religions approach. It sees all human religions as belonging ultimately in some way to Christ. It affirms saving power in all religions and traces that power to the divine presence in that religion.

At the same time, it retains its "Christian" tone or flavor by rejecting other religions as ultimate sources of salvation. This saving insufficiency is explained by affirming that, in some way or other, all religious truth belongs ultimately to Christ.

The representatives differ in how they seek to remove that insufficiency. They all ask, Where are the connecting lines between the Christian faith and the inner religious dynamism of the other religions? Inclusivism does not seek to draw "delineating lines"[11] but "inclusivist lines"—lines that bring religions together, not separate them.

Common to all advocates of inclusivism is the search for ways by which the "non-Christian" faiths may be integrated creatively into Christian theological reflection. In the language of Alan Race:

> It aims to hold together two equally binding convictions: the operation of the grace of God in all the great religions of the world working for salvation and the uniqueness of the manifestation of the grace of God in Christ, which makes a universal claim as the final way of salvation.[12]

The most prominent voices for inclusivism today belong in all likelihood to John Hick and Paul Knitter. But since other chapters deal with their views at some length, I will turn to other representatives.[13]

Raimundo Panikkar (b. 1918), in a dialogue with Hinduism now

11. This language is borrowed from Alan Race, *Christians and Religious Pluralism* (Maryknoll, N.Y.: Orbis, 1982), 38.

12. Ibid.

13. On Hick, see Charles Van Engen, "The Effect of Universalism on Mission Effort"; on Knitter, see Timothy D. Westergren, "Do All Roads Lead to Heaven?" both in this volume.

extending over two decades, exemplifies this approach. Not far from the "fulfilment" idea of liberalism popular among missionaries to India more than half a century earlier,[14] his 1964 title, *The Unknown Christ of Hinduism,* affirms that Christianity and Hinduism both meet in Christ. Christ is present in Hinduism. "The good and *bona fide* Hindu is saved by Christ and not by Hinduism, but it is through the sacraments of Hinduism, through the *Mysterion* that comes to him through Hinduism, that *Christ* saves the Hindu normally."[15]

Challenging the normativity of Christ, Panikkar calls for an "ecumenical ecumenism" among world religions, a search for the shared mystery that he sees as part of every genuine religious experience.

Lately, Panikkar's Christology has taken an even more radical turn. The 1981 revision of *The Unknown Christ of Hinduism* speaks of Christ as "a living symbol for the totality of reality: human, divine, cosmic."[16] No longer willing to speak of the fullness of revelation in the historical Jesus, he speaks instead of Christ as a universal symbol that "all religions recognize in one way or another." Christ, the "Supername," can go by many other names—Rama, Krishna, Purusha. Though unknown and unacknowledged, Christ is at work in Hinduism.

The celebrated Jesuit theologian, Karl Rahner (1904–84), reinforced this inclusivist model in 1961 with his introduction of the term *anonymous Christian.*[17] According to Rahner, it is no longer sufficient merely to concede that values can be encountered in the world's religions. We must admit that these religions are the historically tangible expressions of God's universal salvific will. Every time we reach out beyond ourselves to what is true and good we are responding to a "transcendent revelation" built into our very nature. And, in doing that, we are experiencing and responding to saving grace. We can thus speak of the presence of the grace of Christ outside of Christianity; there are "anonymous Christians" in Hinduism, Islam, and Buddhism.

Inclusivism strongly shows the leftover marks of the Enlightenment and historicism. There is a serious erosion of confidence in the historical Jesus as the historical Christ. The particularity of Jesus of Nazareth evaporates and Christ remains only as a universal Absolute, a spiritual experience of some ultimate Mysterion of common values. In the

14. An excellent treatment of the history of this part of Hindu-Christian dialogue can be found in Eric J. Sharpe, *Faith Meets Faith* (London: SCM, 1977), esp. 19–44.

15. Raymond Panikkar, *The Unknown Christ of Hinduism* (London: Darton, Longman & Todd, 1964), 54.

16. Panikkar, *The Unknown Christ of Hinduism,* rev. ed. (Maryknoll, N.Y.: Orbis, 1981), 27.

17. Karl Rahner, "Christianity and the Non-Christian Religions," *Theological Investigations* (New York: Seabury, 1961), 5:115–34.

manner of Vedanta Hinduism, rapprochement reduces Christianity to a philosophical system.

But the gospel claims to be much more than a collection of integrative ideas. "It is, as Bishop Newbigin says, 'primarily news and only secondarily views'. And if the news is denied, the views hang in the air."[18] Any explicit affirmation of Jesus Christ in inclusivism becomes so minimalist as to make Christology superfluous.

Further, does there not flow from this syncretistic sensitivity to other religions a more ultimate insensitivity to those deep religious commitments? Would we Christians be willing to be called "anonymous Buddhists" or "anonymous Muslims"? On what basis then can we make demands of Buddhists and Muslims that we are not willing to make of ourselves? What keeps inclusivism from the presumption of a kind of "theological prefabrication" that "sweeps the whole of good-willed humanity . . . into the back door of the . . . church"? [19]

Moreover, inclusivism proceeds from the assumption, verbalized by Paul Knitter, that all religions "in all their amazing differences" are still ultimately "more complementary than contradictory."[20] I join David Bosch in asking on what basis we reach such a conclusion:

> Don't we now just compare *what we have decided* is the best in our own religion with *what we have decided* is the best in other religions? What if religions perhaps face in different directions, ask fundamentally different questions? What if they are worlds in themselves with their own centers, turning on different axes, and irreducible to each other or to a common denominator?[21]

Inclusivism, operating with the Enlightenment assumption of the similarity of all religions, does in fact pay minimal attention to differences.

Pluralism

Very close to the inclusivist end of the spectrum, pluralism may be called the Christ-alongside-religions approach.[22] With inclusivism, it strongly affirms religious traditions outside of Christianity. With inclusivism, it spurns the confrontational approach. With inclusivism, it is

---

18. W. A. Visser 't Hooft, *No Other Name* (Philadelphia: Westminster, 1963), 35.

19. David Bosch, "The Church in Dialogue: From Self-Delusion to Vulnerability," *Missiology* 16 (1988): 143.

20. Paul Knitter, *No Other Name?* (Maryknoll, N.Y.: Orbis, 1985), 220.

21. Bosch, "Church in Dialogue," 142–43.

22. I use the term *pluralism* in a very narrow way. In contemporary literature, it sometimes is used as a broad category to cover the whole area of "approach theories." Or it may be used synonymously with syncretism. Or again, it may incorporate views I classify under inclusivism or other categories.

deeply reluctant to claim the absoluteness of Christianity as the answer "over against" what are often perceived as the "deficiencies" in other faith systems.

At the same time, it retains its own distinctiveness from inclusivism. Its major plea is not so much a Christian plea for synthesis and integration as a plea for tolerance as a moral imperative. Its Christian stance does not stand "above" other religions. It does not condemn; it calls for understanding and common cooperation. As did Arnold Toynbee, it can sometimes speak of interreligious "cooperation" to preserve the spiritual dimensions of the emerging "one world."

The short-lived "Christian Presence" movement of the 1960s may offer us one good sample of this pluralist model. It arose at a time when the world church was wrestling with rapid social change and talking of a "nonreligious interpretation" of the Christian message. The Western colonial world, long misidentified with Christianity, was being rapidly dismantled. Could Christianity make peoples of different cultural backgrounds feel at home in this changing, postcolonial setting? What did the church have to do to prove its integrity?

British Anglicans approached the world of religions, appropriating the terminology of the Catholic "worker-priest" movement of France. Christians were to "be present," to enter empathetically into the world's religious systems by walking in another's religious shoes. The model was exemplified in a series of seven books published from 1959 to 1966, under the general editorship of Max Warren, then general secretary of the Church Missionary Society.

In his introduction to the series, Warren sums up his intended goals.

> Our first task in approaching another people, another culture, another religion, is to take off our shoes, for the place we are approaching is holy. . . . We may forget that God was here before our arrival. We have, then, to ask what is the authentic religious content in the experience of the Muslim, the Hindu, the Buddhist, or whatever he may be. We may, if we have asked humbly and respectfully, still reach the conclusion that our brothers have started from a false premise and reached a faulty conclusion. But we must not arrive at our judgment from outside their religious situation. We have to try to sit where they sit.[23]

Judged in the best light as a kind of preevangelism, the Christian Presence movement affirmed the church's growing uneasiness with the confrontational approach of exclusivism. It reminded the church of its obligation to understand before it criticized, to empathize before it condemned.

---

23. Quoted from Kenneth Cragg, *Sandals at the Mosque* (London: SCM, 1959), 9ff.

At the same time, some wondered when, if ever, empathy would give way to encounter. "Somehow, the question which is fundamental to many Christians, 'What must I do to be saved?' is either not asked, or asked at best indistinctly and obliquely, being replaced by the question, 'How can we together recognize the presence of God?'"[24]

That question becomes more acute in the second sample of the pluralist model toward which the Christian Presence movement pointed—the formal dialogue process promoted by the World Council of Churches (WCC) in the 1970s and 1980s.

Evaluating the dialogue movement of the WCC is not easy. Even within the WCC it has been controversial and has changed its shape.[25] The guidelines drawn up by the WCC's Central Committee in 1971 recognized that dialogue may be held with several goals. It has no single pattern. It may be dialogue for the sake of common action in the service of people in pluralist societies. It may serve to promote better understanding. It may seek to promote more authentic indigenization of the Christian faith in different cultures. It must, however, take place in freedom—each partner in the dialogue is to be understood as they understand themselves.

These early guidelines also acknowledged that no agreement yet existed over the theological implications of dialogue. It affirmed that some in the church were concerned that "the emphasis on dialogue will blunt the cutting edge" of witness to the gospel. And, it noted, there were also those who felt that "the community of human and spiritual discourse created by dialogue will further it."[26] In any case, the guidelines affirmed, "Christians enter into all forms of dialogue from the standpoint of their faith in Jesus Christ and their obligation to witness to him."[27]

In the years that followed, the WCC subunit on dialogue convened a number of formal meetings with persons of other faiths. And in 1979 the Central Committee revised its guidelines. They are still in effect today.

Changes are evident. There is less tentativeness about the value of dialogue. Based on the experiences of the decade, there is more encouragement for "sharing in common enterprises in community."[28]

---

24. Sharpe, *Faith Meets Faith*, 108.
25. Stanley J. Samartha, "The Lordship of Jesus Christ and Religious Pluralism," in *Christ's Lordship and Religious Pluralism*, ed. Gerald H. Anderson and Thomas Stransky (Maryknoll, N.Y.: Orbis, 1981), 30–31.
26. Stanley J. Samartha, ed., *Living Faiths and the Ecumenical Movement* (Geneva: WCC, 1971), 51–52.
27. Ibid., 49.
28. "Guidelines on Dialogue with People of Living Faiths and Ideologies," *Occasional Bulletin of Missionary Research* 3 (1979): 161.

Dialogue through discussion has become "dialogue-in-action" and "partnership in common social, economic and political crises and quests." The idea of learning through self-scrutiny continues to be underlined. "Partners in dialogue should be free to 'define themselves'"; there is to be opportunity for "a mutual questioning of the understanding partners have about themselves and others."[29]

The most significant shift could well be a move to isolate dialogue from witness. And, in support of this interpretation, the WCC decided to detach its subunit on dialogue from the work of the Commission on World Mission and Evangelism. One of the stated intentions behind this shift was apparently to take a middle road between dialogue as a *substitute* for mission and dialogue as a *subterfuge* for mission. But the effect of that intention may well have been to produce a larger gap between dialogue and evangelism. And, given the theological assumptions of Stanley Samartha, the shaper of the dialogue format, our concern may be more than calculated guesswork.[30]

Pluralism, as a model, affirms positive values that evangelicals need to emulate—the importance of listening carefully and sensitively to the religious views of others; the need for recognizing that, in hearing others, we may see our own faults and misunderstandings.

Yet, at the same time, dialogue as a form of pluralism can slip easily into inclusivism. We must ask if there are hidden theological presuppositions at work here. What are the assumptions being made about the saving power or value of other faiths? Does the form of the dialogue implicitly demand that we as Christians have an "objective" or "neutral" approach that may force us to minimize our faith commitment to Christ?

Several caution signs and questions arise in evaluating the WCC approach. What, for example, does the 1977 WCC Consultation on Dialogue in Community in Chiang Mai, Thailand, mean when it speaks of meeting Jesus Christ anew in dialogue? Why is the language missing from the 1979 guidelines coming out of that gathering? What does Samartha mean when he asserts that "there is no reason to claim that the religion developed in the Sinai is superior to that developed on the banks of the Ganga"?[31]

As Christians, we must "expect, look for, and welcome all the signs of the grace of God at work in the lives of those who do not know

29. Ibid.
30. For a careful analysis of the history of dialogue in the WCC, consult Paul G. Schrotenboer, "Inter-Religious Dialogue," *Evangelical Review of Theology* 12 (1988): 208–25.
31. Stanley J. Samartha, *Courage for Dialogue: Ecumenical Issues in Inter-Religious Relationships* (Maryknoll, N.Y.: Orbis, 1982), 99.

Jesus as Lord."[32] And we must be willing to do that in interreligious dialogue with a measure of risk. But the methods we adopt for that encounter cannot put at risk our commitment to Jesus Christ. At that point risk involves the loss of assurance of faith. And that loss is too precious a gift to hazard.

Accommodation

A fourth approach might be called, again modifying Niebuhr's language, that of Christ-above-and-in-religions. With inclusivism, it shares a tone that is more integrational than confrontational. With pluralism, it retains a more Christian tone in its affirmation of Christianity as some sort of ultimate answer. It sees religions as insufficient or inadequate apart from Christ. Yet, at the same time, its Roman Catholic roots also move it closer to the exclusivist side of the spectrum. It teeter-totters between two fundamental poles: the necessity of the church for salvation and God's universal love revealed in the dialectic of nature and grace.

From the fifth century through the Middle Ages, the earliest examples of the accommodation model remained structured by the view that "outside the church there is no salvation." Then came the "age of discovery" that unveiled a new world of religions to the church.

Thomas Aquinas (ca. 1225–74) earlier had used his nature-grace dualism to accommodate theology to Aristotelianism. Jesuit missionaries like Matteo Ricci in China and Roberto de Nobili in India saw the same work of grace "completing" Confucianism and Hinduism. And at the Council of Trent (1545–63) a more optimistic attitude toward the "pagan religions" prevailed. A "baptism of desire" (*in voto*) could admit into the church anyone who lived a moral life but could not receive baptism of water (*in re*).

Knitter sees this shift as highly significant, one from an exclusive to an inclusive understanding of the church as the sole channel of grace. "Catholic belief," he contends, "moved from holding '*outside* the church, no salvation', to '*without* the church, no salvation'. The universal possibility of salvation was clearly recognized."[33] Knitter's judgment may be overdone. He himself admits that very few theologians in the post-Tridentine years ventured to suggest that universally available grace might be accessible through the religions.[34] Could we interpret the change more accurately if we saw this history more as a shift

32. Lesslie Newbigin, *The Gospel in a Pluralist Society* (Grand Rapids: Eerdmans; Geneva: WCC, 1989), 180.
33. Knitter, *No Other Name?* 123.
34. Paul Knitter, "Roman Catholic Approaches to Other Religions: Developments and Tensions," *International Bulletin of Missionary Research* 8 (1984): 50, 53.

of emphasis within the Thomistic poles of nature and grace? Could it be that the inclusivist theme associated with nature now received more underlining than the exclusivist character of grace?

The Second Vatican Council (1962–65) took the accommodation model further. According to Edward Schillebeeckx, at least two "monopolistic claims" of the church over non-Christian religions were abandoned.[35] First, neither the church nor religiousness itself were to be seen as the sole avenue to God: "Whatever truth and grace are to be found among the nations, as a sort of secret presence of God, this activity frees from all taint of evil and restores to Christ its maker."[36]

Second, Christianity was now said to have no monopoly on true religiousness. The Declaration on the Relationship of the Church to Non-Christian Religions (*Nostra Aetate*) affirms that "the Catholic Church rejects nothing which is true and holy in these religions." These systems, "though differing in many particulars" from the church, "nevertheless often reflect a ray of that Truth which enlightens all men."[37]

Interpreting these statements of Vatican II is difficult. Those within the Catholic church like Knitter, Panikkar, and Rahner see them moving to the mutually open inclusivism I have detailed earlier. Others, like Avery Dulles, are more conservative in their judgments.[38] I see a strong spirit of antitriumphalism in the documents, a deep desire that the church display her character as a sacramental mystery even among the world's religions. But I also see a Thomistic spirit still providing the framework for understanding other religions, a framework that has not been basically restructured.

Where will this model go in the future? There is obviously strong pressure from many sources to move the accommodation model closer to inclusivism. And there are enough similarities between the two approaches to encourage this shift. Several ambiguities within the accommodation model may foster such a movement. These ambiguities may be expressed as questions.

Just what is the relation between the church as "the all-embracing means of salvation" and that truth and grace found in the world's religions? This question, it seems to me, is an old accommodationist tension. What heightens it now is the new emphasis coming from Vatican II that speaks of religious systems rather than simply believers in other religions (as in the past).

35. Edward Schillebeeckx, *God, the Future of Man* (New York: Sheed & Ward, 1968), 117ff.

36. Walter M. Abbott, ed., *The Documents of Vatican II* (London: Geoffrey Chapman, 1966), 595–96.

37. Ibid., 662.

38. Avery Dulles, *The Reshaping of Catholicism* (San Francisco: Harper & Row, 1988), 42–46.

What is the relation between the affirmation of salvation through Christ alone, as affirmed again by the Catholic magisterium, and non-Christian world religions? Nowhere does Vatican II state explicitly that other religions are a "means of salvation." At the same time, scholars like Thomas Stransky concede that the Council seems to lean that way.[39] Is this struggle for understanding not part of the conundrum of the accommodation model?

Finally, does the accommodation model of Vatican II open the door to a "nonconversionist" understanding of mission? Vatican II has shifted the issue of salvation in some sense from ecclesial affiliation as the "sign" of salvation to the universal, salvific efficacy of Christ himself in all religions. The church has become "the universal sacrament of salvation." In view of this, what could the significance of conversion as a turning to Christ be? And of evangelism as a call to the outsider to come in? Is the "outsider" really outside?

Looking quickly at the proposals of the Christian world outside the evangelical community has its frustrations. The various theologies of religion leave us with more questions than answers. They do not convince. So we continue to cling to our belief, grounded in Scripture, that only through Jesus Christ can people be saved.

But we dare not stop here. Affirming the finality of Christ does not relieve us of the responsibility to explain the relationship between Christianity and other religions. Sadly, the evangelical world seems almost silent on this crucial issue. Apart from a few exceptions like J. H. Bavinck and his exciting "possessio" model,[40] no extensive, systematic model has appeared in recent years.

So evangelical missions scholars have more homework to do. To come up with a satisfactory theology of religions, we will have to include at least the following questions. In some ways, they summarize the issues left behind in my survey.

1. Should Christianity be drawn in a continuous line with other religions? Or is there discontinuity? Or both? Where does the continuity lie? Does Christianity have anything positive to say about other religions?

39. "In *some* way an individual can be saved not despite but in one's community of faith, because *in some way* these religions incarnate sufficient 'religious beginnings (*incepta religiosa)*' of a supernatural response to the revelation in Christ"; Thomas Stransky, "The Church and Other Religions," *International Bulletin of Missionary Research* 9 (1985): 157.

40. John H. Bavinck, *An Introduction to the Science of Missions,* trans. David H. Freeman (Philadelphia: Presbyterian & Reformed, 1960), 169–90, 221–72; Bavinck, *The Church Between Temple and Mosque* (Grand Rapids: Eerdmans, 1966).

2. What does Christianity share with other religions? How do we understand the nature of the religious experience? Are there general characteristics of all religions that Christianity also shows?
3. What is the biblical relationship between conviction and tolerance? Is there a point where tolerance becomes syncretism? Can one oppose religious systems as unbiblical and still participate with adherents of those religions in common tasks—nation-building, opposition to social evils, participation in humanitarian concerns?
4. What kind of belief in Christ is necessary for salvation? Does a person have to be aware of the work of Christ to be the beneficiary of that work? How far does God go to extend the redemption he offers in Christ?
5. How should Christianity best participate in dialogue? What are the presuppositions of dialogue? Are there different kinds of dialogue? What are the legitimate goals of dialogue?

17

Eternity in Their Hearts?

Tite Tiénou

D on Richardson's *Eternity in Their Hearts* has enjoyed broad success among evangelicals in the last few years.[1] Its success is due, in part, to the author's positive evaluation of non-Christian religions. Richardson claims he has found "startling evidence" that non-Christian religions have great value—something often overlooked by evangelicals.

Eternity in Their Hearts rejects the traditionally negative attitudes evangelicals have had of "pagan" religions. The religious beliefs and practices of other peoples, Richardson argues, are often in reality allies

1. The book was first published in 1981 and a second edition appeared in 1984 (Ventura, Calif.: Regal); references are to this revised edition. There are numerous positive references to the book in evangelical missiological and theological literature: see, for example, Clark H. Pinnock, "The Finality of Jesus Christ in a World of Religions," in *Christian Faith and Practice in the Modern World,* ed. Mark A. Noll and David F. Wells (Grand Rapids: Eerdmans, 1988), 159, 164 n. 17, 319; Evert D. Osburn, "Those Who Have Never Heard: Have They No Hope?" *Journal of the Evangelical Theological Society* 32 (1989): 367–72. Bruce A. Demarest and Richard J. Harpel, "Don Richardson's 'Redemptive Analogies' and the Biblical Idea of Revelation," *Bibliotheca Sacra* 146 (1989): 330–40, offer some perceptive critical insights.

of the gospel of Jesus Christ. Long before the various peoples of the world had heard the gospel, God had prepared their hearts. In other words, general revelation has paved the way for the acceptance of special revelation. The messengers of Christ should therefore rejoice because God has already put eternity in the hearts of those who have not yet heard the name of Christ.

But should we really rejoice because the "heathen" are supposedly waiting to embrace Christ? Or is there reason for concern? How firm is the theological foundation of this missiological euphoria? And what exactly is the nature of this eternity that Richardson claims God has placed in "heathen" hearts? In this chapter we will not concern ourselves with the exotic examples Richardson presents as missiological proofs of his views.[2] Rather, we shall answer these questions by examining his theological argument and showing its deficiencies at several vital points.

General Revelation and Eternity in Their Hearts

The term *revelation* broadly refers to God's self-disclosure. Theologians distinguish between two basic kinds of revelation: general and special. General revelation is God communicating to all peoples; special revelation is God communicating with specific people at specific times.[3] Richardson uses the distinction between general revelation and special revelation as the basis for the thesis of his book. He contends that Melchizedek (the enigmatic king of Salem, Gen. 14:18–20; Heb. 7:1–7) and Abraham (progenitor of the Jews, Gen 12:1–3) are types of divine revelation to humankind. Melchizedek represents general revelation and Abraham stands for special revelation. The former is "a figurehead or type of God's *general* revelation to mankind" and the latter is a type of "God's covenant-based, canon-recorded *special* revelation to mankind" (p. 31). Richardson calls general revelation the "Melchizedek factor," and special revelation the "Abraham factor."

2. A critical evaluation of Richardson's examples of the "beautiful interplay between . . . God's general revelation and . . . God's special revelation" (p. 32) requires a separate study. His "proofs," taken from secondary and tertiary sources, remain unconvincing. They sound too much like the often-told stories from missionary "ideological" literature of "benighted heathen" just waiting for the missionaries to come. I am rather skeptical of such "evidence" and I am not a Caucasophobe!

3. Millard J. Erickson, *Christian Theology* (Grand Rapids: Baker, 1986), 153–54, provides the following definitions: "General revelation is God's communication of himself to all persons at all times and in all places. Special revelation, on the other hand, involves God's particular communications and manifestations of himself to particular persons at particular times, communications and manifestations which are available now only by consultation of certain sacred writings." If one agrees with Erickson, then the Melchizedek story can only belong to the category of special revelation.

Refining his thesis, Richardson claims that general revelation is greater than special revelation because it is older and influences one hundred percent of humanity (p. 31). By implication, special revelation would be "lesser" because it is more recent than general revelation and influences only a small percentage of humanity.

Because general revelation affects one hundred percent of humanity, divine truth is universally available. This so-called Melchizedek factor should cause us to rejoice and embolden us for mission because God has not only "prepared the gospel for all peoples [he] also prepared all peoples for the gospel" (p. 33).[4]

Such then, is the nature of the eternity that God has placed in human hearts. The thesis argued by Richardson contends that God, in disclosing his truth to all peoples, has prepared them to respond positively to the gospel message. Such people will embrace Christ, the giver of eternal life, because eternity has already begun its work in their hearts.[5]

If Richardson's understanding of the relationship between general revelation and special revelation is correct, evangelicals will have to modify significantly a number of their traditional theological and missiological ideas. But, Richardson's novel approach fails to satisfy several important questions, among others, three theological issues and one missiological issue. First, if general revelation is greater than special revelation, why would the latter be necessary? Second, is Melchizedek really a type of general revelation? Third, is special revelation limited to the canon? Fourth, does not Richardson's view lead to universalism, despite his protests to the contrary?

To anticipate my conclusions, I will show how fragile the theological basis is for Richardson's optimistic assessment of the fate of those who have not yet heard the name of Christ. My purpose is to work toward a proper theological grounding of evangelical mission. Unless this is done, our euphoria and triumphalism, born out of theological anemia, will be shortlived.

General Revelation and the Melchizedek Factor

To be sure, Richardson should be commended for his positive attitude toward general revelation and his refusal to denigrate the "heathen." Too often, we evangelicals have failed to appreciate the religious traditions of those who have never heard the name of Christ. General revelation must be taken seriously because it comes from God. Must we

---

4. Pinnock, "Finality of Jesus Christ," accepts Richardson's view.

5. Richardson concedes that general revelation is not always "friendly" to special revelation. He calls the "hostile" element of general revelation the "Sodom factor" (pp. 32–33).

do so, however, because Melchizedek is a type of general revelation, and does this mean that special revelation has only a secondary role?

Richardson builds his Melchizedek–Abraham typology on an arbitrary differentiation between general revelation and special revelation. He sees the two as complementary, yet treats them as if they were two distinct modes of divine revelation. In so doing, he has imposed "speculative categories upon the realities of revelation" and has forgotten that "not even the terms *general* and *special* arise in biblical history to describe God's revelation."[6] Rather, categories such as general and special help us to understand revelation's inner workings, not to establish types for evaluating human religions. Had Richardson maintained the unity of God's revelation, he would not have become imprisoned by his own false dichotomy between general and special revelation. By affirming the unity of revelation we can ascribe real value to general revelation and at the same time exhibit hope and sorrow for those who have only general revelation.

There is hope for them because general revelation provides real and authentic truth about God. There is also sorrow because even with revelation (general and special) human beings suppress God's truth and transform it into idolatry (see Exod. 32:19–24; Rom. 1–2).[7]

A rigid distinction between general and special revelation is not the only theological blunder Richardson makes. He compounds his problem by characterizing Melchizedek as a type of general revelation, when in fact he is not. His confusion arises out of his claim that "special revelation is always associated with an inspired canonical record" (p. 156).[8] As his argument goes, the story of Melchizedek must belong to the category of general revelation because it was not preserved by a written canonical record. Such a proposal is theologically untenable for many reasons.

First, Richardson's argument flatly contradicts his own definition of special revelation. The Melchizedek story is recorded in the canon (Gen. 14:18–20), and so it is part of an "inspired canonical record." Therefore, the enigmatic Melchizedek is a type of special revelation, not general revelation.

Second, and more important, his claim that special revelation must be equated with a canonical record will not stand. Fundamentally, the canon is not a statement on what kind of revelation a document con-

---

6. Carl F. H. Henry, *God, Revelation and Authority,* vol. 2: *God Who Speaks and Shows* (Waco, Tex.: Word, 1976), 71.

7. On this idea, see Carl F. H. Henry, "Is It Fair?" 250–52 in this volume.

8. One wonders how, on that basis, the "canonical records" of other religions would not qualify as special revelation. Richardson does not deal with this question, however. He is more interested in comparing and contrasting Melchizedek and Abraham.

tains but a judgment as to which documents should be considered authoritative. Surely the Bible is a record of God's special revelation, but the Bible does not record all of God's specific ways of making himself known to human beings throughout history. The essential difference between general revelation and special revelation is not canonicity. Rather, as the words indicate, the former is available to all people, whereas the latter comes to specific persons in specific places at specific times. It is thus inaccurate to suggest that if an idea is not in the Bible, it cannot be special revelation.

Surprisingly, Richardson recognizes that both Abraham and Melchizedek "received direct communication from God" (p. 155).[9] If that is not "special," what is?

We could end our inquiry here were it not for the fact that Richardson's thesis leads him to comment on two important contemporary issues of missiology: the value of general revelation (do other religions save?) and the final destiny of the heathen (will God save everyone?). Because these questions are treated elsewhere in this book, I shall discuss these ideas only as they relate to Richardson's views.[10]

Is General Revelation Greater Than Special Revelation?

The writer of Hebrews argues that Melchizedek is greater than Abraham. Richardson latches onto this truth and claims that general revelation is greater than special revelation. He concludes his book with the suggestion that missionaries who represent the Abraham factor (special revelation) should acknowledge the Melchizedek factor (general revelation) "with the tithe of credit it deserves" (p. 156) as they communicate the good news of Christ.

If general revelation is so great and if special revelation is the "junior partner," why should anyone change from the first to the second? If we take Richardson's statements seriously, Christians should be in the business of revitalizing general revelation.[11] Missionaries should then help people find the truth hidden in their religions. Therefore, people like my parents in Africa were fools because they never should have left the

9. See also Demarest and Harpel, "Don Richardson's 'Redemptive Analogies'," 338–39.

10. See Millard J. Erickson, "The State of the Question"; David K. Clark, "Is Special Revelation Necessary for Salvation?"; William V. Crockett, "Will God Save Everyone in the End?"; Harvie M. Conn, "Do Other Religions Save?"—all in this volume.

11. Richardson's evangelical commitment prevents him from drawing Richard H. Drummond's conclusion: "The role of the Christian world mission is also to inspire, to stimulate . . . persons to reform and renew not only their own lives but also their own religious traditions"; Drummond, *Toward a New Age in Christian Theology* (Maryknoll, N.Y.: Orbis, 1985), 200. It should be noted, however, that such rejection of pluralism is emotional or sociological, not theological.

old ways—they should have instructed their children about the greatness of their ancestral religion! No appeal to the so-called Sodom factor will solve this problem. It is one thing to see similarities between Christianity and other religions; it is another to get people to agree on what specific elements of a non-Christian religion are from general revelation and which are human perversions. What looks like Sodom to one person seems like Melchizedek to another.

Again, we need not go to such extremes to recognize the value of all of God's revelation. Ultimately the question is not, What kind of revelation do you have? but Do you know God and do you follow him in humble service? God has made himself known in various ways (Heb. 1:1–4) but Jesus Christ, the Son, explains God to us best (John 1:18). While both general revelation and special revelation "speak" of Christ, the latter is much clearer. General revelation is like someone telling a lost traveler, "If you take this road you eventually will get to your destination." Special revelation, on the other hand, is like someone handing a clearly marked map to a lost traveler with the words, "If you follow this map you will get right to where you want to go." I do not know many travelers who would choose the aggravation involved in following the first recommendation. Most would breathe a sigh of relief when given clear directions. Special revelation has the same liberating effect on weary, searching, sin-sick human beings. The problem is that most lost travelers are so caught up in their attempts to find a way home (ancestral religion) that they would rather continue their search than accept clear directions (Christianity).[12]

Does General Revelation Save?

Richardson may have realized that his argument has another conclusion: those without the gospel may be saved through general revelation. He cites the example of the Mbaka of the Central African Republic whose religion made the transfer from ancestral religion to Christianity easy. Lest someone conclude that Mbaka religion alone could have saved them, Richardson tempers his praise for the old religion. He solves his problem by claiming that Mbaka religion is redemptive, not redeeming (p. 59). That is, the general revelation hidden in the people's religion made it easier for them to accept redemption but it does not make it possible for them to be redeemed.

The distinction between redemptive and redeeming is a major problem. Normally, the terms are synonymous in English, and we might ask if such a distinction really is helpful. Richardson defines redemp-

12. Such an observation casts doubt on Richardson's optimistic outlook for missionary activity.

tive as "contributing to the redemption of a people, but not culminating it" (p. 59).[13] This two-tiered approach to redemption points to an unresolved fundamental problem: Can people really know God solely on the basis of general revelation? While we disagree on this question, most evangelicals are emotionally reluctant to answer this question with a clear affirmative.[14] Emotion, however, will not be an adequate reason for a person considering unitive pluralism or other forms of universalism. One needs theological reasons. Commendably, Richardson's distinction means he is unwilling to go so far.[15] Yet, there is no theological reason why someone cannot use Richardson's approach to claim that non-Christian religions do redeem. If we leave such a door open, someone will inevitably walk through. Richardson's book provides no clear reason why we should not continue down the road toward universalism.

If the question is, does general revelation save? the answer is no. Revelation does not save, Jesus Christ does! Yet Scripture never rules out the possibility that some might come to a saving knowledge of God through general revelation. God has chosen not to give us an easy test for determining people's salvation based on what kind of revelation they have. Consequently, no attempt to simplify the complex picture painted by Scripture is adequate. Let us therefore be content with the sobriety of Scripture.

Richardson's *Eternity in Their Hearts* is an example of the theological anemia currently plaguing evangelical missiology. In his attempt to generate excitement about the church's missionary outreach, he (and other missiologists) neglects to grapple with significant theological issues. Instead of Richardson's tidy picture of those waiting to hear the gospel, we must maintain two theological truths in tension. On the one hand, God has made it possible to hear his voice through any culture: we need not destroy other cultures in order to build Christianity. On the other hand, only few people will choose to travel on "the narrow path to life." We must resist the over-optimism of those who say multitudes will follow Christ because they are just waiting for us to tell them to do so. On the contrary, countless people throughout the world are rejecting the gospel message in spite of eternity in their hearts.

---

13. One finds a similar embarrassed attempt to take general revelation seriously, while blunting its effectiveness, in Demarest and Harpel, "Don Richardson's 'Redemptive Analogies,'" 336, who propose that "general revelation does serve a salutary purpose."

14. As well, where does one draw the line between "facilitating" and "culminating"? Richardson, again, is unclear.

15. Richardson (p. 59) merely claims that we all know a person cannot be saved apart from the gospel; but if non-Christian religions have so much value, some people may not be so certain about this claim.

18

Is Hell a Proper Motivation for Missions?

John D. Ellenberger

In 1953, on Norwegian radio, Ole Hallesby startled his listeners: "I am certainly speaking tonight to many people who know they are unrepentant. . . . if you were to fall to the ground dead, you would fall directly into hell." Almost immediately church leaders assailed Hallesby's method of evangelism. "The doctrine of eternal punishment," said Norwegian Bishop Schjelderup, "has no part in the religion of love."[1]

But the doctrine of love must confront "biblical realism" and "the painful reality of hell," as missiologist Peter Wagner puts it.[2] If large numbers of people stand in danger of "judgment and doom" then hell might reasonably be seen as a proper motivation for evangelism.[3]

In this chapter, I will argue that hell was a major motivating factor

---

1. Friedrich Schauer, ed., *Was ist es um die Hölle? Dokumente aus dem norwegischen Kirchenstreit* (Stuttgart: Evangelisches Verlag, 1956), 23, 25–26, quoted in Hans Küng, *Eternal Life?* trans. Edward Quinn (Garden City, N.Y.: Doubleday, 1984), 130.

2. Peter Wagner, *On the Crest of the Wave* (Ventura, Calif.: Regal, 1983), 45.

3. Arnold Cook, "The Missing Motivation," *Alliance Life* 124/22 (8 Nov. 1989): 6–7.

in Jesus' own ministry. But we should not think that Jesus' ministry was primarily driven by a fear of eternal torment for those who rejected his message. Rather, hell was only one part of the human predicament the Bible calls "lostness." Jesus was motivated by a deep compassion for real people mired in a condition they needed to be delivered from.[4] If this is true, then the idea of lostness is significant to his followers—even in our modern world—for Jesus taught at least twice that the model for his disciples' ministry must come from his own (John 17:18; 20:21).

The Motivation of Jesus

When Jesus inaugurated his ministry, he declared that God had sent him "to preach good news to the poor. He has sent me to proclaim freedom for the prisoners . . ., to proclaim the year of the Lord's favor" (Luke 4:18).[5] Jesus chose these kingdom themes to show that God had not forgotten the down-trodden, but cared about human poverty, broken-heartedness, captivity, and lostness. Further, John the evangelist assures us that God's motivation was his love for the entire world. He desired not to send judgment, but to give life, and with it the possibility of escaping death (John 3:16–17).

This same motivation surfaces in six of the "I-have-come-to" statements of Jesus, where he ties his coming to the needs of the human condition.

1. "I have . . . come to call . . . sinners" (Matt. 9:13)
2. "The Son of Man did not come to be served, but to serve, and to give his life as a ransom for many" (Mark 10:45)
3. "The Son of Man came to seek and to save what was lost" (Luke 19:10, compare John 12:47)
4. "I have come that they [the sheep] may have life" (John 10:10—a reference to saving the sheep while they are outside in danger of death and destruction)

4. When Jesus evangelizes, the motivation of lover is clearly paramount. We should note that he reserves his threats of judgment for those who should know better, but do not (e.g., Matt. 10:15, "It will be more bearable for Sodom and Gomorrah . . .").

5. The kingdom theme that Jesus chose reflects several unfolding Old Testament motifs. Among them are (1) God as sovereign ruler over all the nations, (2) the covenant relationship of love and obedience between Yahweh and his people, (3) the hope of the coming of a great new age when God would finally triumph over sin and death. That expectation looked to (a) the coming of an anointed servant (Isa. 42:1–4), (b) God himself establishing his throne in Jerusalem (Isa. 66:1–2, 15–21), and (c) the streaming of the Gentiles to the mountain of the Lord (Mic. 4:1; Zeph. 3:9). For further discussion of kingdom themes, see Donald Senior and Carroll Stuhlmueller, *The Biblical Foundations for Mission* (Maryknoll, N.Y.: Orbis, 1983), 144–45.

5. "I have come into the world as a light, so that no one who believes in me should stay in darkness" (John 12:46)
6. "I have come into this world, so that the blind will see" (John 9:39)

These graphic descriptions of humanity's plight are different images of the same condition: lostness. What motivated God to send Jesus was the love of the Father for lost people of the whole world.

God's love for lost people compelled him to provide a comprehensive solution to the human predicament. Salvation involves far more than an escape from hell. When salvation came to Zacchaeus's house (Luke 19:9), it involved "an effective and practical revolution in his life, inwardly and outwardly,"[6] and incorporation into the family of God. Lostness and salvation, then, have broader implications for the hearer than a mere release from eternal punishment.

Nonetheless, people can reject God's gracious offer—and many do. Jesus never denied an individual's freedom to choose—and to suffer the consequence of judgment (as in Matt. 19:22). The Christian finds no pleasure when a person rejects Christ, and many would gladly eliminate the doctrine of judgment were it not so clearly taught in the New Testament.[7]

The Motivation of the Disciples

No one can deny the dramatic effect of the early church's preaching or its rapid growth. Surely the disciples were highly motivated. But by what? The Great Commission? The warning of eternal punishment? Or a convergence of other factors?

One approach is to interpret the data through the eyes of Jesus' kingdom message and its effect on the early disciples. Jesus' earliest preaching stressed the expectation of the soon-coming kingdom and the need to enter that kingdom through repentance and acceptance of Jesus' good news (Mark 1:15). So later, as the disciples preached, the person of Jesus became the crucial element in that good news. More than anything else, it was his death and resurrection, accompanied as it was by awesome signs in nature (Matt. 27–28), that vindicated Jesus. When Peter preached, he emphasized that the disciples were witnesses of Jesus' resurrection and ascension, and, thus, they were obliged to tell the good news: "God has made this Jesus, whom you crucified, both Lord and Christ" (Acts 2:23–36).

6. Norval Geldenhuys, *Commentary on the Gospel of Luke*, New International Commentary on the New Testament (Grand Rapids: Eerdmans, 1956), 471.
7. C. S. Lewis, *The Problem of Pain* (London: Geoffrey Bles, 1940), 106.

Joachim Jeremias suggests a further reason for the compulsion to preach the gospel. The disciples, he says, believed that the death and resurrection of Christ was the dawn of salvation—the expected age in which God himself would gather the nations to Zion. This ingathering had to wait until *after* Jesus' ministry to the House of Israel was completed, and after his death and resurrection (Acts 15:16–18, quoting Amos 9:11).[8] But one question remains unanswered. If God alone gathers the nations, then why did the early church feel so responsible to go to the Gentiles?

The solution lies in the disciples' understanding of *their own role* in bringing in the Gentiles.[9] The disciples now became convinced that preaching the significance of Jesus would bring the Gentile nations into the kingdom, the prophesied final act before the consummation! In witnessing to the Gentiles, they could become "a part of the final fulfillment. . . . co-operating with God in his gracious anticipation of the decisive hour of redemption . . . the Gentiles accepted as guests at God's Table."[10]

So we conclude that the early church was motivated by two bedrock convictions. First, they were convinced that Jesus was the only answer to humanity's lostness, that there was no other name by which people could be saved (Acts 4:12). Second, they believed Jesus was the promised Messiah (Acts 2:36) and that the end of the age was near. Because the end was upon them, they needed to make disciples of all peoples. This they saw as cooperating with God to accomplish the final act needed to bring back the king and usher in the promised day of the Lord (2 Pet. 3:10–12). The point is that these motivations accepted Jesus' concept of "lostness," yet focused on the hope of redemption.

The Motivation of Paul

Each of Luke's summaries of three of Paul's sermons in Acts 13:26–41, 14:15–17, and 17:22–31 contain similar constant ideas. First, God is Creator, Provider, and Lord of the whole earth. Second, God demands that the nations turn from idols and accept the lordship of the God-appointed Jesus. Third, God has provided proof of Jesus' lordship by raising him from the dead. Fourth, those who resist his offer will endure future judgment.[11] Paul raises the specter of judgment

8. Joachim Jeremias, *Jesus' Promise to the Nations* (Naperville, Ill.: Allenson, 1958), 70–73.

9. Senior and Stuhlmueller, *Biblical Foundations for Mission,* 156–57.

10. Jeremias, *Jesus' Promise to the Nations,* 75.

11. Michael Green, *Evangelism in the Early Church* (Grand Rapids: Eerdmans, 1970), 125–29.

because it is a reality, but his primary focus is on Christ's demand of lordship. As an evangelist, Paul is seeking a change—a first-time change of allegiance to Christ. While the apostle's message is contextualized for his audience, it stands in continuity with the preaching of Jesus and the early disciples. Paul agrees that humanity is lost and needs to respond to the good news.[12]

More significant for understanding Paul, of course, are his letters, which tell us much about what motivated him to ministry. A wide array of factors stirred Paul to invest his life in world evangelism:

1. A sense of obligation to God
   a. A trust committed to him (1 Cor. 9:16–17)
   b. Obedience to the divine commission (Rom. 1:1, 5)
   c. Fear of disappointing his beloved master (2 Cor. 5:11)[13]
   d. Speaking in God's stead (2 Cor. 5:20)
   e. Reward for labor (1 Cor. 3:8–9)
2. A desire to increase God's glory (2 Cor. 4:13–15)
3. The rule of God's love in his life (2 Cor. 5:14–20)
4. A sense of obligation to people (Rom. 1:14–15)
5. A sense of urgency because of the shortness of time (1 Cor. 7:29–30)

The third motivation listed above, the rule of God's love, must be considered primary. The two motivations preceding it are an expression of gratitude for Christ's love. The two following it express love in dedicated service. Paul saw himself as a minister of reconciliation, an ambassador, and a mouthpiece of God (2 Cor. 5:18–20). Thus, for Paul, the rule of God's love was the paradigm by which all motivation was judged.

Do Exceptions to Lostness Hinder Missionary Effort?

A critical issue in motivation arises when we consider the fate of those who have yet to hear the good news. What of that one-third of the world who have never heard the gospel in any form, and another third who have never heard the claims of Christ in a personal way that makes commitment possible?[14] So we ask: (1) Does everybody receive the same degree of punishment? (2) Are there exceptions to lostness? (3) If so, do they cut the "nerve cord" of missionary motivation?

The question whether there are exceptions comes when we ask if

---

12. Paul's speeches in Acts, especially Acts 17:22–31, are discussed in greater detail in Darrell L. Bock, "Athenians Who Have Never Heard," in this volume.

13. Green, *Evangelism in the Early Church*, 245.

14. Warren Webster, "Where'er the Sun," *Onward* (1988): 8.

Jesus' teaching on punishment is just. For example, his parable of the unfaithful servants shows that the severity of judgment depends on the level of revelation the servant had (Luke 12:47–48).[15] "Beaten with many blows" for those who reject God's gracious plan in Jesus, while distressing, is believable. But is it just for the disobedient servant who does not know the master's will—or, who has never even heard his name—to receive even the "few blows" mentioned in the parable? For many, this is one of the most difficult features of the Christian faith.

Paul's message to the spiritually illiterate people of Lystra implies that all cultures have access to the general revelation of God in nature, which shows his kindness, provision, faithfulness, power and goodness (Acts 14:16–17). Creation gives a glimpse of his power and divine nature, and all people will be held accountable for it (Rom. 1:20). So the few blows result because "they disregarded the admonitions of conscience"[16] or as Wayne Dye expresses it:

> Even an unbeliever's inner awareness of what is right for him may be more demanding than he admits . . . and God will use this standard to judge him (Rom. 2:1–8). This explains the words of Jesus: "God will apply to you the same rules you apply to others" (Matt. 7:12). Why? Because you are aware that it is wrong or you wouldn't use it as a standard for others.[17]

Many evangelicals conclude that general revelation serves only to condemn those who never heard: they are without excuse.[18]

If we take this theological idea seriously, then we reach an unfortunate conclusion. Even though some truly seek after God, they, and a preponderance of the world's population, will never see the light of heaven. Many evangelicals question this deduction, and have proposed a range of solutions, some more probable than others. In order to reduce "the problem of percentages,"[19] Norman Geisler proposes a unique solution. He thinks that high infant-mortality rates in the overwhelmingly non-Christian third world have a salvific design: "He takes his elect from those who are under the age of accountability in countries where if they had grown up they wouldn't have heard the gospel and they would have wanted to hear [it]." In other words, he

---

15. Eugene Nida, *Customs and Cultures* (New York: Harper, 1954), 50.

16. Geldenhuys, *Gospel of Luke,* 364.

17. Wayne Dye, "Towards a Cross-cultural Definition of Sin," *Missiology* 4 (Jan. 1976): 32.

18. See Geoffrey Bromiley, "Natural Revelation," in *Baker's Dictionary of Theology,* ed. Everett F. Harrison (Grand Rapids: Baker, 1960), 456.

19. Don Richardson's term used in an unpublished paper: "Hell: Modern Evangelicalism's Closet Doctrine," 1.

takes his elect by taking babies.[20] This is abhorrent. It is inconsistent with the meaning of God's victorious "gathering of the nations" and, more significantly, it undermines the missionary effort to win "as many as possible" (1 Cor. 9:19–23).

A more promising avenue is to ask if natural revelation has a larger role than we have traditionally recognized. The history of Christian expansion is replete with stories of individuals in their pre-Christian states who nonetheless sought after God with a clearer vision of the light than their contemporaries had. For example, there was the Chinese youth in Jakarta, Indonesia, who refused to dust the household idols "because they don't care whether they get dusted or not, and probably they don't hear us when we pray to them either."[21] Another was the Dayak leader in Kalimantan, also in Indonesia, who realized that his charms and fetishes were creations of his own hands, and resolved to worship instead the deity that created his hands.[22] In another part of the world, a Lobi man from Burkina Faso, West Africa, claimed God had told him to put away his fetishes and wait for a messenger who would come to tell him the true way.[23] In Laos, southeast Asia, a Hmong female shaman prophesied about the coming of a messenger who would tell them of the true God.[24]

Some of these perceptive people saw God as Creator and Deity, others did not. But in each case they identified Jesus as the fulfilment of their searching when they heard the gospel message. It took the Chinese youth years of exposure to Christian faith before he fully believed. The missionary who came to the Dayak leader's village spoke of "the God that made you, who made your hands," upon which the seeker recognized that this was the goal of his search. The Lobi African waited ten years, suffering ostracism and persecution, before the gospel came to his village, where he was the first to accept. The Hmong shaman identified the gospel message as the fulfilment of her prophesy, and influenced a "people movement" to Christ which was effective largely because of her considerable prestige.

20. Norman Geisler, "All You Wanted to Know about Hell and Were Afraid to Ask," Pippert Lectures (Alliance Theological Seminary, Nyack, N.Y., 1982).

21. Personal interview by the author with Eddy Susanto, Jayapura, Indonesia, December 1975.

22. Personal interview by the author with Ruth Rudes, missionary of the Christian and Missionary Alliance to Indonesia, August 1990. The event took place in the Apo Kayan area of East Kalimantan, Indonesia.

23. Robert S. Roseberry, *The Niger Vision* (Harrisburg, Pa.: Christian Publications, 1934), 117.

24. G. Linwood Barney, "The Meo—An Incipient Church," in *Readings in Missionary Anthropology,* ed. William A. Smalley, 2d ed. (South Pasadena, Calif.: William Carey Library, 1978), 469.

These incidents suggest that anyone who seeks wholeheartedly will certainly find God (Deut. 4:29). But we must not forget that there were other seekers—we will never know how many—who did not find the true God: the gospel message did not come to them in time! Deen, a leader from Irian Jaya, Indonesia, when he heard the gospel message, led a people movement of his kin-group to follow Christ. This was partly because of the earlier influence of his stepfather, Mugumende, who had been a spiritual seeker, but died without hearing of Christ.[25] "If Mugumende had been here when the gospel came to our valley," his stepson told me, "he would have been the first Christian (instead of me)."

Consequently, we might ask: How will God decide the eternal fate of people like Mugumende? Do we know how much special revelation is necessary for salvation? And how does that inquiry affect missionary motivation?[26]

Some see an unconscious universalist loophole in Matthew's heavy emphasis on *doing* righteousness, but this is unwarranted.[27] The whole tenor of Scripture is contrary to the idea that one who is religious and lives a moral life can earn salvation. Another possibility sees a correlation between unevangelized seekers and Old Testament believers whose salvation came before the advent of Christ.[28] With only limited knowledge, by their belief in God and his holy standard, and by casting themselves upon his mercy for their sin, they were given forgiveness identical to ours. Anderson observes:

25. Alice Gibbons, *The People Time Forgot* (Chicago: Moody, 1981), 212–17.

26. These issues are discussed in this volume by David K. Clark, "Is Special Revelation Necessary for Salvation?" and by William V. Crockett and James G. Sigountos, "Are the 'Heathen' Really Lost?"

27. Senior and Stuhlmueller, *Biblical Foundations for Mission,* 248–49. Senior's proposal that Matthew's emphasis on obedience threatens "to move beyond the bounds of Christian Confession" and "seems to open up the arena of salvation to the world with all humanity judged on the basis of action" is unwarranted. To be sure, the confessional element in Matt. 7:21 takes second place, but this is merely a matter of emphasis, as the following verses, 24–27, indicate. "Building your house" on Jesus' words is another way of saying "to follow Jesus," which involves *both* belief and obedience. So too with Matt. 25:31–46. To suggest that "this represents an opening in the New Testament tradition for assessing the validity of religious traditions and human life outside a Christian context" is to build a doctrine antithetical to the intent of the evangelist. This Senior acknowledges when he admits that "the evangelist remains in a thoroughly confessional framework."

28. This correlation between Old Testament saints and modern preevangelism seekers has followers as far back as Zwingli and, more recently, G. Campbell Morgan. See James N. D. Anderson, *Christianity and Comparative Religion* (Downers Grove, Ill.: Inter-Varsity, 1970), 97–107. More recently, this approach has been espoused by Art Glasser in *Biblical Perspectives on Mission/Biblical Theology of Mission* (Pasadena, Calif.: Fuller Theological Seminary, 1982), 205–7.

Is not this perhaps, the meaning of St. Peter's words in the house of Cornelius: "I now see how true it is that God has no favourites, but that in every nation the man who is god-fearing and does what is right is acceptable to him." . . . does it not mean that the man who realizes something of his sin or need, and throws himself on the mercy of God with a sincerity which shows itself in his life . . . would find that mercy—although without understanding it—at the cross on which "Christ died for all"?[29]

Some say that unevangelized seekers are not the same as Old Testament believers because seekers lived after Christ had come. Millard J. Erickson, however, is not convinced by this kind of argument. He observes that a timeless God "does not necessarily view events sequentially."[30] Wideness of application of this principle varies greatly, from Charles Kraft who feels many have entered the kingdom this way to Erickson who suspects "very few, if any, actually come to such a saving knowledge of God on the basis of natural revelation alone."[31] How wide the application *really* is will be known when the book of life is opened (Rev. 20:12, 15).

Thus, salvation is only through the crucified Christ, and true seekers—those who have experienced conviction, leading, or instruction from the Holy Spirit—will recognize and respond when they encounter the good news. For seekers who never hear, Old Testament believers may be a model God will use to relate them to Christ's saving death. For Mugumende and others like him, perhaps F. F. Bruce has the best insight: "King David knew how fearful a thing it was; but when it came to the crunch, he made the right choice: 'Let us fall into the hand of the Lord, for His mercy is great.'"[32]

Many have feared that if God saved seekers who have never heard the name of Jesus, the "nerve cord" of missions would be cut. In reality, admitting that God is working above and beyond the work of missionaries and pastors enhances our motivation to evangelize the lost in the following ways.

First, it provides a fresh impetus for evangelism. The knowledge that the Holy Spirit has been working in the hearts of people prior to hearing the good news should encourage us. Far from undercutting

29. Anderson, *Christianity and Comparative Religion,* 102.

30. Millard Erickson, "Hope for Those Who Haven't Heard? Yes, But . . .," *Evangelical Missions Quarterly* 11 (1975): 125.

31. Charles Kraft, *Christianity in Culture: A Study in Dynamic Biblical Theologizing in Cross-Cultural Perspective* (Maryknoll, N.Y.: Orbis, 1979), 254; Erickson, "Hope for Those Who Haven't Heard?" 126.

32. F. F. Bruce, writing in the foreword to Edward W. Fudge, *The Fire That Consumes* (Houston: Providential, 1982), viii.

missionary endeavor, it is a dynamic compulsion for world evangelization. So it was with Paul. "I have many people in this city," the risen Lord told him as he encouraged the apostle to be brave in evangelizing Corinth. Paul responded by a longer commitment to that city than any other outside of Syrian Antioch.

Second, it renews our commitment to reach every individual. Because the great majority have not responded to general revelation, they need to be confronted by the claims of Jesus. Believing faith, sparked by the preaching of the sent ones, is the normal pattern (Rom. 10:14–15).

Third, it broadens our understanding of the whole gospel. The good news is not just cognitive information about Jesus, nor is it limited to an escape from eternal punishment. Salvation is much more. It involves being part of the people of God, participating in a covenantal relationship, and working for the *shalom* of the kingdom in all of society. All people everywhere deserve a clearly understood invitation to the fullness of salvation. This is different from the limited message of general revelation or the restricted outlook of fire-insurance religion.

Last, it reaffirms love as the primary motivation. Paul made himself "a slave to everyone, to win as many as possible" (1 Cor. 9:19). He himself was willing to be damned if that meant salvation for others (Rom. 9:1–3). He was a missionary motivated by love, and that love witnessed at every opportunity, endured suffering, and warned about judgment. It was the only response possible when he had been loved so much (2 Cor. 5:14–15).

So the biblical witness, supported by missionary experience, suggests that God works in the hearts of seekers who abandon their pagan religion for the "true light, that gives light to every man" (John 1:9). In view of this, we should labor to bring these seekers fully into the sheepfold of the church and to evangelize others who have not yet responded.

What of Today's Motivation?

The zeal to reach that "last person" from some hidden, unevangelized community is more alive today than ever before. This is evident in the "Unreached Peoples" movement and the drive to evangelize the world by the year 2000. But we must have more than emotion if we are to reach the whole world. Our motivation must flow from a clear understanding of the biblical mandate for world evangelism.

The message for today is the same as the invitation Jesus gave: "The kingdom of God is near. Repent and believe the good news" (Mark 1:15). The good news of the kingdom is that Jesus, and Jesus alone, has come to redeem the lost. People can find salvation only in Jesus, not in Buddhism or any other religion. We who have experienced salvation are now Christ's mouthpiece as he reconciles the world to himself. We go encouraged by the fact that God has gone before us. In addition, the kingdom's presence means that salvation has many dimensions, not simply forgiveness for sins. A renewed awareness of the kingdom dimension of Jesus' teaching has broadened our understanding of the gospel.

The motivation that should stir us today must stem from the same primary impulses that moved the early church. They knew that, as the Father had sent Jesus, so now Jesus had commissioned them to preach to a dying world. They saw their master weeping for the lost and they were driven by the same compassion for those who needed to hear. To them, the task was urgent. The disciples were eager to participate with God in world evangelism—the last great chapter before the coming of Christ (2 Pet. 3:11–12).

But not all Christians are so moved. Signs of danger are all around us. Some have grave doubts about lostness, about calling people of other religions to repent and believe, about conversion. Others have merely lost that pervasive expectancy of the kingdom's nearness and a sense of personal responsibility for the world. In many sectors of the church the horror of lostness is no longer there. The burden for evangelism has fallen prey to a creeping conformity to the majority culture around us.[33]

The people of God must fight these distressing drifts like hell itself, because they deny the very nature of the church. Any church that loses its desire to bring all nations into the kingdom, as Johannes Verkuyl says, "is no longer a church; it has become an exclusive club."[34] The church must recapture its all-consuming passion to gather all nations under Christ's lordship and bring him back as King.

33. See Bryan R. Wilson, "An Analysis of Sect Development," in *The Social Meanings of Religion,* ed. William M. Newman (Chicago: Rand McNally, 1974), 250–70. See also Dean Kelly, *Why Conservative Churches Are Growing* (New York: Harper & Row, 1972), esp. chap. 5, "Traits of a 'Strong' Religion."

34. Johannes Verkuyl, *Contemporary Missiology: An Introduction,* trans. Dale Cooper (Grand Rapids: Eerdmans, 1978), 167.

19

Did Early Christians Believe Pagan Religions Could Save?

James G. Sigountos

The previous chapters have demonstrated that there is little biblical evidence for unitive pluralism and other universalistic views. Rather, the Bible overwhelmingly affirms that those who reject Jesus Christ by adhering to other religions are lost.

But a different kind of argument has been raised to show that people can be saved through other religions. Some writers have reexamined the history of the early church and have concluded that many early Christians were far more "open-minded" toward pagan religion than has been thought. It was only at a later date, they argue, that Christians agreed that only Christianity could save people.[1] There is some truth in their analysis, but it has been grossly overstated. Even the most open-minded Christians in those early days never claimed that non-Christian religions were an alternative route to God.

---

1. Paul F. Knitter, *No Other Name? A Critical Survey of Christian Attitudes toward the World Religions* (Maryknoll, N.Y.: Orbis, 1985), 121–23; Richard H. Drummond, *Toward a New Age in Christian Theology* (Maryknoll, N.Y.: Orbis, 1985), esp. chap. 4, where Augustine (354–430) and Fulgentius (468–533) are the villains who introduce "barbarism" (his term, pp. 41–42) to the church.

Were Ancient Writers Aware of the Problem?

Before we examine ancient writers, we ought to ask whether they would have even understood the issue addressed in this book. In other words, did they face the question of those who had never heard the gospel? We know that they did understand the basic issues, if for no other reason than that pagan authors attacked Christians on this very point. Pagans knew that Christians claimed that God worked only through his chosen people Israel, and thereafter exclusively through Jesus. The fourth-century Roman emperor Julian ridicules Christians because of their claim to exclusivity. He wonders how they can claim Christianity as the only true religion for all humanity, when Christianity's God sent revelation only to a small, insignificant group:

> But that from the beginning God cared for the Jews only and that he chose them out as his portion, was not only stated clearly by Moses and Jesus, but also by Paul . . . [Yet, Paul also] says: "He is not only the God of Jews, but also of the Gentiles. . . ." So then, it is fair to ask Paul why God . . . lavished upon the Jews the prophetic gift, Moses, anointing oil, the prophets, and the law. . . . And finally, also gave them Jesus. But he gave us no prophet, no anointing oil, no teacher, no herald of his coming love for humanity (even though it would arrive late). But he even overlooked us for myriads of years . . . while men in such ignorance served idols, as you call them. . . . For if he is the God of all of us and likewise the creator of all, why did he overlook us?[2]

Early Christian theologians responded to these criticisms in treatises (called apologies). These works reveal that Christians were well aware of pagan religion, and, from the stridency of their condemnations, thought it a serious threat to their own beliefs. So it is fair to appeal to these ancient writers because they were dealing with some of the same kinds of issues we deal with today.

Modern pluralists who attack evangelicals for seeking converts from other religions often claim early Christians as their forerunners. These Christians, they say, had a positive attitude toward pagan religion, an attitude we should emulate and take even further today.

In this chapter I will examine three major challenges posed by the

---

2. Julian, *Against the Galileans* 106A–E. A similar sentiment was expressed by Celsus (Origen, *Against Celsus* 6.78).

Ancient texts are cited from standard editions. For Clement, I have followed Claude Mondésert, and André Plassart, *Clément d'Alexandrie: Le Protreptique*, 3d ed., Sources Chrétiennes 2 (Paris: Cerf, 1976); for Eusebius, *Die Praeparatio Evangelica*, ed. Karl Mras, Die griechischen christlichen Schriftsteller der ersten Jahrhunderte, 2 vols. (Berlin: Akademie-Verlag, 1954–56); for Justin, Edgar J. Goodspeed, *Die ältesten Apologeten* (Göttingen: Vandenhoeck & Ruprecht, 1914). All unidentified translations are my own.

pluralist position. First, pluralists argue, early Christian attacks on pagan religion[3] do not mean that pagan religions are entirely evil. Second, they say early Christians had great respect for classical learning and, therefore, Christians were not exclusivists. Third, the *spermatikos logos*, or universal reason, was supposed to be in every person's heart, and therefore all would have an adequate knowledge of God without Christianity. We will see that, at best, all three of these pluralist claims are exaggerated.

Early Christian Attitudes toward Ancient Religion

Early Christian writers were unremittingly negative in their attacks on pagan religious practices.[4] Some, like Clement of Alexandria (ca. 150–ca. 215), show an embarrassing eagerness to dwell on the most gruesome or titillating details of non-Christian religious myths and ceremonies. Clement describes Zeus as a lecherous man who lusts after any woman he sees and fulfills his desire in every case (*Exhortation* 32.4). None of the other gods or goddesses are any better, "So it is fitting that such gods as yours should be [depicted in your literature as] slaves, since they have become slaves to their passions" (*Exhortation* 35.1). It is no surprise to Clement that devotees of licentious gods would shamelessly hang pornographic pictures and sculptures in their houses (*Exhortation* 60.1). The relationship between worshiper and object of worship is also reciprocal: "Indeed, you believe in idols because you eagerly desire their debauchery; you deny God because you cannot endure self-control" (*Exhortation* 61.4). For Clement, these religions are the product of malevolent demons—who even enjoy human sacrifice (*Exhortation* 42.1)!

If such ridicule were merely an ad hoc collection of propaganda stories, we might argue that Christians were more charitable toward other religions than Clement's abuse indicates. The spectacular examples, however, reflect a deeper and more philosophical rejection of all existing non-Christian religions, one that Christians took over from their past.

Scholars agree that the earliest Christians, who were Jews, inherited the attitude of Second Temple Judaism toward ancient religions.[5] For

---

3. A distinction must be made between ancient religion and ancient philosophy, for, while the line between religion and philosophy was blurred in antiquity, it was never obliterated. More important, ancient writers differentiated between religion and philosophy, and modern patristics scholars have followed their example. See, e.g., Richard P. C. Hanson, "The Christian Attitude to Pagan Religions," in *Studies in Christian Antiquity* (Edinburgh: T. & T. Clark, 1985), 144.

4. Admitted, e.g., by Drummond, *New Age in Christian Theology*, 27.

5. Hanson, "Christian Attitude to Pagan Religions," 144–45; Robert M. Grant, *Gods and the One God*, Library of Early Christianity 1 (Philadelphia: Westminster, 1986), 46.

Jews, all pagan religions were simply idolatry. Idolatry, they argued, had disastrous consequences—consequences that explain why Justin Martyr (ca. 100–165), Clement, and other patristic writers focus on the most scandalous examples of Hellenistic religion.

The author of the Wisdom of Solomon was a Hellenized Jew of the Dispersion, possibly in Alexandria, writing in the last century before Christ.[6] His attitude toward idolatry can be seen in the following quotation:

> For whether they [idolaters] are child-killers as mystery initiates, or secret celebrants of mysteries, or holders of frenzied revels with strange customs, they no longer keep lives or marriages pure, but each treacherously kills the other, or grieves each other by adultery. Everything around them is bedlam: blood and murder, theft and treachery, corruption, faithlessness, tumult, perjury, confusion about what is good, forgetting favors done, pollution of souls, homosexuality, disorder in marriages, adultery, and debauchery. For the religion [*thrēskeia*; compare James 1] of unnamed idols is the origin [*archē*] of every evil and the end result of guilt. (Wisd. of Sol. 14:23–27)

This typical text shows that the evils mentioned by Alexandrian Jews, such as the author of the Wisdom of Solomon, or the earliest Christians, such as Paul or Clement, were no accident. They are caused directly by idolatry, the worship of any god other than the God of the Bible. On this basis, the vile examples brought up by the apologists are not a subsidiary argument. They have appropriated a line of argument from late Judaism via Paul and his contemporaries. Greco-Roman vices demonstrate the bankruptcy of idolatrous non-Christian religions. Wherever idolatry exists, they contend, unthinkable sins are inevitable. No wonder that one major objective in early Christian catechetical training was to ensure a clean break with the pagan past, to turn "from idols to serve the living and true God" (1 Thess. 1:9).[7]

There was another reason why Jews were so concerned about idolatry. Idolatry had eternal consequences. Those who worshiped false gods would "endure the deserved judgment of God" (Wisd. of Sol. 12:26; compare 14:8). They would be punished by the very idols they made, and throughout their suffering they would see the true God that they spent a lifetime denying through their idolatry. The text continues:

6. This example is significant because Drummond, *New Age in Christian Theology*, 26, cites the Wisdom of Solomon as an example of open-minded Jews whose "contacts with Hellenism enabled them to appreciate its good, even its religious good . . . as a good in itself that they could appropriate and learn from for their own sakes."

7. As Drummond must admit (*New Age in Christian Theology*, 27). On Paul, see also Grant, *Gods and the One God*, 46–49.

"Therefore [*dio*, a strong inferential conjunction] the utmost condemnation will come upon them" (RSV). Idolatry brings God's judgment, and the punishment is severe. The link to Romans 1 is obvious: the apostle Paul shares this Jewish fear of idolatry. But do later Christians, who were not Jewish, also hold this view?

Justin Martyr did. Justin is important, for he is an often-cited example of early Christian "broad-mindedness." The reason for Justin's "liberality" is his observation that some who did not know Christ were actually Christians. Accordingly, some cite *1 Apology* 46 and leap to the conclusion that pagans can be saved through their own religions.[8] But such appeals are little more than "prooftexting," for they overlook the context of Justin's words. Justin carefully qualifies those whom he identifies as "Christians."

True, he did say people such as Socrates, Heraclitus, Abraham, and others lived "with the Logos" (46.3). But the crucial concessive clause, "even though they were thought to be atheists [*kan atheoi enomisthesan*]," deserves careful study. What Justin means when he calls Socrates an "atheist" is explained earlier in chapter 5. Socrates was praiseworthy because he recognized that the "gods" of Greece were really evil demons. He was executed because he, *like Justin and the other Christians*, attempted to expose the true nature of polytheistic religion.[9] And this charge of atheism does not apply only to Socrates or Justin. All of the other individuals Justin names rejected the religious status quo of antiquity.[10] Justin's statement, "And they do precisely the same thing to us" (5.4), leaves no doubt that both Socrates and the Christians are being persecuted by the same demons who do not want the sham of their pagan religions exposed. So Justin never said that sincere worshipers of non-Christian deities are Christians. He merely affirms that some throughout human history have stood up to the demonic deception of pagan religion. And he likewise affirms that all who challenged the status quo have paid dearly (*2 Apol.* 8).[11]

Christians in the second and third centuries, then, shared a common horror of idolatry. Idolatry caused both this-worldly evil and punishment in the next. Christians rejected the idolatrous religions of

---

8. E.g., Knitter, *No Other Name?* 248 n. 4; Drummond, *New Age in Christian Theology*, 28.

9. The same argument is repeated in *2 Apol.* 10.

10. As Arthur J. Droge, *Homer or Moses? Early Christian Interpretations of the History of Culture* (Tübingen: Mohr, 1989), 67 n. 64, correctly observes.

11. The only exception to this unrelentingly negative attitude could be in Clement of Alexandria, *Stromata* 5, but I have argued elsewhere that Clement viewed Christ as the key to unlocking the true wisdom of the Greeks as part of a larger strategy of cultural ingratiation; see my *Basil the Great's Rejection of Allegory* (Ph.D. diss., University of Chicago, 1987), 70–72.

their neighbors and eagerly seized examples of others who had likewise attacked the religious status quo of antiquity.

Early believers did not derive all their ideas about ancient religion from their Jewish heritage. One idea in particular went beyond anything the Jews had argued.[12] Christians attributed the origins of pagan religion to malevolent demons. Justin shared the early Christian view that demons were the source of pagan religion (*1 Apol.* 5.3, 44), as did the other apologists.[13] The demonic origins of non-Christian religion also show why patristic writers see no saving value in pagan religion.

Christians had a philosophical weapon at hand that greatly helped their cause. Euhemerus, a Greek writer from about 300 B.C., had suggested that the gods were originally kings. They became gods because grateful subjects deified them, much as Hellenistic and Roman emperors were deified.[14] Most apologists never tired of claiming that all of the pagan gods were, in fact, merely dead heroes. Tatian (ca. 160) and especially Clement and Eusebius (ca. 260–ca. 340) make tremendous use of the idea. Christian use of Euhemerus's ideas fits well with the evidence we have already seen. This explanation is another attack on the validity of pagan religion.

It is no wonder that believers were accused of being "atheists," as Justin recounts. Ancient writers called everyone who denied the existence of the customary deities "atheists." The importance of the word *atheist* is often overlooked. If both Christians and their opponents knew what the term meant, and both sides agreed that it applied to Christians, then all agreed that Christians rejected pagan religion. It is hard to see how Christians saw any positive value in pagan religion. By taking the atheist designation seriously, we realize just how opposed the early Christians were to the religions around them.[15]

12. There is an excellent discussion of this notion in Hanson, "Christian Attitude to Pagan Religions," 164–69.

13. Clement, see 231; Tatian, *Oration* 12.3–4, 14.1, 21.2, 29.1, cited according to *Tatian: Oratio ad Graecos,* ed. Molly Whittaker, Oxford Early Christian Texts (Oxford: Oxford University Press, 1982). References for Theophilus are given by Robert M. Grant, ed., *Theophilus of Antioch: Ad Autolycum,* Oxford Early Christian Texts (Oxford: Oxford University Press, 1970), xvi–xvii, with comments. For Athenagoras, see *Legatio* 26.1–2 and the comments of William R. Schoedel, ed., *Athenagoras: Legatio and De Resurrectione,* Oxford Early Christian Texts (Oxford: Oxford University Press, 1972), xvii.

14. See Grant, *Gods and the One God,* 61, for a good discussion; and Hanson, "Christian Attitude to Pagan Religions," 176–89, esp. 179: "The Christian intellectuals seized with glee upon the theory of Euhemerus and used it as one of their most powerful arguments against contemporary paganism."

15. Evangelicals are not the only ones who see this. For example, Robert M. Grant's *Augustus to Constantine* (1970; repr., New York: Harper & Row, 1990), views the conflict between Christianity and Greco-Roman religions as a major theme in the development of the church (e.g., pp. 79, 82, 96, 103). Grant's summary (p. 312) is telling: "The

Christians in the first three centuries thought that pagan religions were demonically inspired idolatries. Deified heroes became oppressors of the human race. They brought both temporal and eternal harm to humanity. The only way to see any value in them was to view them from within Christianity, which alone had the full measure of truth.

Early Christian Attitudes toward Ancient Philosophy

When pluralists try to show how open-minded ancient Christians were toward non-Christian religions, they cite passages dealing with Greek philosophy. Their claim has some merit, for early Christian theologians were more positive about Greek philosophy than Greek religion. All of the theologians who lived in the Greek-speaking part of the Roman Empire knew ancient philosophy fairly well. For most of them, it served as a "handmaiden to theology." With a few exceptions, they believed that Christianity was compatible with the best in Greek philosophy. But these Christians viewed ancient philosophy in a way that makes it impossible for them to agree with unitive pluralism.[16]

All Greek Christians of the first four centuries argued that philosophers contradicted one another at every turn. Since pagan thinkers could not agree on what truth was, the fathers asserted, they were completely deceived.[17] But Christianity, Justin, Tatian, Theophilus, Origen, and Eusebius all agreed, had a unified system of truth that did not contradict itself. Thus, only Christianity—not pagan thought—could be authentic.

As a result, Greek philosophy is not accepted *en bloc* by early Christians. All Christian writers in the patristic era carefully sift Plato and the others through varying grids. Justin is a good example. He commends every school for something, but, in the end, criticizes them all. He became a Christian, he says, not because of the agreements between Moses and Plato, but because of the differences (*2 Apol.* 13.2).

Eusebius stands in the same tradition as Justin.[18] Yet, by his day, the early fourth century, he is less inclined to be charitable toward Greek philosophy. For Eusebius, the only philosopher worth quoting is Plato. Eusebius has a simple rule for judging the worth of Greek philoso-

---

basic problem was religious, as J. Vogt has insisted. The Christian gospel involved the proclamation of the reality of the one true God and, consequently, the absolute rejection of the gods recognized by the Roman state. The Christians regarded worship of these gods . . . as idolatry and absolutely refused to participate in it."

16. The literature on this subject is vast. The best work is Droge's *Homer or Moses?*

17. Grant, *Gods and the One God*, 170–71.

18. I leave aside the highly critical approaches of Tatian and Tertullian, which can only help my argument. On Tatian, see Robert M. Grant, *Greek Apologists of the Second Century* (Philadelphia: Westminster, 1988), 113–23; on Tertullian, see W. H. C. Frend, *The Rise of Christianity* (Philadelphia: Fortress, 1984), 349.

phers: how closely they parallel the teaching of the Bible (e.g., *Preparation for the Gospel* 14.1.1–3; hereafter cited as *PE,* an abbreviation for the Latin *Praeparatio Evangelica*). Plato follows biblical teaching most closely (*PE* 11–12), yet falls short in several areas (*PE* 13.13.66–14.1.1). Other philosophers are mere babblers, hopelessly lost in contradiction (see esp. books 14–15).

How did Plato find the truth? First, Eusebius states, Greeks are nothing more than plagiarists. To prove this, he quotes statements from the Christian Clement of Alexandria (*PE* 2.1–15) and the pagan philosopher Porphyry (*PE* 10.3.1–25), who both agree that the Greeks generously borrowed their wisdom from others. Pythagoras, who invented the term *philosopher,* was also a plagiarist, and "from the wise men of Greece did he get nothing . . . so on the contrary became the author of instruction to the Greeks in the learning which he had procured from abroad" (*PE* 10.4.15–16).[19] Plato similarly visited Egypt, where he had contact with "barbarian" wise men (*PE* 10.4.20).

More important, Plato plagiarized directly from the Bible. Eusebius several times states that Plato "all but directly translated" a particular section of the Hebrew Scriptures (e.g., *PE* 12.11.1; 12.13.1). Even when there is not complete correspondence, Eusebius thinks he can determine Plato's dependence on Moses. For example, Plato knew the story of Adam's rib in Genesis 2, "although Plato did not understand [its] meaning" (*PE* 12.12.1). He thus has Aristophanes, the comic playwright, retell a revised version of the story in the *Symposium.* The revised story, which is about the creation of male and female from an original androgyne (i.e., a person who is both male and female), bears little resemblance to Genesis 2, until Eusebius interprets both texts allegorically. Then, both stories match up perfectly.[20]

Now that Eusebius has established, to his satisfaction, that Plato shamefacedly plagiarized the Hebrew Bible, another question faces him. Just how much of the Scriptures had Plato appropriated? To find out, Eusebius extensively compares the writings of Plato to the Old Testament in books 11–13 of the *Preparation for the Gospel.* In these books, Eusebius argues that the agreements between Plato and the Bible are so clear and so frequent that one must be borrowing from the other. Since he has already shown that Moses, David, Solomon, and the prophets are earlier than Plato, the only conclusion is that Plato has stolen whatever is good in his philosophy from the Bible.

19. Translation from Eusebius, *Preparation for the Gospel,* trans. Edwin H. Gifford (Oxford: Oxford University Press, 1903; repr., Grand Rapids: Baker, 1981).

20. Eusebius got this line of reasoning from Origen, as Origen, *Against Celsus* 4.39, also equated the garden of Eden with Plato's *Symposium;* see my *Basil the Great's Rejection of Allegory,* 73–77.

But even Plato does not follow the Bible entirely, and Eusebius, just like Justin, uses that fact as the reason why he follows the Bible and not Plato (*PE* 13.13.66).[21]

The implications of this observation are staggering. The true elements in Greek thought, then, come from *special revelation*, not from some kind of universal inspiration. The "openness" of Eusebius and others is no openness at all. Christians affirm that they have the only intact truth. The best that other religions and philosophies have is a secondhand version of Christianity intermixed to varying degrees with human confusion and perhaps even demonic "disinformation." If this is true, what could Christians learn from other religions? They already have the complete truth. Imagine how open-minded modern pluralist scholars would be if they adopted the patristic attitude. They would have to evaluate non-Christian religions by how closely they agree with Christianity. They would be forced to say that the elements that correspond to Christianity in, say Buddhism, are true, while those that are different are false. Of course, unitive pluralists would never take such an attitude because it is based on the one premise they oppose most strenuously: the superiority of Christianity to other religions. No kind of unitive pluralism worthy of the name is possible within such a framework.

The reason why Christians never used the similarities between Christianity and ancient philosophy for mutual dialogue is because that was never their intent. They did try to show that Christianity was not much different from the best of pagan thought. Their purpose, however, was twofold: to defend themselves from pagan attack and to ingratiate themselves with their pagan neighbors. They merely wanted to show that they were good neighbors, not the cannibals or sexual profligates that some gossip-mongers had said they were. Early Christians were subject to sporadic persecution, and so they had a vested interest in living exemplary lives.

Everything changes, though, when Christians are no longer a persecuted minority. As the majority group, they do not need to ingratiate themselves with anyone. By the middle of the fourth century, a generation or so after Christianity received imperial support, the earlier motivations are gone. As a result, the attitude toward pagan thought changes. This shift in thinking can be seen by comparing the works of Eusebius, who was part of a Christian minority, and those of Basil the Great (330–379), who only knew Christianity as the religion of the

---

21. Modern patristics scholars, of course, do not believe that Plato read the Bible. Eusebius's historical errors, though, do not damage the conclusions I draw in the next paragraph.

imperial house. Eusebius's *Preparation for the Gospel* attempts to show, through allegorical interpretation, that stories in Plato and the Old Testament are the same. Basil's *Address to Young Men,* on the other hand, is a document that reduces the study of the classics to a hunt for moralizing tales and rhetorical adornment. There is no serious engagement here with the thought of classical antiquity—Basil merely suggests that pagan literature contains many useful illustrations of Christian beliefs.[22] Most damaging for the pluralist cause is the entirely unrepentant attitude of religious and cultural superiority that permeates Basil's work.

The attitude of Eusebius and others is an example for us. We must be aware of the ideas that surround us. We need to be open to the positive aspects of every human culture, and not just drive a wedge between Christ and culture. But we must also stand with these early Christians who, despite their tolerance of ancient philosophy, still viewed their Christianity as the one privileged and correct vantage point from which to view culture.

The Logos in Early Christianity

The only hope left for any kind of pluralist antecedent in the patristic era is in the idea of the *spermatikos logos*. This "logos," primarily discussed by Justin, is supposed to have "lighted everyone who comes into the world," to use the Johannine phrase. A careful analysis of the extent and value of what the *spermatikos logos* offers is highly revealing.[23]

Justin believed that certain people who lived before Christ were able to see the folly in pagan religion and turn to the true God. But how did they obtain such revelation?

Scholars agree that Justin gives three explanations for why Greeks possess truth: They stole it from Scripture (the "theft theory"), demons who knew spiritual truth inspired their writers, or the Logos (i.e., Christ) inspired them through "seeds" (*sperma*) implanted in them

22. I discuss the attempts of early Christians to ingratiate themselves with the wider culture in *Basil the Great's Rejection of Allegory,* 65–81; the distance between Basil on the one hand and Clement and Origen on the other is discussed on 143–45 and esp. 147–53. The naive comments of Drummond, *New Age in Christian Theology,* 209–10 n. 13, should be read in the light of this latter discussion.

23. This discussion follows the general lines of Ragner Holte, "Logos Spermatikos: Christianity and Ancient Philosophy according to St. Justin's Apologies," *Studia Theologica* 12 (1958): 109–68. Note especially Holte's translations of the important texts in Justin, 131–35, because the older English translations blur distinctions that are crucial for understanding Justin's position; the translations I quote, except for *1 Apol.* 46:4 (which is mine), follow Holte's, with slight modifications indicated. See also Droge, *Homer or Moses?* 65–69 (whose n. 61 led me to Holte), for additional discussion and literature.

(hence *"logos spermatikos"*).[24] If one assumes that the Logos was as seriously active among pagans as he was among Jews and Christians, then one might agree with scholars who say that Justin thought Christianity and Greek philosophy were "almost identical ways of apprehending the same truth."[25] But there is a price to pay for this assertion. It is difficult, if not impossible, to reconcile the *logos spermatikos* explanation with either the theft theory or the idea of demonic inspiration. How could a serious thinker like Justin one minute claim the Greeks were both demonically inspired and plagiarists, and the next that Jesus Christ, the Logos, gave them a system comparable to Christianity? Surely Justin was not confused about an idea of such central importance to him. "Is it not more likely," as Ragner Holte puts it, "that modern scholars have tried to see Justin as an exponent of their own modern theological viewpoint?"[26]

It is true that Justin views Christ, the Logos, as having inspired people outside of Christianity. But Justin lays out the relationship between the limited truth Greeks have and the full revelation Christians possess:

> Our doctrines, then, appear to be greater than all human teaching, because the complete truth has come to be in Christ, the one who appeared for our sake, body, reason, and soul. For whatever either lawgivers or philosophers uttered well, they elaborated according to their share (i.e. fragmentary knowledge) of Logos by invention and contemplation. But since they did not know all that concerns Logos, which is Christ, they often contradicted themselves. (*1 Apol.* 10.1–3)

Greek philosophers had only a partial idea of the truth, while Christians had a complete version. The proof is that, for Justin, Christian teaching is consistent with itself, while Greek philosophies contradict each other. In fact, the truth possessed by non-Christians was so fragmentary and limited that Justin could compare it, even in Socrates, to the reasoning capacity of a child.[27] So the revelation was, at best, fragmentary.

But to say it was fragmentary does not imply that the revelation was false. In *1 Apology* 46, Justin claimed that Socrates was a Christian. That same passage provides the purpose for the *logos sper-*

24. Holte, "Logos Spermatikos," 111.
25. Henry Chadwick's phrase, from *Early Christian Thought and the Classical Tradition* (Oxford: Oxford University Press, 1966), 11, quoted by Droge, *Homer or Moses?* 52; on the history of scholarship see Holte, "Logos Spermatikos," 109–16, and Droge, *Homer or Moses?* 52–53, esp. 53: "It would be a grave misjudgment to assume that Justin's main intention was to reconcile Christianity to Greek philosophy."
26. Holte, "Logos Spermatikos," 113.
27. Ibid., 141.

matikos revelation. "Therefore, those who lived before Christ, and lived far from the Logos were wicked, and enemies of Christ, and murdered those who lived with the Logos. But those who live with the Logos, both now and in the past, are Christians, and are free from fear and disturbance" (46.4) With this statement, Justin concludes his argument for the culpability of all humanity. The chapter opens with the statement "lest someone . . . challenge us that all those who had lived before [Christ] were not accountable" (46.1), clearly indicating that the issue before him was whether those who could never have known the name of Christ were responsible. The summary statement in verse 4 answers the opening challenge in verse 1. By stating that the Logos had granted a "seed" of understanding to everyone, and that a few Greeks and a large number of "barbarians" (i.e., Israelites) had lived in accordance with the Logos, Justin shows that all had a fair chance even before Christ came. The *logos spermatikos,* limited and fragmented as it was, allowed some to become Christians. But many rejected the light so offered to them. They were enemies of God and murdered those who attempted to live according to the Logos. This kind of revelation, then, bears a striking resemblance to Romans 1—all had light, but the light was largely rejected. So all are culpable.[28] Only a few philosophers, Socrates, Heraclitus, Musonius and those like them, withstood the attacks of those who wanted to suppress the truth.

Justin's use of the *logos spermatikos* idea, then, does not conflict with the general patristic view outlined in this chapter. Entire philosophical systems are not inspired by the *logos spermatikos.* Rather, it only implants a small number of basic theological and moral ideas.[29] The *spermatikos logos* idea means that all who lived before Christ had enough revelation to enable them to reject pagan gods and immorality, and to reach out to the true God, the God of the Christians. The fact that multitudes did not act in accordance with the revelation they had is not God's fault.

Pluralists are correct that early Greek Christians were more open-minded than their Latin counterparts. Theologians such as Justin and Eusebius thought that some pagans had responded to general and special revelation and had become Christians even though they did not know the name of Jesus. But these early Christians were not as open-minded as modern pluralists would have us believe. Greek Christians

28. Both Holte, "Logos Spermatikos," 129–30, 163; and Droge *Homer or Moses?* 68, see the connection to Romans 1.

29. Holte, "Logos Spermatikos," 163. We should also remember that later writers back away from Justin's ideas, in favor of the theft theory.

saw a "great gulf fixed" between Christianity and non-Christian religions. Those who wanted to be Christians had to first make a clean break with their pagan past. They had to measure their pagan philosophical thought by the yardstick of God's complete truth, the Bible. All early Christians recognized that those who adhered to non-Christian religions, no matter how sincerely, were lost.[30]

30. If unitive pluralists wish to argue that the patristic tradition was wrong to reject pagan religion, that is their right. But let us at least start our discussions from a historically sound analysis. Once we clear away the anachronisms, the real issue becomes whether any form of traditional Christianity can meet the challenges of the twenty-first century.

Part

Concluding Remarks

20

Is It Fair?

Carl F. H. Henry

After all is said and done, is it fair?

Skeptics have emblazoned that question over many elements of biblical teaching: Adam and Eve's creation with a sin-penetrable nature; Adamic headship of the human race; divine election of the Hebrews and preferential prophetic revelation; God's incarnation once-for-all in Jesus of Nazareth; irreversible eternal condemnation of human beings who in this life reject the divine Redeemer.

These critical demurrals reflect at bottom a rejection of the supreme sovereignty of God, a disavowal of the elective-decree of a self-revealed deity of holy love, and a repudiation of his eternal plan of creation, redemption, and judgment.

Through the centuries Christian orthodoxy has patiently countered such assaults. One or another of the chapters in this volume has commented on them. Yet every generation copes with such renouncements as if they were wholly new, and as if no one had confronted them.

This chapter discusses God's fairness by focusing—as many commentators do—on the final destiny of those who have "never heard." After all is said and done, is it fair—so the query is often phrased—that the unreached heathen should perish?

The inquiry has four prongs. Each term—heathen, unreached, perish, fair—bears importantly on the answer.

1. Who precisely are the "heathen"?
2. Is any human being totally "unreached" by truth about God and his ways?
3. Just what does "perish" suggest in respect to humanity's final destiny?
4. How is "fairness" to be defined, and by whom?

Of these items, the third concern—what it means for human beings to perish—has already been anticipated in earlier chapters.[1] We are not talking only about physical death. Finite creatures, after all, are not intrinsically imperishable. Whatever perpetuity we have—contrary to Plato—is not inherent in our soul-life but rather is dependent upon external factors. Naturalism speculates that evolutionary nature alone provides the supports of life. But Christianity insists that the living God is the source of creation-life, of redemption-life, and of resurrection-life. Although humans are creatures of dignity, they nonetheless are not imperishable gods, and their survival in eternity and the nature of that survival is conditioned on God's sovereign will.

Who Are the Heathen?

The first of the four prongs jolts us with a reminder that the term *heathen* has multiple meanings. Originally, anyone who did not worship the God of Israel was considered heathen. Later the term was applied to anyone not a Jew, Christian, or Muslim. But the modern avalanche of nominally religious people has created the categories of heathen Jews and heathen Christians. Thus the term *heathen* now applies not only to uncivilized pagans or to agnostics and atheists, but also to irreligious people generally. The term has come, in fact, broadly to mean anyone who worships idols or has perverse priorities. In that case it might embrace masses of moderns, including some of our neighbors, who in turn may have deep suspicions about us. For our purposes, heathen refers to those who have never heard the good news that God offers sinful humanity divine forgiveness on the ground of the substitutionary death of Jesus Christ. The crucial point is not that the heathen are a class of illiterate barbarians, but that they comprise a multitude of people that have never heard the gospel, either because they lived in pre-Christian times, or because they reside

1. Particularly in Scot McKnight, "Eternal Consequences or Eternal Consciousness?" and Timothy R. Phillips, "Hell: A Christological Reflection."

in inaccessible locations, or because they somehow escape the net of missionary outreach.

It is noteworthy that many people decide whether they can believe in God's justice or fairness on the basis of their answer to this question: Will a just God eternally doom human beings who have never heard the name of Jesus?

The case of Old Testament Jewry is not here at issue. Although the covenant people knew the Redeemer's name expressly only in eighth-century prophecy (Isa. 9:6 [Heb. v. 5]), and were unaware that divine incarnation was in view, already from the time of Abraham they knew that God would provide a Savior. Old Testament redemption emphasizes that salvation is not a human achievement; the Mosaic sacrificial typology anticipated a divinely provided atonement for the sins of the penitent. Jesus reminded Nicodemus that refusing to accept the Old Testament revelation left him responsible (John 3:3–15).

The heathen who have "never heard," by contrast, stand outside the channel of revealed religion. They lack knowledge of a historically provided atonement that requires personal faith in the suffering Servant as a condition of salvation.[2]

In assessing those who have never heard Christ's name, evangelical orthodoxy challenges a common misunderstanding, namely, that those who have never heard of Christ are divinely condemned for rejecting him. People who have never heard the gospel will not be condemned for rejecting Christ. Evangelical theologians concede—even insist—that it would be unjust to condemn those who have never heard for their lack of response to an unknown offer of grace. To say that those who have never heard are condemned for rejecting Christ overstates and needlessly confuses the issue. Only those who know the good news and reject it are guilty of spurning the divine offer of grace.

Is Anyone Totally Unreached?

Yet those who have never heard the gospel are not spiritually guiltless. Human beings are judged in God's sight for the response they make to whatever light they have—and no human being is without light. The human species is created in the *imago Dei*. God has endowed all humanity with categories of morality and reason and, moreover, has ensconced humans as responsible caretakers of the cosmos. He has endued all humankind with some inescapable knowledge of

2. Children who die before the age of accountability fall into a different category. They are embraced by covenant-theology as members of the family of faith. Other communions hold that, just as children are counted guilty in Adam without volition of their own, so God accounts them justified in Christ without personal exercise of faith.

divinity. Judgment day will not overtake any man or woman as a total surprise.

The living God universally confronts all human beings in general revelation—in nature and history and in the human mind and conscience. The Logos of God lights every human self (John 1:4, 9). Long before the Logos became enfleshed in Jesus the Nazarene, the eternal, cosmic Christ everywhere challenged humankind's unbelief, convicting a fallen and rebellious humanity of sin and coming judgment. Even before any human being hears the name of Jesus Christ, the eternal Logos confronts all human beings internally with the Creator's claim on human conscience and life and consigns mutinous humankind to a fearsome sense of impending judgment (see Rom. 1:18–32).

God's universal revelation was not aimed to condemn the human race, but was given rather "so that men would seek him and perhaps reach out for him and find him" (Acts 17:27). Although Scripture teaches that all humans are sinners, the hypothetical possibility existed that Adam and his progeny might have perfectly kept the moral law and would thereby have enjoyed ongoing fellowship with God on the basis of sinless obedience. But Scripture testifies that all have sinned and that God punishes nobody undeservedly. The notion that apart from redemptive revelation some persons might repent of sin and throw themselves on the mercy of God has no express biblical support; repentance and faith are gifts of the self-revealing God who has provided a Savior.

The intensity of human rebellion no doubt varies from person to person, the measure of insurgency being reflected in the biblical warning that final divine judgment includes "few blows" and "many blows" (Luke 12:47–48). Yet every person is held accountable for his or her response to available and accusing light. The one thing that humans cannot do is to extinguish the light that shines in their moral darkness and relentlessly exposes their rebellious condition. Those who have heard the gospel certainly have had more light than those who have never heard, but all are judged for light obscured and deflected.[3]

The biblical passages that most pointedly clarify universal knowledge of God are Acts 17 and Romans 1. Although pagans are unillumined by special revelation and therefore do not comprehend God's redemptive offer (1 Thess. 4:5; 2 Thess. 1:8), their sinful constitutional condition nevertheless does not involve a total ignorance about God.

---

3. Although involvement in the Adamic fall and in personal rebellion does not mean that human beings are as fully wicked or devoid of civic justice as they might be, nonetheless their participation in the fall eliminates any reason for divine acceptance on the basis of human works. In their revolt against the light of general revelation, human beings act out of selfish motives and obscure the character of God.

To be sure, what survives the fall and human rebellion is not a universally shared knowledge, one that pagans incorporate as such into the nonbiblical religions and that the Christian religion embodies and develops. No ubiquitously dispersed common ground exists between the presuppositions and content of the heathen religions and the biblical revelation. Indeed, the nonbiblical religions and biblical religion are so contrary that the Greeks viewed Paul's teaching as new doctrine about a foreign divinity (Acts 17:18–19) of whom Paul himself declares the Greeks to be ignorant (Acts 17:23). Paul can even say that the Gentiles "exchanged the truth of God for a lie" (Rom. 1:18, 25).

Yet Paul does not fault God's universal revelation, for that revelation makes effective contact with every human being (Rom. 1:20) and yields individual knowledge of God (Rom. 1:21). Much as fallen humanity seeks to stifle and nullify the all-powerful Creator's revelation, that revelation cannot be wholly obliterated, despite humanity's distortion of it and its active contrary will. The human race's rebellion against inextinguishable divine light establishes human culpability and invites judgment.

Does General Revelation Provide Genuine Knowledge of God?

The question of divine fairness also arises when theologians discuss the character of divine revelation. The debate here concerns whether God's universal revelation issues in genuine knowledge about the deity. Quite in a Barthian mood, G. C. Berkouwer grossly exaggerates the pagan ignorance of God. General revelation, he affirms, never passes over into genuine knowledge.[4]

But, in that case, can God hold all humankind blameworthy? If human beings are incapable of drawing valid conclusions about deity from God's universal revelation, and therefore have no genuine knowledge at all about God, can they fairly be considered culpable? If in fact humankind cannot know anything trustworthy about God and his will through general revelation, would it not be morally intolerable for God to judge humankind guilty of revolt?

One may properly question the validity of nonbiblical religions, and view them as apostate systems that distort general revelation; one can, moreover, justifiably greet the natural theology of the Roman Catholic scholastics with skepticism; one can applaud a determination not to allow general revelation to dwarf or to supplant special revelation; one can even insist that Christ is at the center of all genuine

---

4. G. C. Berkouwer, "General and Special Divine Revelation," in *Revelation and the Bible*, ed. Carl F. H. Henry (Grand Rapids: Baker, 1976), 15.

divine revelation if one here has in view the eternal Logos. But the fact that some scholars misjudge the epistemic consequences of sinful revolt against general revelation supplies no good reason for understating or overstating them. Bruce A. Demarest rightly declares that it is "irresponsible to abolish altogether a valid concept . . . on the grounds that it has been abused."[5]

Psalm 19 affirms that God's revelation in the created order continually confronts the human race. In general revelation God discloses himself as the all-powerful, wise, and just Creator and Preserver of the universe and as its Judge. In Galatians 4:8, 1 Thessalonians 4:5, and 2 Thessalonians 1:8 what Paul asserts is not that unregenerate humanity possesses no knowledge whatever of God; what he affirms, rather, is that—apart from special salvific revelation—humankind lacks knowledge of God's offer of redemptive grace.

The notion that general revelation provides only a misty pseudo-knowledge of God would, as Demarest rightly contends,[6] impugn God's justice "for condemning a person on the basis of ignorance." Contrary to Berkouwer's disavowal of any positive epistemic value of general revelation for sinful humankind, the Protestant Reformers Luther and Calvin insisted on a twofold intelligible revelation of God: one given universally in nature, in history, and in the human mind and conscience, and the other—a special redemptive disclosure—given in Hebrew history and prophecy and supremely in Jesus Christ as scripturally attested.

How Much Information Does General Revelation Provide?

Cornelius Van Til, proponent of evangelical fideism, holds that humans as created bearers of God's image know innately that God is Creator, Preserver, and Judge of all: "All men know God, the true God, the only God. They have not merely a capacity for knowing him but actually do know him."[7] Awareness that God exists is therefore prephilosophical. In some passages Van Til seems to imply that the unregenerate sinner's only knowledge of God is psychological and not intellectual. He insists that the natural order yields fallen humans no knowledge of God. Van Til argues that because human beings are sinful they strive to stifle every remnant of knowledge of God, whether from the external world or from the depths of mankind's psychological constitution.

5. Bruce A. Demarest, *General Revelation: Historical Views and Contemporary Issues* (Grand Rapids: Zondervan, 1982), 145.

6. Ibid., 147.

7. Cornelius Van Til, *The Defense of the Faith* (Nutley, N.J.: Presbyterian & Reformed, 1967), 87.

Van Til shares the apostle Paul's view that fallen humanity responds perversely to God's general revelation. But he holds that none of God's revelation in nature gets through as an objective datum, even fragmentarily. The universal external revelation serves only to condemn human beings, not to illumine them; only after regeneration does one truly apprehend God in external nature and history. Only by interpreting reality theistically can humans gain trustworthy knowledge of the deity.

The few truths perceived through general revelation not only cannot be related into even a rudimentary natural theology, but are immediately suppressed by human psychological and epistemic violence. The apostate structure of unbelieving knowledge poisons all revealed truth and denies its veracity by assimilating it into a rebellious worldview.

Van Til's motive—to this extent commendable—seems to be to exclude a natural theology, defined as a universally shared body of doctrine held by sinful humanity preparatory to special revelation. But while properly avoiding the excessive claims of natural theology, Van Til unfortunately exaggerates fallen humankind's epistemic inability, and thereby does less than justice to scriptural representations regarding the humanly received content of general revelation. The Bible depicts general revelation as an intellectual content that confronts humanity both externally and internally, and as conveying cognitively reliable data to all, even if persons differ somewhat in their admission and retention of elements of that revelation. Nobody is without some objective knowledge conveyed by general revelation, a knowledge that renders every person guilty for revolt against light, in view of humankind's attempted suffocation of that revelatory content.

General revelation, however, does not provide sinful humanity with a comprehensive, reliable view of God. Because of humanity's sinful condition, a proper understanding even of the content of general revelation rests in the divinely inscripturated special revelation. Scripture objectively identifies valid and invalid claims made by rebellious sinners on the basis of the supposed *indicia* in nature and humankind.

If Van Til fails to do full justice to the epistemic potency of general revelation in the experience of sinful humankind, Demarest seems to overstate that potency, by translating general revelation into a globally shared body of information about the Deity.[8] But Demarest at least

8. In *Integrative Theology* (Grand Rapids: Zondervan, 1987), Bruce Demarest and Gordon Lewis insist commendably that general revelation involves knowledge of God implanted universally in human moral and psychological constitution and that this knowledge establishes accountability and renders rebellious humanity guilty of spiritual mutiny. They emphasize that there is a universal, continuous, and clear divine revelation to all humankind, that all humanity perceives this revelation, and that all are accountable for transgression. They concede that the moral law is a divine given and

recognizes what Van Til somewhat obscures, and Berkouwer even more so, that divine condemnation of sinful humankind presupposes some objectively reliable knowledge of God that rebellious human beings can consciously reject.[9] Demarest's repeated insistence that general revelation penetrates the human mind everywhere with objective knowledge is sound. Also sound is his insistence that sin is inexcusable because sinners consciously spurn God and thus have no right to plead ignorance. "Since knowledge of God is mediated to all by general revelation, human accountability to God is firmly established."[10]

---

not derivable from any religious or social milieu (p. 71). They reject natural theology in the manner that Thomas Aquinas formulated it, that is, without any reliance whatever on divine revelation, and simply by empirical observation of the universe, one can mount a logical demonstration of the existence of God. Yet they do not reject natural theology per se. Indeed, they contend that "the reality of natural theology . . . is explicitly and repeatedly taught in Scripture" (p. 75), although Scripture does not explicitly support Thomas Aquinas's fivefold "proof" of God's existence from observed data (p. 76). They mount no demonstrative alternative, but somewhat amorphously encourage a recognition of "the cumulative impact of all external and internal data and the valid elements in all lines of reasoning based on them." Somewhat guarded is the statement that "a universal ability to *know* some objective truth about creation and the creator is implied in a natural theology as a product of common grace" (p. 83). They affirm that contemplation of the universe yields "conclusions about God's character and moral requirements" (p. 66), a position that theologians who stress the limits and tentative nature of empirical observation question. If we examine more closely such limited additional knowledge, which Demarest and Lewis hold to be conveyed by the modalities of general revelation, it includes not only knowledge acquired "by rational contemplation of the natural world" mediated through sense perception but "areas of agreement" with non-Christian philosophies also (pp. 69–70). "Paul at Athens established the truth about God as creator and as giver of the moral law by recovering distorted common ground in the writings of one of the Stoic pantheists' own poets" (p. 88).

9. Demarest and Lewis acknowledge that sinful humanity volitionally distorts both innate and acquired knowledge of God. Yet they espouse "cultural points of contact" (ibid., 89) and tell us that Christians may profitably seek in comparative religions, anthropology and psychology supplementary theological data that does not flatly contradict Christian doctrine (p. 73). Instead of finding an overlapping point of contact in the teachings of biblical and nonbiblical theology and philosophy, however, and contending that despite the fall a universally shared body of truth and morality survives in human thought and practice, another option—and in my view a preferable one—is that of locating the point of contact not in divergent religious or philosophical systems but in the *imago Dei* that ineradicably structures every human self. On this alternative every person would, despite the fall and its consequences, retain some valid knowledge of God and his will, yet such knowledge cannot be extended into a universally shared system of truth and morality. The world philosophies and nonbiblical religions are indeed a response to general revelation, but a response forged by humankind in revolt rather than in obedience. A distorted view of God that consequently lies at the heart of these schemas has reductive and distortive results involving every affirmation about the nature of reality and the human condition.

10. Ibid., 246.

Must God Redeem All?

How people are saved through Jesus Christ also depends on the knowledge-ignorance question. General revelation attests God's eternal power and moral majesty and renders rebellious humankind guilty. But it declares nothing of God's redemptive grace and the atoning work of Jesus of Nazareth that provides salvation for sinners. The question arises, therefore, whether a just God will condemn humans who have never heard of Jesus Christ.

Augustine took to task early Christian apologists who stretched general revelation to include special revelation and who argued that the Logos provided a knowledge of Christ to some who had embraced Greek philosophy and non-Christian religions.

Demarest has moved away from his earlier view in *General Revelation* that a sovereign God might intervene in the lives of persons who, out of a deep sense of need, throw themselves on divine mercy.[11] The "overwhelming" biblical data, Demarest concedes, is that all humanity is lost and needs to trust Christ for salvation.

In fact, Scripture testifies that God has dealt with fallen angels differently than he does with humankind. He has provided no redemption—and hence made no offer of redemption—for Satan and rebellious spirits whom he consigned to judgment without mercy (2 Pet. 2:4). The condition of angels for whom no divine redemption is provided is similar to that of fallen and unredeemed humans who have never heard the name of Christ the Savior. Angels are judged solely for what they have done with the light of God's general revelation; so also are unregenerate humans who have never heard the gospel. God is not obliged to save any morally rebellious creature. His nonprovision of redemption for some fallen humans does not compromise his justice, any more than does his nonprovision of redemption for all fallen angels. God is not obliged to redeem all or any rebels; his elective intervention is a voluntary expression of holy love.

Nowhere does the Bible teach that God plans to save all human beings; it indicates rather that God in his sovereign will elects certain individuals in Christ (John 6:37; Eph. 1:4–5). Some would seek to invert predestination by conditioning it on foreseen faith or good works, but biblical salvation rests distinctively on God's merciful intervention and not on human merit.

Is God Unjust?

The justice of God is questioned also by some critics who protest that election-love is discriminatory and therefore a violation of justice.

11. Ibid., 260.

But all love is preferential or it would not be love. The nonelect are condemned not because they are nonelect but because they spurn God's universal revelation in nature and history and in the human conscience and mind.

The modern misjudgment of God flows easily from contemporary theology's preoccupation with love as the core of God's being, while righteousness is subordinated and denied equal ultimacy with love in the nature of deity.

The very content of justice, as well as the character of love, is today in debate. Traditional biblical justice is rivaled by permissive, modern, Western alternatives, as well as by restrictive Sunni and Shiite Muslim justice and other misconceptions. Current liberal or humanist notions vigorously dispute the justice proclaimed by the God of biblical orthodoxy. Naturalists see justice simply as a reflection of cultural pressures, of the prevalent standard of social obligation, or of evolutionary advance, without a fixed transcendent basis.

God's justice is not based on empirical considerations but reflects his own essential nature: he is intrinsically just (Ps. 85:11 [Heb. v. 12]: "Righteousness looks down from heaven"). Not only is God unswervingly faithful in keeping his promises and covenant-commitments, but he is infallibly consistent in his normative self-determination. God does not stand under justice as a norm but is himself the norm. Justice is the foundation of his throne (Ps. 89:14 [Heb. v. 15]). Justice is a predicate of God, not of fallen finite creatures whose measure of justice is warped. God's justice is the norm for kings and for all roles of authority.

To the biblical writers it is unthinkable that God would pervert justice (Job 8:3: "Does God pervert justice? Does the Almighty pervert what is right?"). For God is eminently just (Neh. 9:33: "In all that has happened to us, you have been just"). Psalm 7:9 [Heb. v. 10] declares that he is "the righteous God, who searches minds and hearts"; Isaiah 45:21 states that "there is no God apart from me, a righteous God and a Savior; there is none but me"; and Zephaniah 3:5 says that "the Lord . . . is righteous; he does no wrong. Morning by morning he dispenses his justice."

God is Judge of all the earth and his judgment is infallible (Gen. 18:25: "Will not the Judge of all the earth do right?"; Deut. 32:4: "All his ways are just"; Job 34:10: "Far be it from God to do evil, from the Almighty to do wrong"). His justice is the touchstone of human behavior, for all humanity is answerable to his revealed standards. He seeks justice throughout the social order, as well as in individual life; he requires that we "act justly and . . . love mercy and . . . walk humbly" (Mic. 6:8).

Even a pagan society retains some sense of justice. The citizenry is capable of justice in the sense of satisfying ordinary legal norms and defining civic duty. In the Bible justice means fulfilling one's duties to God and to humanity under God. The Bible's wisdom literature contains many passages that describe or define the just person. Jesus Christ "the Holy and Righteous One" (Acts 3:14) would be no partner in a less-than-just manifestation of grace, whether in withholding it entirely from fallen angels or extending it in elective love. The gospel is the final righteous declaration by God. It involves the substitutionary death of "the Holy and Righteous One" who expressed God's electing grace.

To accuse God of misconduct, to fault him and disparage his elective grace, is to forget that God himself is the standard of truth and justice and love. Scripture nowhere derives its doctrine of truth, justice, and love from heathen sources. The perversion of truth, justice, and love is what makes humans heathen. God's fairness is demonstrated because he condemns sinners not in the absence of light but because of their rebellious response. His mercy is demonstrated because he provides fallen humans with a privileged call to redemption not extended to fallen angels. He continues to extend that call worldwide even while some rebel humans spurn it as unloving and unjust and prefer to die in their sins. All are judged by what they do with the light they have, and none is without light.

21

Are the "Heathen" Really Lost?

William V. Crockett and James G. Sigountos

A few years ago a fashionable, mainline church invited a missionary surgeon to speak. Later that evening they honored him with an elaborate dinner, lauding his sacrificial service on the remote mission station where he worked. Things were going well until someone asked him to describe a typical day.

"I usually do surgery in the morning," he said, "and examine people after lunch, much as I did here." Then he paused. "Of course, the whole time I try to tell them about Jesus and their need of a Savior."

The questioner shifted awkwardly. "You don't think everyone needs to convert to our religion, do you?"

"I certainly do," said the doctor, "that's why I'm out there. Without Christ, I believe they will be lost eternally."

As you might guess, the dinner gathering was stunned by his

An abbreviated form of this chapter appeared in *United Evangelical Action* 50/1 (Jan.–Feb. 1991): 8–9, under the title "Acceptable in God's Sight? Must We Evangelize Those Who Have Never Heard?"

answer. How could anyone, they wondered, seriously believe that God intends to toss people of other religions into hell?

Through No Fault of Their Own?

Today, a growing number of Christians are abandoning the traditional teaching that salvation is found in Christ alone. They look around and see thousands of millions of people—good people from other lands with other faiths—who had no opportunity to hear the gospel. They wonder about the Ethiopian mother who carried her children across barren lands, looking for milk and bread, until her sickly body collapsed in exhaustion. They ask about those who die clutching amulets or religious fetishes, praying for release from their misery. Are we to suppose, they ask, that our merciful God simply translates these wretched people from one hell to another?

These are disturbing pictures. We understand how scholars like John Hick, who had a "born-again" experience, have forsaken their evangelical roots. Hick, Paul Knitter, and a host of other theologians have called on the church to abandon its ethnocentric, barbaric attitudes toward adherents of the great world religions.[1] Admit it, they say, faithful Muslims, Hindus, and even animists are as acceptable to God as we are.

How do evangelicals handle such challenges? The truth is, not very well. The problems posed by liberal scholars are often sidestepped or ignored. Some even perceive a glibness in the way we answer questions about the fate of those outside the gospel. But if evangelicals seem callous or insensitive, it is not because of an uncaring spirit. Many struggle over the issue. In the end, however, we surrender our own ideas to the authority of Holy Writ, which insists that all who reject Jesus Christ are lost. Thus, for the evangelical, the fate of those who have never heard is not a question of passion, but of biblical teaching.

For example, when the apostle Paul confronts this question, he says he is not ashamed of the gospel because "it is the power of God for the salvation of everyone who believes" (Rom. 1:16). But what about those who have never heard? They are without excuse, says Paul, because they rejected God when he came to them in nature (Rom. 1:18–32) and when he spoke to them in the secret chambers of their hearts (Rom. 2:6–16). Paul's point in Romans 1–4 is that *all* people everywhere are sinners and need to be saved by God's grace.[2]

---

1. See further, Millard J. Erickson, "The State of the Question"; Charles Van Engen, "The Effect of Universalism on Mission Effort"; and Timothy D. Westergren, "Do All Roads Lead to Heaven?"

2. These passages are more fully treated in Aída Besançon Spencer, "Romans 1: Finding God in Creation"; and indirectly by Douglas Moo, "Romans 2: Saved Apart from the Gospel?"

Some, of course, object that we in the West have had the opportunity to hear the gospel, but others "outside" have not. Such a situation, they complain, is unfair.

Evangelicals are divided on how to respond.[3] On one side are Reformed theologians who hold that God desires to save only the elect.[4] God is not obliged to save every rebellious sinner. We should be thankful he deigns to save anyone. Other evangelicals find Reformed theology inadequate.[5] They argue that God desires to save all people (2 Pet. 3:9) and genuinely offers salvation to everyone, even though most will reject it. But those who do seek God with all their hearts will find him—regardless what seeming accidents of geography or ancestry there might be.

Yet, how can we say that God offers salvation to people who have never heard the name of Jesus? This second group of evangelicals suggests that general revelation provides enough light to bring about salvation for those who have never heard. More precisely, it is not general revelation that bestows salvation, but the work of Christ on the cross. All evangelicals acknowledge that salvation comes only through the name of Jesus. "Salvation is found in no one else," records Luke, "for there is no other name under heaven given to men by which we must be saved" (Acts 4:12). So, even though seekers after God might find him through the light of general revelation, they obtain mercy because of the gracious provision of Christ.

Naturally, the idea that a person can find saving grace without actually hearing the name of Jesus is not new. At every period in history, great saints have held this view. Christians such as Justin Martyr (ca. 100–165), John Chrysostom (ca. 347–407), Huldrych Zwingli (1484–1531), and John Wesley (1703–91) believed that God would save the unreached who earnestly sought him—even though they might never have heard the gospel.

But salvation through general revelation is entirely different from what Hick and Knitter espouse.[6] They think non-Christian religions

3. The two positions are laid out in David K. Clark, "Is Special Revelation Necessary for Salvation?" The reader should note that the contributors were free to adopt either position. Both positions are well represented in this book, a fact that testifies to the diversity in evangelicalism on the issue of fairness. The issue is a thorny one and it is not surprising that several contributors (Timothy R. Phillips, "Hell: A Christological Perspective"; Aída Besançon Spencer, "Romans 1: Finding God in Creation"; and Tite Tiénou, "Eternity in Their Hearts") prefer to leave the matter in the hands of God.

4. A good example of this argument is Carl F. H. Henry, "Is It Fair?"

5. Evangelicals who take this position are listed in David K. Clark, "Is Special Revelation Necessary for Salvation?" n. 7. Those whom Clark Pinnock calls "lenient" hold similar positions, see Pinnock, "Acts 4:12—No Other Name under Heaven," n. 2.

6. A point well made by David K. Clark, "Is Special Revelation Necessary for Salvation?" 42–43.

can save—and this evangelicals reject. We follow the lead of the apostle Paul in Athens (Acts 17:16–34), who genuinely tried to convert the Greeks from their pagan religions.[7] Thus, when evangelicals say that salvation may come through general revelation, they mean only for those who have never heard. Those who hear and reject the gospel are lost. And those who do embrace the light of general revelation must be willing to turn from their dead idols to serve the living God (1 Thess. 1:9). General revelation, then, creates in them a desire to reject their pagan religions; it does not help them see the saving significance of their own.

Cutting the Nerve Cord of Evangelism

Nevertheless, evangelicals who expect some to find God through general revelation are faced with a difficult question. If God saves people apart from missionaries, does this not cut the "nerve cord" of missionary motivation? After all, if people can be saved without missionaries, why send them?[8]

We send them, of course, for the same reason we commission ministers and evangelists to preach the gospel in our own lands. Just because people have heard the gospel, or have in some way been touched by the Spirit of God, is no reason to turn our backs on them. Christ himself commissioned his followers (Matt. 28:16–20) to make disciples of all nations by baptizing and instructing them. Our Lord's vision was of disciples making other disciples. Seekers who find God through general revelation are like the blind groping toward a dim light: they will remain isolated and undiscipled until a missionary comes. So while a few seekers may find grace, they will never form a church, never praise the name of him who saved them, never experience the warmth of Christian community, and never lead anyone else to Christ.

Actually, the existence of "implicit Christians," as we might call them, should increase motivation. These seekers after "glory, honor and immortality" (Rom. 2:7) have already responded to the living God and are waiting eagerly to hear more about him. If hundreds of such seekers lived in a given locale, a strong church would spring to life, giving glory to God and evangelizing their pagan neighbors.

7. See the fuller discussion of Darrell L. Bock, "Athenians Who Have Never Heard," although Bock opposes an implicit-faith view.

8. This objection has been answered extensively several times in this book. The implicit-faith view has its problems, but diminishing missionary motivation is not one of them. In addition to the argument that follows, see David K. Clark, "Is Special Revelation Necessary for Salvation?"; Clark H. Pinnock, "Acts 4:12—No Other Name under Heaven"; and John D. Ellenberger, "Is Hell A Proper Motivation for Missions?"

This last observation may settle a debate among evangelicals on the "implicit-faith" view. Some, like Augustus H. Strong, Millard Erickson, and James I. Packer, believe that few, if any, will respond. Others, such as Charles Kraft and Clark Pinnock, hope for multitudes. Missionary experience might provide a clue as to how many implicit Christians there might be. If there are such people, we can assume they would quickly embrace the gospel. Thus, the number of immediate converts who had been waiting for the gospel would give us a rough idea of the number of implicit Christians. Missionaries have often spoken of individuals—sometimes even entire villages—who responded immediately to the gospel.[9] They seemed to have been waiting to hear from the God they always believed in. But examples of this are rare. A few missionaries may report unusual success in pioneer work, but most find that people quickly reject the gospel in favor of their traditional religions.

Evangelicals, however, should not fasten their attention only on the parochial issue of whether there are implicit Christians. The question is certainly worth examining, but, equally, we should recognize that there are wolves outside the door. The real challenge comes from those who demand we stop seeking converts from other religions. These people would have us believe that Christianity is no better than any other great world religion. They ask us to reduce Jesus Christ from the Savior of the world to a kind of symbol for all truth in human religion. They want us to place the incomparable salvation offered us in Jesus on the same level as "enlightenment." Such a religion, while keeping the trappings of the church, would drain the Bible of its authority and undermine historic Christianity.

As Christians, we must resolve to reach those who have never heard the gospel. Despite the reproach of an increasingly secular world, we must continue to plant churches among all peoples, so that everyone may have a chance to glorify the One who created them and sent his Son to purchase their redemption.

Where Do We Go from Here?

Evangelicals, then, have responded firmly to those who challenge our exclusive position on salvation. We cannot abandon the clear teaching of Christ and the apostles, regardless how we might feel about certain aspects of that teaching. When we examine the biblical arguments that purport to show the possibility of salvation apart from

---

9. Several helpful examples are in John D. Ellenberger, "Is Hell a Proper Motivation for Missions?" 223–24. The observation that only individuals and small groups come to Christ this way accords well with the Old Testament. R. Bryan Widbin, "Salvation for People Outside Israel's Covenant?" 82, notes that, while Israel acknowledged *individual* God-fearers, she denied that any other *nation* followed Yahweh.

Christ, we find them inadequate. The New Testament writers simply did not believe pagan religions could save. Nor did the classical thinkers of Christianity consider other religions an alternative pathway to God. We also find that we cannot accept the theological proposals of liberal missiologists, because they cannot be reconciled with our foundational commitment to the ultimate authority of Scripture.

Yet, as we ponder the fate of those who have never heard, we recognize that our task is not finished. We cannot remain a chorus of "naysayers," but must, as in other areas of theological endeavor, provide a positive response. If we fail, those outside our number may justly dismiss us as another group of shrill obscurantists. Several tasks remain, therefore, that require positive, constructive answers.

First, we still need an evangelical theology of religions.[10] This will require us to steer between two extremes. At one end are those who assume all truth resides in Christianity; non-Christian religions lack truth entirely. But several Christian scholars have forced us to realize that other religions do indeed have a measure of truth in them. How, then, should we account for these true elements? Did people long ago deduce such ideas from a natural theology or by logic? Was there some kind of primeval revelation? Has God revealed himself in ways we have been unwilling to acknowledge? All these remain unanswered questions. The other extreme claims that non-Christian religions are just as valid as Christianity. But such a view produces devastating results, as the earlier chapters in this book have shown. Thus, it is easy to state the two extremes—but far harder to actually plot a course between them.

These issues will not go away because contextual theologians will continue to raise them. The problem is, if we place too little value on the religions of the world we create theologies that are not authentic, indigenous witnesses to the gospel. These theologies will be irrelevant and will cause people to stumble over culture rather than Christ. On the other hand, if we place too much value on the world's religions we will be drawn down the path toward "Christopaganism"—which is not Christianity at all. Either approach will prove disastrous in the third millennium.

Second, we must face the difficult questions that relate to fairness. We should ask how far the implicit-faith view goes. For example, we know from experience that missionary preaching wins people to Christ. If you send missionaries to a land with ten thousand people, a certain number of them will accept the message. Don't send them and

10. Observed by Harvie M. Conn, "Do Other Religions Save?"; and by Clark H. Pinnock, "Toward an Evangelical Theology of Religions," *Journal of the Evangelical Theological Society* 33 (1990): 359–68.

those same people will never hear and never experience the joys of Christ. So it stands to reason that more missionaries (or more proclaimers in our own lands) means more people entering the kingdom. For whatever reason, people do not always respond immediately to the gospel message—some, like James the brother of the Lord, need to hear it many times.

This raises the issue of potential Christians. How many more would have accepted the gospel given the chance? Would God not know whose heart was sensitive and whose was not? And come judgment day, would he not welcome those potential Christians as his own? After all, they would have responded had they the chance.

Perhaps, though, this objection is more inspired by our American ideas of egalitarianism than by Scripture. Does fairness mean that all get a chance, or must fairness mean everybody gets the same number of chances? How many chances must God grant an individual, whether through general or special revelation, before it is deemed "fair"? Moreover, we need to ask whether preaching always produces converts. Muslims, for example, have proved highly resistant to the gospel. But these observations, in truth, still leave us with unanswered questions. The problem of potential Christians remains.

Third, we in North America must encourage our colleagues in non-Western churches to lead the way. Is it not reasonable to expect that theologians in the non-Western world, who are closer to these problems, would be better able to grapple with these complex questions than we? The increasing number of well-trained Christians overseas makes such a solution possible. Perhaps the most helpful thing Western Christians could do is to provide sabbatical time and research support for these scholars.

Finally, Western countries face an increasingly practical problem. The questions dealt with in this book have, historically, been problems for missionaries. By the end of the century this will no longer be the case. Already pastors are facing many of the questions raised in this book. And these questions are not theoretical. Large groups of people continually emigrate to the West, and increasingly we see them in our communities.[11] These new immigrants have a religion, and it is not Christianity. The pluralistic nature of modern society decrees that their religion isn't so bad. Our ideals of freedom and self-determination imply that we should be tolerant. It will not be easy to explain to the neighbors of these immigrants why we are trying to convert them to Christianity.

As evangelicals, we need to "get our house in order" before the

---

11. A point well documented in Colin Chapman, "The Riddle of Religions," *Christianity Today* 34/8 (14 May 1990): 18–19.

influx of other religions reaches its peak. We must be prepared not only to defend the idea of sending missionaries, but also to make clear why we evangelize among the growing communities of Muslims and others in our midst. The pressure from our own society to be "tolerant" will dwarf the present efforts of theologians like Hick and Knitter. It will be far more difficult to explain why we are being "intolerant" than it will be to explain why we send missionaries.

So the issues raised in this book are not merely academic, and not only for missionaries. As Western countries become increasingly pluralistic, Christians will confront these same questions in their back yards. Christian leaders must begin now preparing the church to face the challenges ahead. As this book has shown, the survival of the evangelical church depends on how we deal with religious pluralism and the uniqueness of Christianity.

Suggestions for
Further Reading

Abraham, William J. *The Logic of Evangelism*. Grand Rapids: Eerdmans, 1989.

Allen, Edgar L. *Christianity among the Religions*. Boston: Beacon, 1960.

Anderson, J. N. D. *Christianity and World Religions: The Challenge of Pluralism*. Downers Grove, Ill.: Inter-Varsity, 1984.

Ariarajah, S. Wesley. "Religious Plurality and Its Challenge to Christian Theology." *Perspectives* 5/2 (Feb. 1990): 6–9.

Atkinson, B. F. C. *Life and Immortality: An Examination of the Nature and Meaning of Life and Death as They Are Revealed in the Scriptures*. Taunton, England: Goodman, 1962.

Bauckham, Richard. "Universalism—A Historical Survey." *Themelios* 4 (Jan. 1979): 48–53.

Bavinck, J. H. *The Church Between the Temple and the Mosque*. Grand Rapids: Eerdmans, 1966.

———. *An Introduction to the Science of Missions*. Philadelphia: Presbyterian & Reformed, 1960.

Bettis, Joseph Dabney. "A Critique of the Doctrine of Universal Salvation." *Religious Studies* 6 (Dec. 1970): 329–44.

Blue, J. Ronald. "Untold Billions: Are They Really Lost?" *Bibliotheca Sacra* 138 (1981): 338–50.

Bosch, David. "The Church in Dialogue: From Self-Delusion to Vulnerability." *Missiology* 16 (1988): 131–47.

———. *Witness to the World.* London: Marshall, Morgan & Scott, 1980.

Braaten, Carl. "The Uniqueness and Universality of Jesus Christ." In *Mission Trends No. 5: Faith Meets Faith,* ed. Gerald H. Anderson and Thomas Stransky, 69–89. Grand Rapids: Eerdmans, 1981.

———. "The Meaning of Evangelism in the Context of God's Universal Grace." *Journal of the Academy for Evangelism in Theological Education* 3 (1987–88): 9–19.

Brown, Harold. "Will Everyone Be Saved?" *Pastoral Renewal* 11 (June 1987): 11–16.

Brownson, William. "Hope for All." *Perspectives* 3/8 (Oct. 1988): 13–15.

Byrne, Peter. "John Hick's Philosophy of Religion." *Scottish Journal of Theology* 35 (1982): 289–301.

Camps, Arnulf. *Partners in Dialogue: Christianity and Other World Religions.* Maryknoll, N.Y.: Orbis, 1983.

Castro, Emilio. "Mission in a Pluralistic Age." *International Review of Mission* 75 (July 1986): 198–210.

Chapman, Colin. "The Riddle of Religions." *Christianity Today* 34/8 (14 May 1990): 16–22.

Clark, David K., and Norman L. Geisler. *Apologetics in the New Age: A Christian Critique of Pantheism.* Grand Rapids: Baker, 1990.

Cobb, John B., Jr. *Christ in a Pluralistic Age.* Philadelphia: Westminster, 1975.

Conn, Harvie M. *Eternal Word and Changing Worlds.* Grand Rapids: Zondervan, 1984.

Cracknell, Kenneth. *Towards a New Relationship: Christians and People of Other Faiths.* London: Epworth, 1986.

Cragg, Kenneth. *Sandals at the Mosque.* London: SCM, 1959.

Craig, William. "'No Other Name': A Middle Knowledge Perspective on the Exclusivity of Salvation Through Christ." *Faith and Philosophy* 6 (Apr. 1989): 172–88.

Crockett, William. "Wrath That Endures Forever." *Journal of the Evangelical Theological Society* 34 (1991): 195–202.

D'Costa, Gavin. "The Pluralist Paradigm in Christian Theology of Religions." *Scottish Journal of Theology* 39 (1986): 211–24.

Demarest, Bruce. *General Revelation: Historical Views and Contemporary Issues.* Grand Rapids: Zondervan, 1982.

Demarest, Bruce, and R. J. Harpel. "Don Richardson's 'Redemptive Analogies' and the Biblical Idea of Revelation." *Bibliotheca Sacra* 146 (1989): 330–40.

Demarest, Bruce, and Gordon Lewis. *Integrative Theology.* Grand Rapids: Zondervan, 1987.

Driver, Tom F. *Christ in a Changing World: Toward an Ethical Christology.* New York: Crossroad, 1981.

Droge, Arthur J. *Homer or Moses? Early Christian Interpretations of the History of Culture*. Tübingen: Mohr, 1989.

Drummond, Richard H. *Toward a New Age in Christian Theology*. Maryknoll, N.Y.: Orbis, 1985.

Dunn, Edmond J. *Missionary Theology: Foundation in Development*. Lanham, Md.: University Press of America, 1980.

Dye, Wayne. "Towards a Cross-cultural Definition of Sin." *Missiology* 4 (Jan. 1976): 32.

Edwards, David L., and John R. W. Stott. *Evangelical Essentials: A Liberal-Evangelical Dialogue*. Downers Grove, Ill.: Inter-Varsity, 1988.

Erickson, Millard J. "Hope for Those Who Haven't Heard? Yes, But. . . ." *Evangelical Missions Quarterly* 11 (Apr. 1975): 122–26.

Evans-Pritchard, E. E. *Theories of Primitive Religion*. London: Oxford University Press, 1965.

Foulkes, Irene W. "Two Semantic Problems in the Translation of Acts 4:5–20." *Bible Translator* 29 (1978): 121–25.

Fudge, Edward W. "The Final End of the Wicked." *Journal of the Evangelical Theological Society* 27 (1984): 325–34.

———. *The Fire That Consumes*. Houston: Providential, 1982.

Gibbons, Alice. *The People Time Forgot*. Chicago: Moody, 1981.

Grant, Robert M. *Augustus to Constantine*. New York: Harper & Row, 1970.

———. *Gods and the One God*. Library of Early Christianity 1. Philadelphia: Westminster, 1986.

Green, Michael. *Evangelism in the Early Church*. Grand Rapids: Eerdmans, 1970.

———. *The Meaning of Salvation*. London: Hodder & Stoughton, 1965.

Greenberg, Moshe. "Mankind, Israel and the Nations in Hebraic Heritage." In *No Man Is Alien*, ed. J. Robert Nelson, 15–40. Leiden: Brill, 1971.

Griffiths, Michael. *The Confusion of the Church and the World*. Downers Grove, Ill.: Inter-Varsity, 1980.

Hahn, Ferdinand. *Mission in the New Testament*. Studies in Biblical Theology 47. Naperville, Ill.: Allenson, 1965.

Hanson, R. P. C. "The Christian Attitude to Pagan Religions." In *Studies in Christian Antiquity*, 144–229. Edinburgh: T. & T. Clark, 1985.

Harris, Murray J. *From Grave to Glory: Resurrection in the New Testament, Including a Response to Dr. Norman L. Geisler*. Grand Rapids: Zondervan, 1990.

———. *Raised Immortal: Resurrection and Immortality in the New Testament*. Grand Rapids: Eerdmans, 1983.

Hebblethwaite, Brian, and John Hick. *Christianity and Other Religions*. Glasgow: Fount, 1980.

Heim, S. Mark. *Is Christ the Only Way?* Valley Forge, Pa.: Judson, 1985.

———. "Thinking about Theocentric Christology." *Journal of Ecumenical Studies* 24 (1987): 1–16.

Hesselgrave, David. "Christian Communication and Religious Pluralism: Capitalizing on Differences." *Missiology* 18 (1990): 131–38.

Hick, John. *God Has Many Names.* Philadelphia: Westminster, 1982.

———. *God and the Universe of Faiths: Essays in the Philosophy of Religion.* New York: St. Martin's, 1973.

———. "Pluralism and the Reality of the Transcendent." *Christian Century* 98 (21 Jan. 1981): 45–48.

———. "The Philosophy of World Religions." *Scottish Journal of Theology* 37 (1984): 229–36.

Hick, John, and Paul F. Knitter, eds. *The Myth of Christian Uniqueness: Toward a Pluralistic Theology of Religions.* Maryknoll, N.Y.: Orbis, 1987.

Hillman, Eugene. *Many Faiths: A Catholic Approach to Religious Pluralism.* Maryknoll, N.Y.: Orbis, 1985.

Hocking, W. E. *Rethinking Mission: A Layman's Inquiry after One Hundred Years.* New York: Harper, 1932.

Holte, Ragner. "Logos Spermatikos: Christianity and Ancient Philosophy According to St. Justin's Apologies." *Studia Theologica* 12 (1958): 109–68.

Horst, Mark. "The Problem with Theological Pluralism." *Christian Century* 103 (1986): 971–74.

Hughes, Philip Edgcumbe. *The True Image: The Origin and Destiny of Man in Christ.* Grand Rapids: Eerdmans, 1989.

Jeremias, Joachim. *Jesus' Promise to the Nations.* Naperville, Ill.: Allenson, 1958. Repr., Philadelphia: Fortress, 1982.

Kantzer, Kenneth S., and Carl F. H. Henry, eds. *Evangelical Affirmations.* Grand Rapids: Zondervan, 1990.

Kitagawa, Joseph. "The History of Religions in America." In *The History of Religions: Essays in Methodology,* ed. Mircea Eliade and Joseph Kitagawa, 1–30. Chicago: University of Chicago Press, 1959.

Knitter, Paul F. "Roman Catholic Approaches to Other Religions: Developments and Tensions." *International Bulletin of Missionary Research* 8 (1984): 50–54.

———. *No Other Name: A Critical Survey of Christian Attitudes toward the World Religions.* Maryknoll, N.Y.: Orbis, 1985.

Kraemer, Hendrik. *The Christian Message in a Non-Christian World.* Grand Rapids: Kregel, 1983.

Kraft, Charles. *Christianity in Culture: A Study in Dynamic Biblical Theologizing in Cross-Cultural Perspective.* Maryknoll, N.Y.: Orbis, 1979.

Küng, Hans. "What Is the True Religion?" *Journal of Theology for Southern Africa* 56 (Sept. 1986): 4–23.

Lightner, Robert P. *Heaven for Those Who Can't Believe.* Schaumberg, Ill.: Regular Baptist, 1977.

Marshall, I. Howard. *I Believe in the Historical Jesus.* Grand Rapids: Eerdmans, 1977.

Meeks, Wayne A. *The First Urban Christians: The Social World of the Apostle Paul.* New Haven: Yale University Press, 1983.

Morris, Leon. *The Apostolic Preaching of the Cross.* Grand Rapids: Eerdmans, 1956.

Moule, C. F. D. *Origins of Christology.* Cambridge: Cambridge University Press, 1977.

Neill, Steven. *Crisis of Belief.* London: Hodder & Stoughton, 1984.

Nelson, J. Robert. "Christian Theology and the Living Faiths of Men." In *Christian Mission in Theological Perspective,* ed. Gerald H. Anderson, 109–24. Nashville: Abingdon, 1967.

Netland, Harold A. "Exclusivism, Tolerance and Truth." *Missiology* 15 (1987): 77–95.

Newbigin, Lesslie. "Religious Pluralism and the Uniqueness of Jesus Christ." *International Bulletin of Missionary Research* 13 (Apr. 1989): 50–54.

———. "The Gospel among the Religions." In *Mission Trends No. 5: Faith Meets Faith,* ed. Gerald H. Anderson and Thomas Stransky, 3–19. Grand Rapids: Eerdmans, 1981.

———. *The Gospel in a Pluralist Society.* Grand Rapids: Eerdmans; Geneva: WCC, 1989.

———. "Can the West Be Converted?" *International Bulletin of Missionary Research* 11 (Jan. 1987): 2–7.

Orlinsky, Harry M. "Nationalism-Universalism and Internationalism in Ancient Israel." In *Translating and Understanding the Old Testament,* ed. Harry T. Frank and William L. Reed, 206–36. Nashville: Abingdon, 1970.

Osburn, Evert D. "Those Who Have Never Heard: Have They No Hope?" *Journal of the Evangelical Theological Society* 32 (1989): 367–72.

Packer, James I. "'Good Pagans' and God's Kingdom." *Christianity Today* 30/1 (17 Jan. 1986): 22–25.

Panikkar, Raymond. *The Unknown Christ of Hinduism.* London: Darton, Longman & Todd, 1964.

Percy, John O., ed. *Facing the Unfinished Task: Messages Delivered at the Congress on World Mission.* Grand Rapids: Zondervan, 1961.

Peters, Ted. "Confessional Universalism and Inter-Religious Dialogue." *Dialog* 25 (1984): 145–49.

Pinnock, Clark. "Toward an Evangelical Theology of Religions." *Journal of the Evangelical Theological Society* 33 (1990): 359–68.

———. "Fire, Then Nothing." *Christianity Today* 31/5 (20 Mar. 1987): 40–41.

——"The Finality of Jesus Christ in a World of Religions." In *Christian Faith and Practice in the Modern World: Theology from an Evangelical Point of View,* ed. Mark A. Noll and David F. Wells, 152–68. Grand Rapids: Eerdmans, 1988.

Punt, Neal. "All Are Saved Except." *Christianity Today* 31/5 (20 Mar. 1987): 43–44.

Race, Alan. *Christians and Religious Pluralism.* Maryknoll, N.Y.: Orbis, 1982.

Rahner, Karl. "Christianity and the Non-Christian Religions." In *Theological Investigations,* 5:115–34. New York: Seabury, 1961.

Richardson, Don. *Eternity in Their Hearts.* Ventura, Calif.: Regal, 1984.

Robinson, John A. T. *Truth Is Two-Eyed.* Philadelphia: Westminster, 1979.

———. *In the End, God.* London: James Clarke, 1950.

Rowley, H. H. *The Missionary Message of the Old Testament.* London: Carey Kingsgate, 1944.

Samartha, Stanley J. "The Lordship of Jesus Christ and Religious Pluralism." In *Christ's Lordship and Religious Pluralism,* ed. Gerald Anderson and Thomas Stransky, 19–36. Maryknoll, N.Y.: Orbis, 1981.

———. *Courage for Dialogue: Ecumenical Issues in Inter-Religious Relationships.* Maryknoll, N.Y.: Orbis, 1982.

Samartha, Stanley J., ed. *Living Faiths and the Ecumenical Movement.* Geneva: WCC, 1971.

Sanders, E. P. *Jesus and Judaism.* London: SCM, 1985.

Sanders, John E. "Is Belief in Christ Necessary for Salvation?" *Evangelical Quarterly* 60 (1988): 241–59.

Sanneh, Lamin. *Translating the Message: The Missionary Impact on Culture.* Maryknoll, N.Y.: Orbis, 1989.

Schillebeeckx, Edward. *God, the Future of Man.* New York: Sheed & Ward, 1968.

Schrotenboer, Paul G. "Inter-Religious Dialogue." *Evangelical Review of Theology* 12 (1988): 208–25.

Senior, Donald, and Carroll Stuhlmueller, *The Biblical Foundations for Mission.* Maryknoll, N.Y.: Orbis, 1983.

Sharpe, Eric J. *Comparative Religion, A History.* London: Duckworth, 1975.

———. *Faith Meets Faith.* London: SCM, 1977.

Shedd, W. G. T. *The Doctrine of Endless Punishment.* New York: Scribner, 1886; repr., Minneapolis: Klock & Klock, 1980.

Stipe, Claude. "Anthropologists versus Missionaries: The Influence of Presuppositions." *Current Anthropology* 21 (1980): 168.

Stott, John. *Christian Mission in the Modern World.* Downers Grove Ill.: InterVarsity, 1975.

Stott, John, and Robert Coote, eds. *Down to Earth: Studies in Christianity and Culture.* Grand Rapids: Eerdmans, 1980.

Stransky, Thomas. "The Church and Other Religions." *International Bulletin of Missionary Research* 9 (1985): 154–58.

Thomas, Madathilparampil M. "The Absoluteness of Jesus Christ and Christ-Centered Syncretism." *Ecumenical Review* 37 (1985): 387–97.

Toon, Peter. *Heaven and Hell: A Biblical and Theological Overview.* Nashville: Nelson, 1986.

Tracy, David. *The Analogical Imagination.* New York: Crossroad, 1981.

———. *Plurality and Ambiguity.* New York: Harper & Row, 1987.

Travis, Stephen H. *I Believe in the Second Coming of Jesus.* Grand Rapids: Eerdmans, 1982.

——. *Christian Hope and the Future.* Downers Grove, Ill.: Inter-Varsity, 1980.

——. *Christ and the Judgement of God: Divine Retribution in the New Testament.* London: Marshall Pickering, 1986.

Van Til, Cornelius. *The Defense of the Faith.* Nutley, N.J.: Presbyterian & Reformed, 1967.

Van Winkle, D. W. "The Relationship of the Nations to Yahweh and to Israel in Isaiah 40–55." *Vetus Testamentum* 35 (1985): 446–58.

Verkuyl, Johannes. *Contemporary Missiology: An Introduction.* Grand Rapids: Eerdmans, 1978.

——. "Mission in the 1990s." *International Bulletin of Missionary Research* 13 (Apr. 1989): 55–58.

Visser 't Hooft, W. A. *No Other Name.* Philadelphia: Westminster, 1963.

Von Balthasar, Hans Urs. *Dare We Hope "That All Men Be Saved"?* Trans. David Kipp and Lothar Krauth. San Francisco: Ignatius, 1988.

Wright, Christopher J. H. "The Christian and Other Religions: The Biblical Evidence." *Themelios* 9 (Jan. 1984): 4–15.

Yandell, Keith. "Some Varieties of Relativism." *International Journal of Philosophy* 19 (1986): 61–85.

Index